The International Political Economy of Transformation in Argentina, Brazil, and Chile since 1960

The International Political Economy of Transformation in Argentina, Brazil, and Chile since 1960

Eul-Soo Pang
Colorado School of Mines
Golden, Colorado

First published 2002 by
PALGRAVE MACMILLAN
Houndmills, Basingstoke, Hampshire RG21 6XS and
175 Fifth Avenue, New York, N.Y. 10010
Companies and representatives throughout the world.

PALGRAVE MACMILLAN is the global academic imprint of the Palgrave Macmillan division of St Martin's Press, LLC and of Palgrave Macmillan Ltd. Macmillan® is a registered trademark in the United States, United Kingdom and other countries. Palgrave is a registered trademark in the European Union and other countries.

ISBN 0-333-91972-6 hardback

This book is printed on paper suitable for recycling and made from fully managed and sustained forest sources.

A catalogue record for this book is available from the British Library.

Library of Congress Cataloging-in-Publication Data

Pang, Eul-Soo
    The international political economy of transformation in Argentina, Brazil, and Chile since 1960 / Eul-Soo Pang.
        p. cm. – (International political economy series)
Includes bibliographical references and index.
ISBN 0-333-91972-6
    1. Argentina – Economic policy. 2. Argentina – Economic conditions – 1945– 3. Argentina – Politics and government – 1955–1983. 4. Argentina – Politics and government – 1983– 5. Brazil – Economic policy. 6. Brazil – Economic conditions – 1945– 7. Brazil – Politics and government – 1964–1985. 8. Brazil – Politics and government – 1985– 9. Chile – Economic policy. 10. Chile – Economic conditions – 1970–1973. 11. Chile – Economic conditions – 1973–1988. 12. Chile – Economic conditions – 1988– 13. Chile – Politics and government – 1973– I.Title. II. International political economy series (Palgrave (Firm))

HC167.S67 P36 2002
338.9–dc21   2001036351

10 9 8 7 6 5 4 3 2 1
11 10 09 08 07 06 05 04 03 02

Printed and bound in Great Britain by
Antony Rowe Ltd, Chippenham and Eastbourne

Contents

List of Tables

Acknowledgements

Every author owes intellectual debt to someone. Since 1986 when I moved from the University of Alabama at Birmingham to the Colorado School of Mines to establish the Latin American Center for Minerals and Energy Development, I have had numerous opportunities to travel to Latin America and the Caribbean and learn from policy makers, business leaders, and academics of various countries. During these years, much of what I have learned about the ABC countries and observed first hand has gone into this book. In Latin America, many academics often take up positions as government officials; hence, their perspectives are invaluable, tested by time and enriched by public-sector experience. I envy their opportunities to combine intellectual pursuit with policy making and implementation. As their friend, I would like to believe that when we discussed policy issues I played a role in policy making as well, however indirectly it might have been. I am grateful for those opportunities as their friend and consultant. I will not cite all of their names, but should mention that friends like Juan Antonio Zapata and Alejandro Bulgheroni (along with Juan Martin, Patricio, M riana, and Alex Paz) of Argentina, Antônio Carlos Pojo do Rêgo, Ana Studart, João Paulo Machado de Peixoto, Augusto de Oliveira, Marquinho de Carvalho, Adonis de Carvalho, Ozires Silva, Breno Augusto dos Santos, Luciano Borges, and Roberto C. Villas Boâs of Brazil, and Mario Meza M., Alejandro Hales, and Mario Maturana of Chile are truly my teachers in helping me understand, unravel, and appreciate the history of the ABC countries, especially their cultures and their political economies. Dr. Carlos Bakota of the US Department of State has been a valuable mentor to this project through the years. And Peter Andrews at Palgrave Macmillan has done a superb job of turning Korean English into a readable prose. I thank them for their contributions; without them this book would not have been possible.

Finally, I must mention that during the years of travel to Latin America, I have had the best sounding board to this book: my wife, Laura, who is an accomplished Latin Americanist, and the conversations with her have helped me understand the nuances of the state, the behavior of the Latin elite and their culture, and the peculiar aspects of Latin America's international political economy that she dissects so well. I duly recognize her contribution to this book.

May 2002
Keystone, Colorado

Abbreviations

ADESG	Associação dos Diplomados da Escola Superior de Guerra
ADIC	Asociación de Industriales de Córdoba
AFP	Administrador de Fondos de Pensión
AFTA	ASEAN Free Trade Area
ALN	Ação Libertadora Nacional
ANP	Agência Nacional de Petróleo
APEC	Asia Pacific Economic Conference
ASEAN	Association of Southeast Asian Nations
B-A	bureaucratic-authoritarian
BB	Banco do Brasil, S/A
BCCI	Bank for Commerce and Credit Internacional
BEFIEX	Benefícios Fiscais a Programas Especiais de Exportação
BIS	Bank for International Settlements
BNDES	Banco Nacional de Desenvolvimento Econômico e Social; formerly known as BNDE
BNH	Banco Nacional de Habitação
BRADESCO	Banco Brasileiro de Descontos, S.A.
BRASPETRO	Petrobrás Internacional, S/A
CACEX	Carteira de Exportação, Banco do Brasil
CAPRE	Coordenação das Atividades de Processamento Eletrônico
CEF	Caixa Econômica Federal
CEPAL	Comisión Económica para América Latina (Spanish and Portuguese acronym for ECLA)
CGT	Comando General de Trabajo; Comando Geral do Trabalho; also Confederação Geral de Trabalho
CIEPLAN	Corporación de Investigaciones Económicas para América Latina
CINCPAC	Commander-in-Chief, Pacific
CNPq	Conselho Nacional de Pesquisa Científico
CNV	Comisión Nacional de Valores
COBAL	Companhia Brasileira de Alimentação
CODELCO	Corporación del Cobre de Chile
CORA	Corporación de Reforma Agraria

CORFO	Corporación de Fomento de la Producción de Chile
COSIPA	Companhia Siderúrgica Paulista
CSN	Companhia Siderúrgica Nacional
CUT	Central Única de Trabalhadores; Central Unica de Trabajadores
CVRD	Companhia Vale do Rio Doce
DOCENAVE	Navegações do Rio Doce
E & P	exploration and production
ECLAC	Economic Commission for Latin America and the Caribbean; formerly, ECLA
EMBRAER	Empresa Brasileira Aeronaútica
EMBRATEL	Empresa Brasileira de Telecomunicações
EMPREMAR	Empresa Marítima
ENAMI	Empresa Nacional de Minería
ENCAR	Empresa Nacional de Carbón
ENTEL	Empresa Nacional de Telecomunicaciones
ELETROBRÁS	Centrais Elétricas Brasileiras, S/A
ESG	Escola Superior de Guerra
EU-15	European Union with 15 members
FDI	foreign direct investment
FIESP	Federação de Indústria do Estado de São Paulo
FRAP	Frente de Acción Popular
FREPASO	Frente Pais Solidario
FTAA	Free Trade Area of the Americas
FURNAS	Furnas Elétricas
GATT	General Agreement on Tariffs and Trade
GC	global corporation
GDP	gross domestic product
GLC	government-linked companies of Singapore
GOU	Grupo de Oficiales Unidos
IAPI	Instituto Argentino de Producción Industrial
IDB	Inter-American Development Bank; also IADB
IEERAL	Instituto de Estudios Económicos sobre la Realidad Argentina y Latinoamericana
IGO	inter-government organization
IMF	International Monetary Fund
INAMPS	Instituto Nacional de Assistência Médica e Previdência Social
INDAP	Instituto de Desarrollo Agraria y Pastoral
INGO	international non-governmental organization
INPI	Instituto Nacional de Propriedade Industrial

INTERBRÁS	Petrobrás Comércio Internacional, S/A
INTERNOR	Internor Trade Inc.
IPE	international political economy
IRI	Instituto di Reconstruzzione Industriale
ISI	import-substituting industrialization; also import substitution industrialization
LBA	Legião Brasileira de Assistência
MERCOSUR	Also MERCOSUL in Portuguese; Mercado Común del Cono Sur; Southern Cone Common Market
MIR	Movimiento Izquierda Revolucionario
MITI	Ministry of International Trade and Industry
MNC	multinational corporation
MR-8	Movimento Revolucionario 8
NAFTA	North America Free Trade Area
NIEO	new international economic order
NTB	non-tariff barrier
NUCLEBRÁS	Empresas Nucleares Brasileiras, S.A.
ODEPLAN	Oficina de Planificación
OECD	Organization of Economic Cooperation and Development
OPEC	Organization of Petroleum-Exporting Countries
PCC	Partido Comunista Chileno
PDC	Partido Demócrata Cristiano
PDT	Partido Democrático Trabalhista
PEMEX	Petroleos Mexicanos, S.A.
Petrobrás	Petroleo Brasileiro, S/A
PFL	Partido Frente Liberal
PJ	Partido Justicialista
PMDB	Partido Movimento Democrático Brasileiro
PORTOBRÁS	Empresa de Portos Brasileiros, S/A
PPD	Partido por la Democracia
PPP	purchasing power parity
PRSD	Partido Radical Social Demócrata
PS	Partido Socialista
PSDB	Partido Social Democrata Brasileiro
PT	Partido dos Trabalhadores
R & D	research and development
RFFSA	Rede Federal Ferroviária, S/A
SAFTA	South American Free Trade Area
SBPC	Sociedade Brasileira para Progresso Científico
SEGBA	Servicio de Energía y Gas de Buenos Aires

SEI	Secretaria Especial de Informática
SEPLAN	Secretaria de Planejamento e Coordenação da Presidência da República; now, Secretaria de Planejamento e Orçamento da Presidência da República
SERPRO	Serviço de Processamentos de Datos
SEST	Secretaria de Orçamento e Controle de Empresas Estatais
Sidebrás	Grupo Siderurgia Brasileira
SINAPAS	Sistema Nacional de Assistência Previdencial e Assistência Social
SNI	Serviço Nacional de Informações
SOE	State-owned enterprise
SUDENE	Superintendência de Desenvolvimento do Nordeste
TELEBRÁS	Telecomunicações Brasileiras, S/A
TELEMEX	Compañia Telefónica de México, S.A.
TELESP	Telecomunicações de São Paulo, S/A
UCR	Unión Cívica Radical
UMNO	United Malays National Organizations
UP	Unidad Popular
URV	Unidade Real de Valor
USAID	United States Agency for International Development
USIMINAS	Usina Siderúrgica de Minas Gerais
VASP	Viação Aérea de São Paulo, S.A.
WB	World Bank
WTO	World Trade Organization
YPF	Yacimientos Petrolíferos Fiscales

Introduction

This book is about the processes of the transformation of the Latin American political economy from the early 1960s to 2002, the epochal transition from the state-centric to the market-oriented systems of economy and polity. How Argentina, Brazil, Chile, and Mexico have responded to the need to modify their non-market, statist economy and populist polity has set the course for the rest of the continent to follow. To be more efficient and productive, the ABC countries have embraced neoliberal reforms that shrank their state and transformed their statist economies into more market-friendly systems. Chile was the first country to embrace the tenets of globalization and market economic principles, followed by Argentina in the early 1990s, and finally by Brazil since the mid-1990s. By the dawn of 2002, Argentina was the first one to fold the neoliberal experiments. Brazil may be the next and Chile may survive.

At various times between 1964 and 1990, all three countries were under military-directed bureaucratic-authoritarian rule that sought to cautiously combine a market-driven growth policy with nationalistic objectives. Chile pursued in earnest the purest form of market economy policy. Argentina experimented with a neoliberal policy briefly in the late 1960s, then was overwhelmed by its internal war, and soon abandoned it altogether under intense domestic political pressures. Brazil's military gave much lip-service to the free-market doctrine but in practice adopted the most closed economic system on the continent. In social arenas, the military regimes in Argentina and Brazil continued, with some modifications, the populist policies that they inherited from the civilian governments which they had over-thrown in 1964 (Brazil) and in 1966 (Argentina). In Chile, the Pinochet regime (1973–90) was flagrantly antipopulist and scrapped all populist programs during its rule.

What has driven this epochal transformation from the statist, populist, and authoritarian economy and polity to more open, market-driven and liberal democratic regimes will be carefully analyzed in the book. There are two historical turning points for this transformation from the state to the market. The first is internally driven and ideological: between 1950 and 1970, the dominant ideology of Latin American development was shaped by the United Nations Economic Commission for Latin America, or CEPAL in Spanish and Portuguese. The *cepalismo* promoted an inward-looking development model that called for closed import-substituting industralization (ISI) for manufacturing, statist finance and investment policy, distribution-drive populism, and xenophobic nationalism. The state took the commanding heights, while the market was subdued and even relegated to the secondary role in nation-building and economic development. Marxism, dependency thinking, and *cepalismo* all melded into a unitary Latin American developmentalist ideology. Statism and ECLA preaching promoted, according to one Venezuelan economist, the notion that "development was equivalent to the deliberate direction of the process of import substitution industrialization through the use of planning."[1] This model began to falter in the late 1960s, and by the onset of the first OPEC-provoked petroleum price hike in 1973 the ECLA-statist-populist model was moribund.

The second impetus for the transformation of Argentina, Brazil, and Chile from the state-centric to the market-driven system began in the late 1960s but ran in full force after the Latin debt crisis of the early 1980s. The stagnant socialist and social democratic economies in Europe, Asia, and Latin America prompted policy makers and academics to question the validity of the ISI-*cum*-populist model. The petroleum crisis of 1973 provoked an internal debate within the Brazilian military and its technocratic community on the viability of the Brazilian model, as the external debt crisis of 1982 set off the process of soul-searching throughout the continent, especially in Mexico, Brazil, and Argentina.

The so-called Washington Consensus emerged by the mid-1980s, promulgating the remedial and reconstructive measures for the heavily indebted Latin America, ranging from such state-shrinking policies as trimming public spending, reconstructing macroeconomic policy foundations, and cutting social programs to rebuilding a market-driven economic regime through liberalizing international trade, deregulating the domestic market, and privatizing the plethora of state-owned enterprises (SOEs) that had served as the locomotive of economic growth in the continent. Banks would not renegotiate the Latin debt without significant commitment to the structural reforms and no fresh money could be had, if the reform and adjustment measures endorsed by the Washington Consensus were not fully embraced. Thus, the great rush for privatization, deregulation, and liberalization, the *tripé* of the Washington Consensus, began in Latin America with little thought and superficial enthusiasm only rivaling that for the anticommunism of the Cold War years.

The end of the Berlin Wall in 1989 and the collapse of the Soviet Union in1991 were just a tip of the iceberg globalization. The border-less, stateless, and 24-hour operating financial system and expanding flows of goods and services to the formerly closed areas of Latin America, Eastern Europe, and Asia Pacific became a reality by the mid-1980s and early 1990s. In 1960, the world merchandise trade was $650 billion; in 1980, it surpassed $3600 billion, and in 1997 it almost trebled to $10 615 billion. Equally impressive is the expansion of service trade: in 1980, the world traded in $839 billion. In 1997, it jumped to $2749 billion, or a 327 per cent increase.[2] Revolutionary innovations in informatics, telecommunications, and transportation technologies have facilitated the expansion of global trade. This is an historic transformation on a global scale.

Capital flows across borders are impressive, too. Money begets money, as an old saying goes. In the United States, the holding by Americans of stocks and bonds expanded from $100 billion in 1980 to $3 trillion in 1998.[3] In mid-1999, the capitalization of the New York Stock Exchange Market reached $11.7 trillion, closely followed by Tokyo's $2.69 trillion, London's $2.32 trillion, and Frankfurt's $1.035 trillion.[4] For the six years of 1985–90, the recorded private capital investment flows in the world reached $141 930 million, but by 1996 surpassed $349 227 million. In Latin America, Brazil, Mexico, Argentina, Peru, and Chile were the top five recipients of foreign direct investment.[5] In 1993, foreign direct invest-ment to Malaysia represented 17 per cent of its GDP, while Thailand's FDI soared to 13 per cent of its GDP in 1995. Between 1992 and 1997, global pension funds increased from $6 trillion to $97 trillion, bigger than the entire combined GDPs of the European Union or that of the United States.[6] In 1996, Asia garnered $102.2 billion, while in Latin America the figure was $386 billion of the total. Money crossed borders with little restrictions, flowing into countries where the safety of investment was assured and the return on investment was greatest. Global investors con-sidered Asia as a safer place than Latin America. This global financial spree began in the 1960s, as Asia revamped its economy, liberalizing, deregulating, and even privatizing by the 1970s. Asia escaped the griev-ous impact of the Third World debt crisis, while Latin America could not.

In the 1960s and 1970s, Chile and Brazil refined the military-technobureaucratic system of governance, while Argentina failed to implant such a system. In Argentina, the civil war, or "the dirty war," in urban areas sapped much of the junta's energy, while in Chile and Brazil the military regimes successfully contained rural and urban guerrilla movements. The Pinochet regime in Chile literally wiped out all political opposition within and without the junta. The emaciated left in general, and communists and socialists in particular, were obliged to join forces with the Christian Democratic Party, a center-left group, to create the *Concertación de partidos por la democracia*. In Argentina, the military were engaged in unspeakable crimes of torture and violations of all human decency, including pushing drugged subversives off airplanes into the icy-cold South Atlantic Ocean.[7] Brazil, supposedly the practitioner of the mildest form of military repression among the three, was also briefly engaged in the unspeakable crimes: General Ernesto Geisel in his 1995–96 autobiographical interviews casually revealed that the Brazilian Air Force also dumped an unknown number of "communists" off the planes into the Atlantic Ocean.[8] Geisel did not say how long such practices continued in Brazil.

Democracy, human rights, and open society values were submerged in pursuit of the economic growth that the juntas strove to achieve, and to some Chile and Brazil became the models for other Latin American countries to avoid.[9] To the eyes of others, Brazil and Chile are the models of successful military-technobureaucratic-authoritarianism, while Argentina was a failure. To some extent, the transformation process – the trials and tribulations of how Argentina, Brazil, and Chile have responded to the pressure and challenges from the globalization of the world economy and how they have designed and implemented reform and adjustment programs to take advantage of the opportunities offered by globalization – is the core of this book.

The concept of globalization since the days of the heated debate over dependency has captured the imagination of both academic and non-academic communities. In the 1970s, it was called "interdependency". Some use internationalization and globalization interchangeably. Both phenomena refer to an increasing crossborder integration of political, economic, and socio-cultural relationships that has blurred the distinction of the nation state and eventually leads to the formation of new transnational institutions that thrive on the supranational conduct of relations.[10] Regardless of the nomenclature, there are two schools of thought on globalization: adherents ("hyperglobalizers" and "transformationalists") and resisters ("skeptics").[11] The adherents recognize the existence of the border-destroying global economy, especially in finance and trade and argue that the end of the nation-state systems as the Westphalian framework defines it is upon us. Reinvention of nation states is necessary to compete in the global economy; those failing to modernize and reorganize will be losers in the twenty-first century. The irrelevancy of the nation-state system notwithstanding, the adherent camp advocates the inevitability of new transnational, regional, and global institutions that will manage the global economy. What was *national* is no longer national, but has become *international*. And what was international yesterday is *global* today. Economic changes drive the need to restructure polity. And domestic political imperatives are often shaped by external or internal forces which are beyond the control of a single sovereign government. Susan Strange, Kenichi Ohmae, and Robert Reich are leading examples of the hyper-globalizers while Manuel Castells, David Held, Andre Gunder Frank, Jean-Marie Guéhenno, Daniel Cohen, and James Rosenau are the trans-formationalists.[12] All of them are ardent adherents to globalization.

The resisters or "skeptics" point out that the nation states are hardly dead. In fact, it was a group of powerful states such as the United States, Japan, Britain, and to a lesser extent Germany and France that have pushed for the consolidation of the single, unified global economy. It was a policy-driven objective of a state which stands to gain from a borderless and internationalized economy. While making cogent arguments that the unitary global economy does not exist, the resisters base their views on an excessive *economism*. The ratio of export to production in 1913 was 33 percent, while that in 1995 was 31 percent. Hence, the argument goes that it is a "myth" that the world economy has become genuinely globalized and a single, border-less, transnational entity.[13] To some, globalization has gone too far and the world must take a measured march toward global integration.[14] In fact, Linda Weiss argued that the existence of the "new global ortho-doxy," defined as the disintegration and disappearance of national economies and the political power of nation states, is "misleading."[15] For environmentalists and some anthropologists, globalization is a dirty word, which destroys local community, its ecosystem, and worse, the indigenous way of life the world over.[16]

Regardless of the philosophical divergence, the two camps of the adherents and resisters of globalization agree on the following premises: in today's world the ECLA-statist, socialist-Marxist, and Third World developmentalist models no longer work and technological revolutions in informatics, digitalization, fiber optics and satellites in telecommunications, and transportation have given birth to a new *global* economy, unitary and integrated. Castells poignantly differenti-ates the old internationalization and the current globalization: while both phenomena have similarities, today, information, money, tech-nology, and data can be transferred *in real time* and what has been driving the global economy is a collection of strategically scattered "global wells" of new production systems to service markets of diverse regions.[17] Speed and the shrinking of distance make today's globalization different from yesterday's internationalization. At the moment, the globalization that we see, feel, and know about is brought to us by the integration of world finances, trade, and technology. Cultural change, political modernization, and social reformation have taken place for the last three decades of the twentieth century, factors whose pace has been accelerating and even instantaneous and whose depth is unprecedented in human history. It is this vortex of this global transformation that has reshaped Argentina, Brazil, and Chile.

Academic specialists and United States policy makers have often painted the political economy of Latin America in black and white, most often in bleak colors. This book shows that the fundamental differences in the ideologies and programs of the left and the right since the 1960s remain more obvious in rhetoric than in practice. There is overwhelming evidence to support this view. The number of state-owned enterprises (SOEs), the engines of economic growth and development in Latin America during much of the period under study, tells an interesting story. Both Chile under Marxist Allende and Brazil under the anti-Marxist military expanded the number of SOEs, thus increasing the degree of *statization* to an all-time high. Each also liberally used the SOEs as socio-political tools of job creation for the regimes' followers and supporters.

Also, the notion that democracy is less well disposed for economic growth can be questioned if we look at Brazil: between 1956 and 1960, the country grew at 10 percent a year, while during the period of the "economic miracle" of the military dictatorship (1967–73) the economy grew at an average of 11 percent a year, a small difference of 1 percentage point. Allende's Chile and authoritarian Brazil under the military controlled the credit market. In fact, as much as 80 percent of all commercial credit came from the government. Labor unions in Argentina and Brazil under their military regimes were weakened by internal ideological strife as much as by the vigilance and harassment of the regimes. But they were able to retain much of the populist practices of labor-management relations intact. Argentina still retains a populist-era labor regime. Indeed, SOE unions became more powerful under the Brazilian and Argentinian military.

Also xenophobia was carefully nurtured. Both the left and right in the ABC countries were hostile toward foreign capital and put up ferocious resistance in the name of economic nationalism. Foreign access to the domestic market in the countries was equally restricted. In other words, the military in Argentina and Brazil were as statist as their populist nemeses, whereas this was not the case in Chile. By the early 1990s, "a cocktail of Marxism and [rightwing?] populist nationalism" plagued the state reforms by opposing principal changes, in particular privatization and free trade.[18]

When the civilian regimes took over in all three countries (in 1983 for Argentina, in 1985 for Brazil, and in 1990 for Chile), the will for state reforms and fiscal adjustment was still strong, although cynics believed it to be just a fad. Well before the Washington Consensus, Chile embraced a series of draconian measures of shrinking the [Marxist] state, trimming public spending, reforming social programs, liberalizing international trade, deregulating the domestic marketplace, and finally privatizing state-owned enterprises. But some Christian Democrats have never abandoned the dream of building a "social market economy."[19] And they believed that without it Chile will have no social justice. Argentina resisted the globalization-driven but externally imposed reform and adjustment programs under Alfonsín, but when Menem came into office in 1989 such measures were taken up enthusiastically. Brazil under civilian government had policies of its own, often as xenophobic as the military regime ever was. Reforms were opposed by the left, nationalistic technocrats, the business community, academics, trade unions, and even the national bar association. Globalization forced these countries to open up, remove the obstacles to their economic recovery, and renew growth.

Democracy in all three countries meant that the government had often to listen to ideologically conflictive groups, accommodate divergent demands, and at times allow views to prevail. This democratic process slowed down and even diluted the intensity and the will to reform. The most drastic reform period in Chile was under Pinochet's rule, where no opposition was allowed. In Argentina, Menem's first administration faced little opposition from organized labor and businesses. During the second term, as monetary stability was assured, inflation was eradicated, and the economy began to grow, opposition to Menem increased. And in Brazil, a full-blown democracy since 1985 has weakened the presidency so dramatically that reforms have moved forward at a snail's pace, and in some instances have actually retrogressed. Roberto Campos, the planning minister of the first military government of Brazil (1964–67), aptly joked that the Cruzado plan under the transitional but democratic Sarney government sought to decree the abolition of hyperinflation, while the tribunes who drafted the Constitution of 1988 strove to legalize the end of the nation's poverty.[20] Globalization has forced Argentina and Brazil to adopt passive responses, while Chile was able to pursue active measures to reform its economy and polity. It is the history of the past five decades that have made Argentina and Brazil first resist external pressures and then reluctantly accept the inevitable. Chile tells a different story.

As globalization intensified, the state reforms and fiscal adjustments of the 1980s and 1990s have produced diverse results in the ABC countries, not always salutary. The prospects for their success in consolidating the practices of open society, liberal democracy, and a market-friendly economy for the coming decades are in doubt. Like Albert O. Hirschman, Jorge Dominguez believed that, underneath, Latin America continued to suffer from *fracasomania*, a failure syndrome and a historical legacy of Latin culture.[21] Abraham Lowenthal worried about the "tentative" commitment to fundamental reforms and increasing societal "disappointment with democratic institutions."[22] Jorge Castañeda questioned whether the neoliberal reforms of market and democracy are mutually compatible, drawing from the Mexican experience of the 1994–95 peso meltdown.[23] George Soros, one of the beneficiaries of the free-wheeling global financial markets for the last four decades of the twentieth century, had become nonsanguine about the "tenuous" compatibility between global capitalism and open society values in democracy. The new global capitalism had not resulted in greater democratization.[24] Finally, Paul Krugman, a persistent critic of shallow reforms and gadfly of economic rationalism, predicted that "disappointing growth" in Latin America, Asia Pacific, and other parts of the world would revert the emerging markets back to "statist retrenchment."[25]

Such a backlash can rage on a global scale, if transitional societies and reforming socialist systems are included. These are very gloomy forecasts for the future of Latin America; nevertheless, they cannot be dismissed lightly. This book documents much of the gloom based on recent developments in the decline of partisan politics, a reversion to strong political personalities (retrocaudillismo?), the loss of sovereignty in economic and financial decision-making, and the rampant social malaise of corruption. Corruption alone, if left unchecked, can undermine the current process of democratic consolidation and market transformation. If it is not to be shut out of the benefits of globalization, Latin America needs to invest more in education, public health, and infrastructure to successfully forge ahead in the twenty-first century. So far, however, it has not done so on a scale that its current and future needs justify.

This book is organized in three parts. Part I (Chapter 1) is an historical overview of Latin America's political economy of growth, development, stagnation and reforms since 1930, highlighting the rise of ECLA-structuralist models, the flowering of the bureaucratic-authoritarian regimes, and the transition to democracy and a market economy, or rather a market-friendly economy, all against the backdrop of globalization. Part II (Chapters 2, 3, and 4) analyzes the specific conditions under which Argentina, Brazil, and Chile discarded the statist-populist policies of the 1960s and what the military bureaucratic-authoritarian governments sought to accomplish during the 1970s and 1980s. Beneath the superficial resemblance among the military regimes of the ABC countries, there were fundamental philosophical and stylistic differences, especially in terms of how to resist and accommodate the external or global pressures for democratization and open-market systems. Part III (Chapters 5, 6, and 7) analyzes how the democratic civilian regimes have confronted the opportunities and challenges created by the globalization process.

The responses effected by civilian democratic regimes, especially during the phase of state reforms of the mid-1980s and early 1990s, were not always open, transparent, and beneficial to the long-term interests of the fragile but budding democracy and market. The next decade could be crucial. Argentina already collapsed under the weight of an imperfectly implemented neoliberalism. If no deepening of the reforms takes place and if no investment in new social and physical infrastructure is made, the transformation to the market economy and democracy will be incomplete. Soros might be right and Krugman could be prescient. The conclusion reviews pros and cons of the current policy thrust and alternatives by comparing the experiences of Latin America and Asia Pacific, especially against the backdrop of the Asian financial crisis of 1997–98.

Part I
Latin America in a New Age

1
Latin America in the Age of Globalization

Globalization at work

In 1993, Fernando Henrique Cardoso contributed a chapter to a volume entitled *The New Global Economy in the Information Age*.[1] A year earlier, the authors of the book had used the findings of their research to advise the Yeltsin government of Russia how to formulate its political and economic policies to thrive in the globalized economy. In it, Cardoso was preoccupied with new challenges that the South has to confront, as the 24-hour-a-day, 365-day-a-year world economy becomes increasingly more globalized, borderless, and stateless. The world was moving toward the New Millennium built on the twin foundations of democracy and economic freedom on the one hand, and innovative science and technology on the other. It has been the technological revolution of informatics, telecommunications, and transportation combined with the political and economic revolution of freedom and market that has been driving the processes of globalization.[2] As in the old world system of "dependency," the North dominated the new information. Gone was the Cold War and its intense superpower rivalry, along with the dual hegemonic worlds of the United States and the Soviet Union.

What has replaced the older "dependent" world system modality is a new "democratic-technological-scientific revolution" which has created a series of region-markets such as NAFTA, the EU, MERCOSUR, APEC, and others. Cardoso warns that unless the South joins these protean and revolutionary changes with sound structural reforms and modernization (selective opening of the domestic economy, heavy investment in education and R & D, and a realistic industrial policy), the developing world will be frozen out of the "democratic-

3

technological-scientific" race and will become "inconsequential." Worse, the South will be swallowed up by the North and will become "servants of the rich economies."[3] The "new dependency" defined by Cardoso involves not only an economic hierarchy between those who have embraced the tenets of the global information age and those who have not but also the survival and modernization of the whole of global society, developed and developing.

The global economy

The World Bank reported in 1999 that the world gross domestic product surpassed $30 trillion.[4] In mid-1999, the New York Stock Exchange boasted an asset capitalization of $11.7 trillion followed by Tokyo at $2.69 trillion, London also at $2.32 trillion, and Frankfurt at $1.03 trillion.[5] In a single day, the global financial bourses traded over $24 trillion. Foreign currency traders handled over $1.7 trillion in a single day. In 1989, it was $640 billion. The United States Treasury turned over $26 trillion every eight days. One New York stock broker said: "Now capital has wings."[6] And between 1992 and 2002, the elderly of the world would save $12 trillion. In 1994, tradable bonds, stocks, and currencies reached $41 trillion, growing three times faster than the rate of the world's combined gross domestic product.[7] The adherents of economic globalization see little or no future for the current nation state system. Kenichi Ohmae terms the nation-state irrelevant and "unnatural" in the globalized economy.[8] Ohmae goes a step further: a mismanaged national policy can destroy national wealth and even rob the country of opportunities to take advantage of the global train of economic abundance.[9] To them, the engine of globalization is capital market integration.

In such a $30-trillion world economy, no single nation, including the United States with its $8 trillion-plus GDP, can dominate the global economy, let alone manage it. Jeffrey Sachs estimates the age of the intense phase of globalization, or trade and financial integration of the seamless markets around the globe, to be from 15 to 20 years old,[10] while Susan Strange argues that the process has been unfolding in earnest for three decades.[11] To others, the current phenomenon of globalization dates back to at least 1890 and even to the mid-seventeenth century.[12] In this process of global wealth creation across borders and across cultures, the one obvious victim has been the nation-state.

Traditionally, the nation-state was the creator of wealth and prosperity for the mercantilist capitalism of the fifteenth through the nineteenth centuries.[13] *Within the borders* of the country, the national government set the rules for all economic activities. Powerful colonial empires successfully extended their sovereignty to overseas colonies, but such hegemonic powers were few in history, mostly confined to five or six western European states. The involvement of the state in commercial and political activities was an absolute necessity during this era, while the benefits of economic prosperity through colonial trade and later national industrialization included the pursuit of military ambitions which often went hand in hand with overseas trade activities and even reinforced the long-term national objective of world domination. Often the rise and fall of the great powers are the history of overseas expansion, colonization, the misuse of ill-gotten profits, and a massive expenditure for military adventurism.[14] Wealth bred military powers in history and that is still true to an extent. Colonial and neocolonial trade basically involved the metropolis and its overseas dependencies. The British, French, Dutch, and later American traders sought to exclude each other from their colonial commerce. Wars were fought over trade monopoly. Silver and gold bullion, slaves, and money were exchanged across borders, but its scope was always nation- and state-*bound*. Today, it is different. Financial assets, products, and services cross borders, often produced and financed in several countries and region-markets, thus creating global consumerism. The global trade of goods *alone* surpassed $11 trillion in 1998. In this world of integrated financing and trade, boosted by technology and science and fueled by spreading mass consumerism, the nation-state has been forced to find a new role. Peter Dicken goes further: "The State is dead ... long live the state."[15] The paradox of globalization is that the world economy is too big for a single nation-state to dominate, but the nation-state is too small to provide necessary services and goods to its citizens. National markets have become too small for companies and it has become the national policy of many countries to assist their corporations in securing a larger share of the world market. To some scholars, the nation-state still matters. Unless the national government accepts its changing role, the very survival of the nation-state is at stake, however.[16]

If trade and finance are propelling forces of globalization, there are plenty of downsides to them. The so-called "globaphobia" is nothing new. Industrializing England had Luddites. Karl Polanyi persuasively argued that the self-regulating market, the capitalism of the first half of the twentieth century, resulted in the great depression of the 1930s, the rise of fascist governments in Europe and Asia, global unemployment, resurgent nationalism, and finally the Second World War. The globalization of today has been blamed for "rising unemployment, falling real incomes, mass layoffs, cutbacks in public services, deteriorating working conditions, elimination of small farms and businesses, accelerating destruction of the environment, and loss of democratic control over their governments and societies."[17] Anthropologists worry about the mass destruction of indigenous societies, literally bulldozed out of existence.[18]

The old left, environmentalists, trade unions, and consumer advocates have united forces to oppose the globalization of the world economy. To them, transnational, multinational, and global corporations have replaced the nation-states. The global corporations, the World Bank, the International Monetary Fund, and the World Trade Organization have become too powerful, frequently trampling on the sovereign rights of nation-states.[19] The academic left are concerned with the rapid undoing of the last seven decades of the achievements of social democracy and socialism that had swept the world since the Russian Revolution in 1917 and especially after the end of World War II.[20] This new alliance is convinced that untamed global corporations would destroy everything. Wolfgang Sachs summarizes best the enviro-leftist consensus: "development is [the] cause[s] of rather than solution to our problems."[21] As in Europe, many leftists in Latin America have joined the environmental movement to oppose the relentless advance of multinational corporations, the foot soldiers of the current and future globalization.

Latin America is very vulnerable. Its principal exports have been raw materials, although an impressive array of industrialization projects have been implanted for the past four decades. The expanding trade and investment since 1990 has benefited well from the "most recent globalization" phase. Of the world's top ten hosts for foreign direct investment six were Latin American countries. Collectively, Latin America and the Caribbean garnered $38.6 billion of FDI in manufacturing in 1996. The world total FDI that year was a little over $349 billion.[22] *Latin Finance* has estimated that the total assets managed by international companies in Latin America are valued at $3.7 trillion and that foreigners invested over $110 billion in equity markets, including funds raised overseas. In 1989, Latin America had 1637 publicly listed companies. In 1996, the latest year for which data is available, the continent boasted 1760.[23] Taking a cue from the expanding global equity market, Latin America has taken advantage of this liquidity by selling off a vast number of state-owned enterprises. Privatization has brought in as much as $100 billion to Latin America in the 1990s. Between 1990 and 1997, Brazil garnered $34.4 billion, Argentina $27.9 billion and Chile $902 million.[24]

The globalization challenge, so eloquently expressed by Cardoso of Brazil, poses a double jeopardy to Latin America. It provides an immediate opportunity of attracting foreign direct investment and portfolio capital to stock markets. The Asian experience tells us that there is an implicit danger of attracting too much cash – more foreign portfolio capital than foreign direct investment – to still developing economies, even with the sound macroeconomic fundamentals as in Thailand, Korea, Malaysia, and Indonesia.[25] The second danger is that Latin America needs to invest more in education, health, infrastructure, and basic research in technology and science. As the saturation of the national market will inevitably force the continent to search for new international markets, the competitiveness of Latin America needs to be addressed. Cheap raw materials and equally cheap labor alone will not take Latin America too far into a highly competitive, information-technology-driven twenty-first century. That was precisely Cardoso's preoccupation.

Latin America: then and now

Latin America in the 1960s and 1980s remained among the world's most closed non-communist economies. But the model worked (Table 1.1). Its import-substituting industrialization (ISI) model and its populist social policy became the bedrock of Latin America's statist political economy. The world trade and investment practices were yet to become liberalized, but through multiple sets of bilateral agreements of trade and investment the world's economy was growing and in some areas, like Western Europe and Southeast Asia, small but significant progress was made toward regional integration. During the same decade of the 1960s, countries in Asia Pacific hastily abandoned their import-substituting industrialization policies and adopted neomercantilist approaches of export-promoting industrialization, as the limits of resource endowments and the size of domestic markets constricted a further expansion of the ISI model. Furthermore, Asian states eagerly responded to the then evolving international and global economic order.[26] Latin America continued to close its markets to outsiders.

Table 1.1: Fifteen Latin American and Other Countries: GNPs and Per Capitas, 1970 and 1996

Country	1970 GNP (US$billions)	1996 GNP (US$billions)	1996 Per Capita (US$)	Growth Rate between 1970 and 1996
Argentina	30.7	259.1	8,380	8.35 times
Brazil	35.6	709.6	4,400	19.9 times
Chile	8.2	70.1	4,860	8.5 times
Colombia	7.2	80.2	2,140	11.1 times
Costa Rica	0.985	9.1	2,640	9.2 times
Dominican Republic	1.5	12.8	1,600	8.6 times
Ecuador	1.7	17.5	1,500	10.2 times
El Salvador	1.0	9.9	1,700	9.9 times
Guatemala	1.9	16.0	1,470	8.4 times
Mexico	38.3	341.7	3,670	8.93 times
Panama	1.1	8.2	3,080	8.2 times
Paraguay	0.595	9.2	1,850	15.4 times
Peru	7.3	20.0	2,420	2.7 times
Uruguay	2.3	18.5	5,760	8.0 times
Venezuela	13.4	67.3	3,020	5.0 times
Japan	204.0	5,149.2	40,940	25.3 times
Switzerland	21.0	313.7	44,350	15.1 times
USA	1,012.0	7,433.5	28,020	7.3 times
World	2,808.0	29,519.0	5,130	10.4 times

Source: World Bank, *1998 World Development Indicators* (Washington, DC: World Bank, 1998), pp. 12–13.

It is worth mentioning that international political economy (IPE), defined herein as the interaction and intersection of the states and the markets on a global scale, is regulated *at present* on two levels – one still lingering in inter-state levels and another in the emergent supra-state region-market level. The days of the politics of inter-state relations defining the national and international markets are rapidly coming to a close; and the economics of new supra-state, regional, and global market places have redefined the politics of a nation-state. The nation-states ceased to be the "managers" of their economies.[27] Region-markets and region-states will regulate the economic life of the new millennium.

The genesis of the Latin American state and IPE

The political economy of the Latin American states was not consolidated until the second half of the nineteenth century. The economy had been in the hands of colonial landholding and mercantile families, whose political ties with the metropolis by the mid-eighteenth century were already weakening. Independence permitted the colonial land-holding and mercantile elites to stitch a new alliance with the world's other metropolises, Britain, France, and, by the onset of the twentieth century, the United States. Europe and the United States constituted the biggest markets for Latin America.

Between 1850 and 1930, the political and economic developments in Argentina, Brazil, and Chile evolved around the great familiocratic oligarchies of land, the Catholic Church, the military, foreign merchants and bankers, railroad builders, transatlantic shippers, and insurers who together constituted the new ruling elite, or, better yet, the elites of export economies. The market access to the new metropolis required restructuring the domestic politics to accommodate the new inter-state and inter-market relationship. Oligarchies owned and ran the country; Britain and the United States, in particular, turned Latin America into neocolonial appendages of raw material producers to feed their industrial machines that now supplied the world market. In this internationalizing setting, Argentina, Brazil, and Chile were practically colonies of Britain. Mexico valiantly resisted the aggression, wars, and temptations from its northern neighbor. But by Porfirian times (1877–1911), it too succumbed to the sphere of pervasive North American capitalism. Railroads, telegraphs, and other public works put in place during this era were prompted by the demands of the new metropolitan markets, not by the eccentric needs of Mexican society. The same can be said about other Latin America countries.[28]

This neocolonization engendered the rise of a new international political economy of inter-American relations. The US served as the de facto "state" for Latin America, while the entire hemisphere became the "market" for US products and services. The authoritarian state in Latin America constituted an integral part of this larger international political economy as a mere policy enforcer and stabilizer for the system. And the internationalization of the Latin American market as an extension of North American hegemonic capitalism and later multinational corporate domination constituted one pillar of the twentieth century IPE. By the 1980s, the Asian, especially Japanese, and the overwhelming European investment in raw material production, processing, manufacturing, and financial sectors began to counterbalance the US hegemony. The response from the United States was the establishment of region-markets, first NAFTA in 1994 and then FTAA, or the Free Trade Area of the Americas, to be established by 2005.

A variety of authoritarian states and their offspring

Between 1890 and 2000, Argentina, Brazil, and Chile, and, by extension, much of Latin America, came to know four distinct state systems: bourgeois-authoritarian (1890–1930), populist-authoritarian (1930–60), statist bureaucratic-authoritarian (1960–90), and, since 1990, the market-friendly open democratic states. This periodization roughly corresponds to that of Latin American economic history: the era of export economy based on agricultural, mineral, agropastoral, and forest products between 1850 and 1930; the period of inward-looking growth based on import-substitution industrialization[29] of 1930–60, spurred by such cataclysmic situations as the depression of the 1930s and the Second World War; the period of deliberate developmentalist and statist tutelage with overt and covert populist overtones; and, finally, the structural reform *cum* market-friendly economy since 1990. Chile is an exception, for it began the fourth phase of economic opening in the mid-1970s. To each of these periods, the Latin American state was forced to realign the existing political systems and structures of the economies.

The political economy of the bourgeois-authoritarian phase was one of the external dependency in the classical sense: the international economy turned Latin America into an exporter of unprocessed raw materials while the state subjugated its national policies to benefit the industrial core economies of the North Atlantic world. The populist era brought in highly politicized xenophobic times of economic nationalism to satisfy the needs of domestic markets by a series of import-substituting measures coupled with the proliferation of state-owned enterprises (SOEs), supplanting multinational corporations (MNCs) and creating domestic private monopolies. The state gained both economic and political power of its own with a bloated state bureaucracy and generous social programs for workers and the middle classes.

The closed economy with myriad import restrictions and a hostile investment environment drove foreign money away, kept the existing foreign investment at bay in the name of *economic* independence and *economic* nationalism, and bred a new domestic industrial bourgeoisie. The so-called ISI alliance of the *dirigiste* state, industrialists, workers, the armed forces, and other xenophobic groups encapsulated the national autonomy. MNCs and domestic private corporations, key players in the market, were effectively checked in Argentina and Brazil, and neutralized in Chile during the brief socialist-Marxist rule of 1970–73.

The third phase, statist bureaucratic-authoritarian (B-A), reshaped populism as a power ideology, while retaining the nationalistic economic policies *with strong populist features* intact. Bureaucratic-authoritarian governments were dominated by the military, civilian career technocrats, and institutions of economic policy making and implementation, in a close alliance with domestic and international corporations.[30] The B-A regimes restricted foreign direct investment to certain areas, while seeking external financing for their development projects. Borrowed money granted the B-A regimes the autonomy of financial management and responsibility, while foreign direct investment gave to the investor, not to the state, the freedom of choosing a project. Almost all Latin American countries adopted a jumble of laws restricting the movement of private foreign and domestic capital, although it had low domestic savings to satisfy the cravings of the B-A regime's building mania. Tapping money overseas, or "external savings," as Delfim Netto used to say, was the way.

The principal feature of the B-A political economy was the consolidation of state power and autonomy in political and economic decision-making, while the state expanded its dependence on external capital, technology, and the market. As such, B-A regimes occurred in those countries with a degree of development and modernization of import substitution.[31] This economic model eventually collapsed by the 1980s, as the accelerated globalization of the world economy resulted in the primacy of private, this time, global capital, which instead chose to make direct investment in cross-border manufacturing and financial markets. The economic globalization simply overwhelmed the Latin American state machine. The economic universe changes faster than the political universe. Thus, the antiquated states drove foreign direct investment away and encouraged the flight of domestic capital. Between 1983 and 1988, world trade expanded by 5 percent annually, while foreign direct invesment during the same period increased by 20 percent per annum. And the best projection for the 1990s was that foreign direct investment from OECD countries would increase by 220 percent. The changing investment climate and trends of the global economy drove Latin America, cut off from easy money, to open up. As the world of the 1990s used new regimes of trade and investment, Latin America geared up for the new day.[32]

Politically, a B-A regime is "exclusionary."[33] It sought to exclude the populist sectors from the political processes while sharing parts of the economic benefits with them. The state was also undermocratic, both in Marxist and liberal senses of the word. Rarely did it allow free elections as the means to renew its legitimacy. Instead, it mandated itself to rule. If elections were allowed they were manipulated and often flawed, as in the case of Brazil (1964–85). The Chilean and Argentinian regimes discarded the national congresses altogether, thus having no need to hold even token elections. The Brazilian military kept the national congress and state legislatures open, although the legislative branches suffered constant harassment and interventions from the military, such as the systematic suspension of political rights of too vocal opposition deputies and senators. The emaciated judicial system came under easy domination of the military in all three countries. In the ABC countries, new authoritarianism represented the political will of the post-populist alliance of the military-civilian technocrats, international capital, and national industrial bourgeoisie, Peter Evans's "the triple alliance." Together they pursued the regime's objective of advancing industrialization and obtaining economic self-sufficiency.[34] Brazil was the only one of the three that also promoted exports, while retaining the historic ISI objectives. Eventually, this balance could not be sustained as globalization speeded up. Furthermore, it should be pointed out that the Brazilian military "were not enamored of free market models," in spite of their frequent pronouncements in favour of capitalism.[35]

The degree of linkages and integration with global financial capital and export markets by each of the three countries also determined the degree of political styles of governance and the stability of regimes. The more a country's economy depended on external capital and an overseas market, the more political relaxation was allowed. Brazil was the export champion among the three military regimes, and its dependence on external financing exceeded those of Argentina and Chile combined. For this reason, the style of the Brazilian military governance was more open and even relaxed thus allowing the continued operation of the legislative system. Argentina and Chile did not have to accommodate the international community by making such a concession, for their economies were more insulated from external pressures.

Fernando Henrique Cardoso considered the B-A regime an outgrowth of modernization. He cautioned that the concept should be used sparingly; a response by the military to limit and undo the leftist (populist) development model and to reorient the state and economy back to the capitalist development path with a restructured but docile bureaucracy set the regime's key public policy objectives.[36] How did this statist bureaucratic-authoritarian regime come about? And how was its political economy structured? Guillermo O'Donnell, Fernando Henrique Cardoso, and others argued that after decades of intense modernization such as the ISI push for inward-looking economic development and the nationalist-populist politics of redistribution, a series of political, economic, and social structural crises set in. Civil society responded with the forging of a military-dominated B-A regime.[37] This is what happened in Brazil in 1964, Argentina in 1966 and again in 1976, and Chile in 1973.

In 1988, O'Donnell updated his now celebrated B-A regime theory first unveiled in 1973. As Latin American countries went through intense political mobilization and incorporation of the populist sectors into the state system, their economies were also undergoing an equally intense transnationalization or globalization. Increasingly, the continent had to depend on external finances, technologies, and information to implement its nationalist-populist economic and social programs, an untenable situation over time. Historically, the savings and capital accumulation rates were low in Latin America.[38] The domestic savings were not sufficient to finance the grandiose development projects. Furthermore, the availability and application of foreign direct investment capital could not satisfy the needs of the Latin American state. As the state consumed more and borrowed more, it saved less and invested even less. The accumulation of capital, concentration of resources, distribution of wealth, and consumption of surplus functioned erratically, creating structural disequilibria. Exports fell and a shortage of foreign exchange deepened the economic crises. The Latin American dependent capitalism was out of synch with the globalization of the world economy. The economy ceased to reproduce or grow. When the state that depended on the support of the populist coalition could no longer lavish extravagant or flamboyant social programs, the political power base began to erode. Economic crises bred social crises, and the armed forces, the national guard, and the national police intervened to restore law and order. The structural reforms and restoration of political stability became their chief preoccupation.

Both in Argentina and Chile, researchers have shown that the macroeconomic imbalances and disequilibria led to the breakdown of the nationalist-populist state, including political party and trade union leadership.[39] The popular sector sought to expand, if not defend, their political space by undemocratic means; hoarding and uncalled for markup of prices among small and medium-sized companies became the norm; workplace discipline collapsed as strikes, stoppage, and violence escalated; the coercive power of parties and unions corroded, as they failed to deliver benefits; and, finally, the disaffected opted for urban guerrilla warfare, riots and even coups to correct the disequilibria. In an empirical sense, the crises that ushered in B-A regimes in Argentina, Brazil, and Chile were similar in their origins, but their intensity and historical etiology differed. The illusion of the self-sufficiency of the B-A regime was soon replaced by the need to borrow externally, which in turn increased the regime's dependency on the global financial market, thus corroding the autonomy of the regime. Gradually, this integration with the global marketplace became difficult to control and even impossible to resist. The changes in the global economic arena of the 1960s through the 1980s were felt as intensely in all three countries, and once statist, populist, and B-A regimes fell one after another.

Incompatibility of the B-A regime with the global economy

The convergence and divergence of populist and conservative forces, the intersecting of the state and the market, and the transformation of the domestic economy were more common in Latin America when the "left, center and right" were never clearly definable and where boundaries were never well delineated. Often political ideologies, economic cultures, and history have played a greater role in the region's political economy. To the conservatives of Western Europe and the United States, the state was the sum of a "representative democracy" of property holders. The enlarging of citizens' participation in political processes should be ideally left to the free market and its distributive role, that is, how fast and how many property holders the market could create and how well the state could enforce laissez-faire rules.[40] The more citizens became property holders, the stronger the state's democracy. The better the state implemented market-friendly rules, the more laissez-faire freedom each individual enjoyed. For this reason, conservatives called for separating the state from the class-based capitalist market system. The state and the market should function harmoniously but each should not intervene in the other. But, in reality, market failures were prone to occur and state interventions were inevitable, as the ruling elite sought to save the economic status quo.[41] This is precisely how the political economy of the B-A regimes in Argentina, Chile, and Brazil defined their roles. Chile was the most successful of the three; Argentina was the most thorough in persisting in

ISI; and Brazil was the least orthodox by mixing ISI policies with export-promotion objectives.

Core groups and actors in B-A regimes

The bureaucratic-authoritarian regimes in Argentina, Brazil, and Chile included both new and old players. Similarly, the rules of the game selectively retained the old and added new recruits to the regimes. Core groups that made up the internal and external members of the B-A regimes in the ABC countries came from Evans's "triple alliance" – the domestic capital, the state, and multinationals. The alliance between military-dominated states and the markets was never formal but implicit. And no less important actors were middle-class professionals, top echelon career civil servants, especially those in the country's diplomatic service, and policy planning staff largely drawn from university professorial ranks. In each country, the role of the core groups differed. In Brazil, the MNCs played a lesser role to the state and the SOEs, while in Argentina the multinationals dwarfed both SOEs and national private firms.[42] In Chile, the Pinochet regime treated the Trade and Production Confederation, the national association of industrial and commercial chambers, which by the mid-1980s held a seat in the government council of economic decision makers, in a deferential manner. In all three countries, retired military officers either held key posts in SOEs or worked for major multinational and national companies, thus completing the networking between the market and the state.

Although Argentinian, Brazilian, and Chilean universities were known for their leftist radicalism and stout opposition to the military, they produced a good number of technocrats for the B-A regimes. A technocrat is often an academic specialist on economics and finances with political savvy, who eventually rises to the highest level of elected or appointed office. And I might add that technocrats mastered the art of compromise, often working with civilian and military opposition by overwhelming them with their technical expertise.[43] In Argentina, Domingo F. Cavallo, an economics professor at the University of Córdoba, became president of the Central Bank in the last years of the military regime of the early 1980s.[44] In Brazil, António Delfim Netto and Mario Henrique Simonsen, ministers of finance and planning during the 1960s and 1970s, were faculty members at the University of São Paulo and the Fundação Getúlio Vargas in Rio, respectively. In

Chile, the University of Chile and the Catholic University were the major suppliers of economists and technocrats to the military regime. Hernán Buchi and José Piñera are some of the best technocrats of Chile. Many of the "Chicago Boys" were also faculty members at these institutions and technocrats.[45]

Political economy of reform and adjustment

In Argentina and Chile, the governments have been able to forge national consensus that has brought the major factions and parties to support the economic policy of reform and adjustment. In Chile, the left joined the government at the expense of its historical commitment to revolutionary militancy. In Argentina, Menem's policy effectively co-opted the militant labor and the moderate left to support the reform, while locking out leftist terrorists. In Brazil, Fernando Collor de Mello, a governor of an obscure Northeastern state, was elected president in the 1990 election, defeating the candidates of the traditional parties. He introduced a host of draconian reforms and was able to plant the seed of the state reform that is in place today. The untimely removal of Collor from office rudely interrupted the momentum of state modernization, but his successor, Itamar Franco (1992–94), was able to hold on to both the right and the left keeping them in check by avoiding the implementation of potentially inflammatory policies such as massive privatization and rapid deregulation of the domestic market.[46]

The breakdown of the old political practices and values played a momentous role in reshaping Latin America. Politicians of traditional parties did not fare well in elections, or were replaced by a new crop of unconventional politicians willing to forge new electoral bases at the grassroots level, often reaching out beyond a party's ideological confines. In Argentina, a provincial politician from La Rioja, one of the poorest parts of the country, and someone outside the mainstream Peronism, secured the party's presidential nomination and went on to win the election in 1989.[47] In Chile, the Christian Democratic Party (PDC) elected a president twice (1989 and 1993) only as one of the several center-leftist parties in the national coalition of the *concertación* wherein the CD ideology no longer dominates.[48] In Peru, two candidates from the dominant parties of the 1950s lost the election to a Japanese-Peruvian who built his campaign with the grassroots support of evangelical churchgoers. Similar trends of unconventional electoral victories by outsiders were seen in Venezuela, Ecuador, and Colombia.[49] The elections of Carlos Salinas de Gortari and Ernesto Zedillo Ponce de León, neither of whom were the first pick of the dominant party's dinosaurs of Mexico in 1987 and 1994, added another piece of undisputed evidence that the traditional parties in a successful transitional political economy were no longer firmly in command.

"Cosmopolitical"[50] economy of Latin America

The growing trends of the globalization of the Latin American economy and the rapid advent of region-markets would play a role in defining the relationship between the state and the market for the 1990s and onward.[51] These changes brought new players on the scene. The globalization of crossborder financial markets as the result of the liberalization and deregulation of banking practices and investment rules throughout the Third World altered the way to do business. At the same time, the power of central banks diminished as well as changed.[52] Major private companies in Latin America obtained investment capital in New York, London, Paris, Zurich, Singapore, Hong Kong, and Tokyo, where money was cheaper and where the central banks promoted international lending as a state's globalization strategy. In this connection, one can convincingly argue that if a Latin borrower could go to overseas lenders then a country's monetary policy no longer belonged to the central bank.[53] The power to control the internal stock of money had not only been eroded but had always been undermined by the quick transferability of megabyte money.

Such a change came hard and expensively in the 1980s, when Mexico, Brazil, and Argentina declared insolvency and defaulted on their external debts (the default was not official but de facto). The rise of 1 percent in the US interest rate added another $1 billion to the annual interest payment by Mexico and Brazil, which held in excess of $100 billion each of external debts. In part, the debt crisis came about, as the US interest rates in the late 1970s soared to double digits; that in turn attracted a flood of money from the international financial markets to the US. This reduced the lending to Latin America and other developing countries. The Reagan administration resorted to external borrowing to finance its conventional military buildup as well as star wars programs, while keeping tax rates low at home. This stimulated the massive inflow of foreign money into the US that could have gone to Latin America. It became clear that no country's economy by the mid-1980s, especially its finances and fiscal policy, was autonomous, insulated, and even sovereign.

The concept of sovereignty is often defined by the power to "base political authority on the principle of territorial exclusivity" and to compel others to abide by one's will.[54] This Westphalian concept collapsed under the weight of global financial integration. By the early 1990s, none of the ten largest banks in the world was American. The first nine were Japanese and the tenth German. The largest US bank, Citicorp, ranked twelfth.[55] The Daichi Kankyo, the world's largest, had capital ($446.9 billion) equivalent to Brazil's GDP, and the tenth (the Deutsche Bank) boasted capital ($302 billion) over seven times Chile's GDP of $42 billion. In direct and indirect ways, these global banks collectively had an impact on any Latin American country's economy equal to, if not more than that of, the US Federal Reserve. And many Latin American banks tied the lending rates to such global rates as LIBOR (London Inter-bank Borrowing Rate) or the US Federal Reserve rate. Now financial globalization was complete.

Latin America in the age of economic multipolarity

The US economy had been under assault by the globalizing tendencies of the world economy and its key actors. The devaluation of the US dollar in relation to the Japanese yen – by mid-1995, the dollar sank to the historic low of 80 yen – and other European currencies had devastating effects on the US economy and especially its fiscal policy. Prominent US academics and government officials had predicted since the mid-1980s that the dollar's devaluation would make US goods cheaper and more attractive: hence, Japan would import more. This would lead to a significant reduction of the trade deficit against Japan. Instead, the devaluation made the yen-based assets of Japanese companies double their value in dollar terms, thus making it possible for Japanese corporations to finance and expand their overseas operations in cheaper dollars and hence outbid and outspend US rivals in Latin America, Southeast Asia, and Sub-Saharan Africa. Doom sayers or Japan bashers even suggested that Japan would take over key US assets at home, hollowing out the American economy.[56] The former chairman of the Federal Reserve commented that the Reagan administration "had fallen into the market trap of seeming to promote depreciation of the dollar as an elixir for our problems."[57] An elixir or not, the yen's appreciation debased the US currency and in the process dethroned the

US as the world's financial leader. This was more than the politics of exchange rates. It was the signal that no longer was the US able to dominate the world economy, let alone Japan's. Globalization does not discriminate.

The demise of the US dollar brought about both positive and negative consequences to Latin America. The political economy of development in Argentina, Brazil, and Chile in the days of the cheap dollar and the strong yen and equally strong Deutsche Mark confronted the state policy makers afresh with the need for reform and adjustment. While the US no longer remained the hegemonic power for Latin America's economic and financial markets this brought about a new beginning for Latin America. In theory, expanding trade and the cheaper dollar should have helped Latin America's external debt. But this did not happen, because almost all of Latin American exports are conducted in dollars. Latin America has not adopted the basket of currencies, as in Asia Pacific, to hedge the dollar against the yen and the mark. The danger of remaining in the dollar zone for Latin America is disconcerting. For the time being, however, the advantages outweigh the disadvantages. The monetary and economic stability of Argentina, Brazil, Mexico, and Panama are based on linking their currencies to the dollar.[58]

To a large extent, the macroeconomic reform and policy adjustments in Latin America were conditioned by these new global dynamics among the world's strong currencies and weak currencies. Thus, the international political economy of the 1980s and the early 1990s changed forever the role of the government in monetary policy in Latin America, the United States, Japan, and Europe. The government no longer had to depend on fiscal policy to pull its economy through. Countries with low domestic savings can always borrow. Since 1990 economic development and growth in Latin America and Asia Pacific have depended not only more on a country's ability and agility to attract international capital and increase its exports to the world's major markets, but also on a new economic structure that can absorb the jarring impacts of the currency fluctuations and interest rates in the global financial marketplace.

In the late 1980s and early 1990s, as much as 60 percent of Japan's trade surplus was derived from the US. Asian countries ran chronic deficits with Japan and a perennial trade surplus with the US. It was their US trade surplus that financed their deficits with Japan.[59] Therefore, Japan's short-term and long-term economic well-being depended on how *long* the US market remained *open* to its exports and

Asian exports. Japan's acceptance of the 1985 Plaza accord of devaluing the dollar, or appreciating the yen by 10 percent overnight and 30 percent in three months, was a strategic move to thwart the growing protectionist sentiment in the US Congress and American society at large. It was better for Japan to give in to the US demand and instead finance Japan's economic expansion in Southeast Asia with the cheap dollar. Japan now exported to the US markets from its Asian platforms as well as from Japan proper. In hindsight, the Reagan administration made the mistake of the century. Latin American had been caught in the currency battles of the titans and had no power to influence the outcome. This was the first lesson of financial globalization.

Part II

From Populism to Military Rule and Democracy

2
Argentina: the Birth of Latin American Populism

The road to populism

In the political economy of industrialization, Alexander Gerschenkron asserted that the state traditionally played a strong and directive role over the market. Industrialization occurred under a strong autonomous state. To industrialize, the state must divert national income from consumption to investment. Furthermore, the Harvard economic historian dwelled on the significant "tension between the prevailing economic conditions and the promise offered by rapid industrial development."[1] How and in what form this is accomplished depends on the history and political and economic culture of a given country. The transition from agrarianism to industrialism in Argentina took place while the state was still weak and not autonomous. Argentina possessed all the requisites of becoming a corporatist state by the 1880s, as the state was indisputably dominated by the principal economic interests of export agriculture. Transforming such an economy that was highly advanced in organization and linked to (even depended on) the outside market, Europe, into an autonomous industrialized economy became the national political obsession. Because liberal democracy failed to distribute national wealth equitably, a variety of anticapitalist and anti-elitist movements vied to replace the old regime. Populism triumphed by the eve of the First World War as the Argentinian response to the economic inequity and social injustice of capitalism strove to establish a populist state by stamping out the domination of political power by the elites of the export economy.[2]

Populism was a reactionary anticapitalist response during the century of the 1880s through the early 1980s. Historians have pointed out that while populism occurred in rural areas in the United States, it was a dominantly *urban* phenomenon in Latin America. Although the attraction of the populist ideology was pervasive throughout the continent, it became the bedrock for national politics in some countries. Mexico, Argentina, Venezuela, Uruguay, Costa Rica, and Brazil had a sustained period of populism, while other countries such as Peru, Chile, Bolivia, and Nicaragua intermittently experimented with populist policies or elected populist regimes to power for a brief period. In this chapter, the international political economy of Argentina, the grandfather of Latin America's populist tradition, will be examined. What happened to Argentina during its populist apogee (1913–89) was not unique, however. Argentina set the pace for Latin America in form, substance, and style of populist practices. Because it was the richest country in South America, its populist policy was more lavish than others. More importantly, the ideology was a sustained societal response of the underdeveloped economy to the real and perceived threat posed by the capitalist core of the world economy. Argentina was also the home of the earlier dependency thinking. The founder and advocate of cepalismo was Raúl Prebisch, an Argentinian banker and founder of CEPAL.

Most often, populism is defined as an urban working-class movement joined by disaffected upper- and middle-class professionals and led by a charismatic leader with the common objective of co-sharing state power with populist classes to expand their political base through electoral manipulations, to implement a growth strategy via nonmarket approaches, and to redistribute the national income through a variety of social equity-oriented programs. In some societies, populist policies promoted reformist objectives without destroying the existing state sector. In others, to borrow the World Bank criteria, new populist regimes restructured the existing state systems and established between the state and the market almost revolutionary but *clientelistic* political, economic, and social relationships. In this sense, populism ideologically straddled the right and the left, thus conjuring the connotation of the "populist left" and the "populist right" at once.[3] The philosophical dilemma for populism was how to distance itself from communism and fascism, while retaining many of the same public policies and looking after the interests of the same urban working-class and lower-middle-class clientele.

Latin America had many populisms. Alan García of Peru sought to remain populist (Aprista variety), while dissociating himself from the Latin American left and while strengthening his ties to the Socialist International. Also vigorous debate raged among the Latin American left over the exact relationship between Castrorite communists in Cuba and populist goals in Latin America. The Ortega brothers in Nicaragua desperately sought economic and military support from Cuba and the Soviet Union, but the timing was wrong. Socialism was at the twilight of its life and neither Cuba nor the Soviet Union came to rescue the Ortegas. A free election booted them out of power. The fact that populism could be exploited by Vargas, Perón, García, Castro, and the Ortegas all at once demonstrates the elusiveness of the ideology and at the same time its chameleon-like versatility to adapt to anticapitalist and anti-elitist situations.[4]

Alfred Stepen went one step further: he described the military regime of Peru, especially the Velasco rule (1968–72), as sufficiently "inclusionary" and "reformist" to qualify for military populism. The development ideology of the officer corps reflected much of the continent's archetypal populist tendencies such as *dirigiste* state planning, pro-urban labor, pro-middle and pro-lower classes, state paternalism in social programs, and frequent state intervention in the economy.[5] Jorge Castañeda blamed the destruction of the communist parties in Argentina, Chile, Mexico, and Brazil on populism and its variations such as Peronism, Getulism, the ideology of the Partido Revolucionario Institucional of Mexico, and socialism.[6]

This was the core strength of populism in Latin America, its cross-ideological and multiclass appeal, and its ability to stay in power, immune to external economic and political pressures. It was a political economy system that thrived in pre-globalization times. Political scientists emphasize the mass mobilization and party/state incorporation (or merger in the Italian case) dimensions of populism as the two parts of the paradigm shift in Latin America's political economy. Others point out that some military regimes such as Peru's (1968–75) exhibited "inclusionary" tendencies in the mobilization of both urban and rural masses into the nascent political system.[7]

It was the economic realm where the hard battles were fought by populists and their adversaries. The rise and fall of Latin American populism that stretched for almost a century was profoundly influenced and shaped by the inter-state relations and globalization of the world economy. Economists frequently associate Latin American populism with a set of policy objectives with the following characteristics: state-led and state-managed growth goals and income redistribution, which often led to the proliferation of state-owned enterprises which served both economic and socio-political purposes; populist goals achieved by "nonmarket" policies such as import-substituting industrialization, wherein the state was the pivotal force, while "inflation" and "deficit" financing of development projects and social programs, and ignoring or resisting "external constraints" by insulating the domestic market were the key features.[8] Argentina fit all four characteristics and then more.

The economic policies of populism worked well from the 1930s through the 1960s, the period that coincided with the growth of relative economic insularity, little or no progress in international free trade practices, and the expansion of national economies along the lines of allegiance in the context of the Cold War. It was only during the 1970s that the globalizing tendencies of the national and regional economies in the United States, Japan and Western Europe began to accelerate, leaving Latin America's closed nonmarket economies still behind the new liberalizing trends in the emerging global economy. Only then did Latin American populism begin to show its tattered face, and by the early 1980s, led by Chile, Latin America began to reject the populist legacy en masse and revert back to the neoliberal market economy model, which was substantially different from the pre-1929 genre.

The making of a populist Argentina

No other country in the world, including the former Soviet Union, has been to both economic paradise and hell and managed to revert to a market economy as successfully as Argentina. Argentina spent more than seven decades with the economic model that eventually failed its 32 million citizens. The salvo of the Russian Revolution was fired the year after Hipólito Yrigoyen was sworn in as Latin America's first populist president in 1916. By 1989, the populist legacy of Argentina was completely wrecked by the personal excesses of Juan Domingo Perón, the prince of the Justicialista Party.

In the 1930s, Argentina ranked among the world's top five richest countries in per capita terms. By the end of the Second World War, the country still ranked among the top ten. In 1991, according to Carlos Saúl Menem, then president of Argentina, it ranked eighty-fifth.[9] The calculation of the World Bank, however, showed that Argentina's ranking was considerably higher than President Menem suggested. It ranked twenty-fourth ($93.3 billion) in the gross domestic products (GDPs) of the 125 countries that the Bank monitored. In per capita, Argentina ranked fortieth ($2370) among the World Bank's reporting group. In the Western Hemisphere, it held the eigth place in the 1991 per capita ranking. Only the United States ($21 790), Canada

($20 370), Trinidad and Tobago ($3610), Brazil ($2680), Uruguay ($2560), Venezuela ($2560), and Mexico ($2490) were ahead of Argentina.

In 1981, the country's per capita was $3286. Between 1980 and 1991, the growth rate of Argentina was negative, or –3.2 percent. The only other country in the Western Hemisphere which outpaced Argentina's negative growth performance was Guyana which recorded –3.3 percent.[10] The popular dictum of the 1980s being the "lost decade" was closer to home in Argentina than Brazil or Chile. Between 1984 and 1990, Argentina registered three years of negative growth: –6.6 in 1985, –1.9 in 1988, and –6.2 in 1989. The last year Alfonsín was in office, 1989, the country showed a decline in three: fishing (–9.2 percent), manufacturing (–7.1 percent), and construction (–24.4 percent).[11] And curiously, if populism preaches the anti-status quo and champions reform, Menem's abandonment of the decades-long legacy was politically astounding, or even revolutionary. He had to adopt a market economy to blow life into the moribund Argentinian economic corpse.

The early or sunrise phase: 1880–1930

The mass disenchantment with the nineteenth century's unbridled capitalism, especially the variety that Britain had nurtured and pervasively imposed throughout its formal colonies and informal dependencies such as Latin America set the stage for the rise of Argentinian populism. More so than other Latin American economies, Argentina's growth between 1880 and 1930 was truly stunning. During the first three decades of the twentieth century, the growth of Argentina was better (4.6 percent) than that of Canada (3.4 percent), Brazil (3.3 percent), the United States (2.9 percent), and Australia (2.6 percent).[12] The political influence of the Positivists and the Generation of 1880 laid the groundwork for establishing a modern state and the era of unlimited material growth that strengthened the tightly-held authoritarian rule by the oligarchy of the export economy – and owners, railroad companies, stockyard operators, meat packers, bankers, insurers, and maritime shippers.

This "order and progress" firmly placed Argentina as the leader of the South Atlantic, and by the 1910s, the economic prosperity successfully pitted Argentina against the United States as a rival power in the struggle for the hegemony over Latin America. Over 90 percent of Argentina's exports constituted agricultural products – beef and wheat

– and 85 percent went to Western Europe. International investment during this period increased phenomenally, as Argentina became the only Latin American country that did not default its external debt at that time. Britain, in particular, was bullish on Argentina's economic future and invested in that economy with a vengeance. This kind of capitalism, however, was neither kind to the Argentinian working class nor exhibited *noblesse oblige* of social justice, though Britain's state policy of internationalization paid off handsomely.

The period from 1913 to 1930 ushered in the "gilded age" for the South Atlantic republic, deepening its dependency on Britain and at the same time begetting an incipient industrial economy. The British Isles imported about 30 percent of all Argentinian goods, while the United States consistently absorbed less than 9 percent per annum. Over half the international investment came from the British, while Italians, Spaniards, and other peoples from the Mediterranean world, including the Arabs, provided much of Argentina's workforce. While the rich got richer and the poor got poorer, political and social reforms were much debated but were slow to come. The lacuna of the domestic political and social conscience for equity for the workers was further compounded by an acute impact of the pre-World War I depression, when the Bank of England raised its interest rate in 1913. A year later, the First World War disrupted the much needed export expansion for the sagging Argentinian economy. As exports declined, urban unemployment began to soar, distant landowners received less profits from the exports, and an inflow of fresh foreign capital ceased.[13] The economy built on exports was too volatile and depended too much on external events for growth and prosperity. The Argentinians felt helpless and wanted more control over their destiny.

This was the first crisis of Argentinian capitalism. As a peripheral but fully integrated player in the world's raw materials market, Argentina was the first to feel the adverse impact of policy changes such as the interest rates in England. The global linkage was there, though not as apparent and real as in the 1980s and 1990s. The election of Hipólito Yrigoyen, the candidate of the Unión Cívica Radical (UCR), or Radicals, was a palpable but nationalistic response to international capital. It was an anticapitalistic expression of the frustrated Argentinians, victims of the capitalist world system then in the hands of the British. The first Yrigoyen administration (1916–22) was marred by crippling internecine political fights between the traditional oligarchies and the newly emerging UCR middle- and lower-class alliance. Also during the 1910s and 1920s, Argentina was laying foundations for its industrial economy. On the eve of World War I, Argentina was the ninth largest trader in the world, eighth in exports and tenth in imports. For the ten-year period of 1913–23, the number of factories increased from 48 779 to some 61 000. The value of the industrial production soared from 1.9 billion pesos to 2.9 billion during the same period. The most notable achievement was the establishment of the national oil monopoly and Latin America's first oil SOE, Yacimientos Petrolíferos Fiscales (YPF) which lasted until 1993, when it was privatized.[14] The YPF was a mantra of Argentina's national energy sovereignty and independent industrial policy.

Unlike the earlier industrialization in Western Europe and the United States, that of Argentina occurred during the periodic economic crises in the capitalist core. The First World War, the Depression of 1929, and the Second World War represented such crisis points, during which time Argentina was forced to industrialize. This import-substituting industrialization was unplanned, externally imposed, and spontaneous. It was a somewhat disorganized and hurried process. As in Brazil and Mexico, Argentina's textile industries captured as much as half of the domestic market from European and American competitors. Typically, these market expansions occurred first in such major and dynamic economic hubs as agriculture and mining centers – Santa Fe in Argentina, São Paulo in Brazil, and Moneterrey in Mexico.[15] This circumstantial or imitative industrialization in Argentina often resulted in the duplication of the core's manufacturing systems, down to the adoption of technologies.[16] As happened elsewhere in Latin America, when each crisis was over and Europe and the United States resumed their exports of manufactured goods, the industrialization of Latin America faltered and the renewed competition from the capitalist core forced infant industries out of business altogether.

By the end of the 1920s, Argentina once again reverted to the old mode of exporting raw materials and importing manufactures. Between 1923 and 1935, the number of Argentinian industrial establishments shrank by 37 percent and their workforce by a fifth.[17] The disenchantment with capitalism deepened and xenophobic nationalism soared. And there was a dire need to reform the Irigoyen populism.

The classical or golden phase: 1945–66

The second turning point in Argentina's economic history began in 1930. Reeling from the impact of the depression, Argentina signed in 1932 the Roca-Runciman Treaty with Great Britain, in a desperate attempt to shore up its depressed economy. The agreement called for Britain to purchase Argentinian beef at the pre-1931 level, while British exports received preferential treatment in the Argentinian market. In the subsequent years the plummeting price of beef drove many ranchers to ruination. The government of Argentina was determined to avoid the recurrence of the industrial shakeout of the 1920s by imposing stiff tariffs on British products, thus defending the market share for Argentinian manufacturers. The British claimed such a measure was a violation of the 1932 treaty. First the Uriburu junta and later the Concordancia government adopted a firm nationalistic import-substituting policy.[18] The policy emerged out of the dual necessity of preserving jobs in the urban areas and launching a new economic policy in the post-depression era, the era of the disintegrating world economy and rampant protectionism.

The role of the state in the economy after 1930 and especially after 1943 with the rise of Perón to power underwent a dramatic change. Before then, the state's investment in the economy reached about 11 percent (89 percent of which were still private) and was restricted to infrastructure, education, and health. However, after the depression, what defined the Argentinian state was its new ascending economic role. State intervention, a corollary to its ability to invest in the general economy, increased by recapitalizing such existing SOEs as the YPF, creating new entities such as the Fabricaciones Militares, and establishing federal and provincial regulatory agencies that supervised the private sector economy. By the end of World War II, the state portion of the investment rose to 25.3 percent of the total and by the end of the decade a whopping 35.3 percent.[19] This trend of the expansionist trajectory of the populist state continued through the years of political vagaries of several coups, attempted coups, and crippling labor strikes. In fact, many regulatory measures introduced in the 1930s and the early 1940s prepared the way for the rise of Peronism and the creation of the Latin American populist Leviathan.

Perón to power

The guiding ideology of Perón's GOU (the acronym has several expansions: Group of United Officers; Group of Organic Unity; Government, Order, Unity; and Group Working for Unification), contrary to the official United States allegation at that time, was not fascism, nor even pro-Nazism.[20] The country was still manipulated by the traditional elites, in cahoots with international capitalists. The railroads were controlled by the British and French; the meat-packing businesses were in the hands of US firms; public utilities were owned and operated by US and Swiss companies; the automobile industry was run by Americans, and construction companies were either German or Dutch. A full 45 percent of the country's industry was foreign owned. The civilian regimes since 1930 had given lip service to democracy, but in fact they perfected the fraudulent electoral processes, intervened in provinces at will, and brutally suppressed the masses. What the GOU advocated was a strong and autonomous state that could not be manipulated by key domestic and foreign economic interests, conservative nationalism that would secure complete and full independence for the nation, and a revolution that would fundamentally change the country's economic and political fabric. One Argentinian historian pointed out that because the GOU harbored some of the same aspirations advocated by fascism it did not make the members Nazis. There is no doubt that Nazi Germany was the object of GOU adulation and respect, however.[21] Perón carefully cultivated the support of labor leaders, only after being rebuffed and rejected by traditional political party leaders. By the end of the war, Perón emerged as the unchallenged champion of organized labor, if not its most ardent spokesman. Under his aegis, new unions were created for wine, utilities, and sugar workers. He also strengthened the existing unions of railroad and dock workers by granting generous government support.

"Third way" of development

The nationalization and introduction of state control of key industries began to take off as the first of Perón's many nationalistic projects but in a "third way" (neither capitalist nor communist) of a development model. Import-substitution was going to be intensified and deepened. Awash with plentiful foreign reserves accumulated during the Second World War, Perón embarked on a series of projects sponsored under the "Act of Economic Independence." Between 1947 and 1952, railroads, utilities, port facilities, meat-packing plants, petroleum and natural gas, and other foreign-owned industries were either bought out or nationalized. The government built no fewer than 37 hydroelectric power plants and the pipeline from Comodoro Rivadavia to La Plata to feed the YPF refineries, an attempt to secure Argentinian self-sufficiency in energy needs and accelerate the nascent industrialization.[22] Similar expansion plans in Mendoza and elsewhere took place. The Argentinian Institute of Industrial Promotion (Instituto Argentino de Producción Industrial [IAPI]) was responsible for the grain trade, but in practice functioned as the government's chief planning agency and systematically rechanneled surplus from the grain export into myriad industrialization projects.

By the end of Perón's first term, the Argentinian state emerged powerful and autonomous, the objective that the GOU had espoused and that was the prerequisite for all successful industrialization that Gerschenkron observed in Europe. In a curious way, the crux of Peronism embodied the ideas of the GOU: the state sponsorship of industrialization at the expense of the traditional agrarian sector, and the corporatist alliance between the state and labor. The state must control the market. In practice, the Argentinian calculus of economic growth and prosperity represented strong support of the state.

Where the private sector could not compete effectively against foreign companies, the state intervened by either imposing stiff regulations and restrictions on international capital, or creating an SOE to keep private competitors out of the market while granting the government corporation a national monopoly. Perón and his xenophobic power base – organized labor, the nationalistic middle class, and parasitic national industrialists – closed the national market, fully implemented the ISI policy, and radiated the Peronist influence into Uruguay, Bolivia, and southern Brazil, thus continuing the historical challenge to the US regional hegemony. To the diehard Peronists, this was the Argentinian mission, consolidating the revolution within and without the borders of the country. Argentina was not suffering from an illusion of power. It had power to become the regional hegemon in the South Atlantic.

Initially, the United States supported Perón's ISI policy. American businessmen saw opportunities in selling capital goods, granting credit, and even transferring technologies under license, so long as Argentina would allow the free entry and exit of capital and profit. Worldwide ISI with accessible markets would not be bad for US foreign trade. Americans defined the global ISI as import-substitution for light and consumer industries, as foreign exchange priorities for capital goods imports, and as freedom for profit expatriation. In a direct challenge to the US vision, the Argentinian government instituted a comprehensive ISI policy with strict control over foreign exchange flows, banning the import of all capital goods, adopting industrialization policies for light, intermediate, and heavy industries, and restricting profit expatriation.[23] Combined with high national content rules, this policy virtually closed Argentina to US businesses and banks.

The economic chauvinism of the Peronist revolution was rather short-lived, however. The movement that "dignified the worker" was short of cash. The decline of grain prices in the early 1950s, flaring inflation, a yawning public deficit, and declining workers' wages contributed to social unrest and even imparted a national depression in the Argentinian psyche. Furthering the process of collapse were the death of Evita Perón, difficulties with the Church compounded by the dictator's indiscretion with a teenaged girl, the legalization of divorce, and the end of compulsory religious lessons in public schools. The state could no longer afford to invest lavishly in industrial projects, or extravagantly grant favors and perks to the workers as before. Also the United States opposition to the Peronist "Third Way" of development was mounting, especially after the expropriation of the properties of Chevron in Argentina. The General Confederation of Labor (CGT) was crippled by factionalism, further debilitating the rank and file of the Peronist, or by now Justicialist, movement. A military coup in 1955 forced the dictator into exile, first to Paraguay and Panama briefly, after which he settled down in Spain until his triumphant return to power in 1973. Organized labor (CGT) was formally disbanded in September 1957, fragmenting itself into 62 Peronist and 32 independent unions.[24] This extreme form of the fragmentation of organized labor demonstrated the empowerment and autonomy of the unions, not their subjugation to the state.

Argentina in the world economy

The end of Perón's first period in office opened up the Argentinian market for the penetration of international capital. The civilian governments that followed the junta allowed international investments but in certain sectors only: automobiles, chemicals, and a few others. As much as $750 million flowed into the country during this period, primarily from the world's largest multinationals such as GM, Fiat, Ford, IBM, Renault, Firestone, Olivetti, Coca-Cola, etc. Even so, the nationalistic restrictions were too much to attract Argentina's fair share in the exploding world economy. Less than 5 percent of the total foreign direct investment (FDI) in Latin America went to Argentina, or a seventh of the FDI that Brazil attracted. In 1975, about a quarter of the US direct investment went to developing countries. Between 1946 and 1959, 529 new MNC subsidiaries were set up in the developing world, but 1549 between 1960 and 1970. About one half of these creations were American.[25] Argentina missed the opportunity to garner a larger slice of the growing world economic pie. Populist economics and global capitalism were incompatible.

Argentina's ISI policy effectively closed the domestic market to all foreign manufactured goods. This forced US manufacturers to transfer their operations to those countries with large internal markets. Once in place, the MNCs were under pressure from the local governments to increase their production capacities by using domestic inputs. The automobile industry in Argentina was told to use domestic inputs incrementally, rising from 30 percent to 95 percent, but still lower than Brazil's 100 percent local content requirement. Furthermore, the one-time accepted economic theory that MNCs bring capital, technology, and jobs did not prove to be correct. Studies showed that the profit expatriation often surpassed what MNCs invested in a given year. Such findings further drove local governments to tighten regulations and added new restrictions. Argentina was the champion of using such regulatory intervention, the classic pattern that all nationalist-populist regimes in Latin America would adopt.[26]

Globalization as a United States policy

In some cases, state intervention was necessary in the face of real or imagined fear of a multinational takeover of the national economy. In 1966, MNC sales represented 14 percent of the regional GDPs. Furthermore, the United States government offered tangible tax advantages for those firms investing in developing countries. Between 1962 and 1975, US MNCs could defer their overseas tax obligations until the profits were expatriated home, and until 1980 those corporations trading in the Western Hemisphere were granted preferential tax treatment by the United States. There were also two other tax advantages in investing overseas. The US charged no import taxes on goods produced overseas by US MNCs and the system of generalized preference after 1976 allowed the duty-free import of foreign manufactured products from certain countries that included practically all Latin American countries, except for Cuba. No wonder that more than 83 percent of all US manufacturing investment in developing countries was made in Latin America.[27] To discourage and even penalize those governments nationalizing US properties without compensation, the US Congress adopted a punitive law and amendments sponsored by Sen. Bourke Hickenlooper of Iowa and Rep. Henry González of Texas. Instead of helping US MNCs, these laws prompted Argentina and Jamaica to demand the recall of the US ambassadors. Some even attributed the overthrow of Arturo Frondizi in 1959 to his willingness to negotiate with six US oil firms in Argentina, suggesting possible US government involvement.[28] The not too subtle presence of the US as the hegemon of the world and the wielder of the Big Stick in commercial and economic diplomacy, long after the Good Neighbor policy fell into disuse, began to backfire on US MNCs in Latin America. As the Cold War relaxed and the US–Soviet détente began to take shape and hold firm, the host countries became less willing to show sensitivity to the United States interests. In fact, by the early 1970s Argentina was virulently anticommunist; yet the Soviet Union emerged as Argentina's major trading partner.

The final or sunset phase: 1976–89

In 1972, urban guerilla wars between the military regime and the civilian opposition, between Peronist followers and the left, and among Peronist factions were in full swing; the national debate evolved around how to deal with "the total war," the name that the Argentinian military gave to the civil war. The armed forces were divided ideologically between the moderates and hardliners. The return of the old dictator was the only way out to maintain political civility. The military stepped down, permitting first the election of a stand-in (Hector Cámpora), and then in 1973 Perón and his third wife Isabel de Perón were elected president and vice-president respectively. The septuagenarian general was no longer himself and was advised by less than competent politicians. Contrary to general expectations, Perón veered to the right and began to assault the leftwing faction of his own movement. There was no peace to be had; the urban guerrilla war intensified and became internationalized by attracting combatants from other Latin American countries.

Castañeda termed the return of the general "tragicomic."[29] The following incident illustrates why thoughtful observers like the Mexican political scientist believed Perón had outlived his usefulness to Argentina and to Latin America. In March 1972, Celso Furtado, former minister of planning in the João Goulart government of Brazil (1961–64), visited with the general in Madrid. Goulart, then in exile in Uruguay, thought that the return of the general to Argentina was imminent and a visit by his representative could cement a possible alliance among the continent's populists and perhaps would pave the way for his own return to power. Perón spent two hours talking about how he could prevent the US from dominating Latin America, how he could reduce the Argentinian debt from $1.2 billion to $80 million, and, more incredibly, how Argentina should prepare for the coming World War III. Once the US was removed from the continent, Perón said, then Europe would give all the money and technology Latin America needed to develop its economy. Astounded by Perón's loss of touch with reality, the Brazilian politely asked where Perón was getting his information. The general said Spanish and German think tanks. Furtado concluded that the general lived in a fantasy world and information frozen in time. As the Brazilian bid farewell to the general, Perón said, "Give my best to Allende." The incredulous Furtado could say nothing.[30] The general was confusing Goulart with Allende. Perón's performance as president lived up to the assessment by Furtado and Castañeda.

The death of Perón in 1976 and the ascent of his third wife, Vice-President Isabel Martínez de Perón to the presidency in hindsight were a bane to Argentina. The press even invented the word "la presidenta," in part as a jest and in part as the need to refer to the female head of state in daily reports, since the Spanish language did not prepare for such an eventuality. But the task and responsibility, more importantly, the political stamina to reconcile the warring factions of her dead husband's followers, overwhelmed the former cabaret dancer. Runaway inflation (50 percent per month), stagnating productivity, and frequent strikes added to the loss of millions of workers' hours; petulant anti-foreign investment laws, and, more saliently, self-recrimination of the Argentinians simply forced the country to the brink of anarchy. Urban terrorism by a variety of political persuasions thrived, spawning a cottage industry of kidnaping and contributing to further social unrest and discontent. The "presidenta" depended more and more on CGT leaders for policy guidance and even daily operations of the government, completely relegating her duties to her closest adviser, a soothsayer, minister of social welfare, and, some said, her paramour.[31]

The military regime in search of ideology

The military intervened once again, the seventh time in the twentieth century, this time to overthrow a woman in office. The macho coup makers were led by General Jorge Videla, the army commander. Unlike the 1966 coup, also led by an army general (Juan Carlos Onganía), the junta faced a different set of circumstances in March 1976. The foundations for the populist political economy were crumbling. Labor fought among themselves, fragmenting into a hundred groups. The middle class, agricultural interests, and industrial groups were tired of the second Peronist legacy of anarchy and were actively seeking military intervention. The officers, especially junior officers, were concerned with runaway terrorism and the country on the verge of collapse. Argentina could become a Lebanon of the Americas. In brief, there were the classical preconditions for the rise of a bureaucratic-authoritarian regime that O'Donnell described. Furthermore, unlike Onganía, Videla was still in active service when he volunteered to save the country. General Roberto Viola, the army chief of staff and a personal friend of Videla, pledged to protect the new president from any internal coups.[32]

When the junta assumed power in March 1976, the country's economy was in chaos. The junta's first and foremost task was to restore law and order and then rebuild the national economy. Its policy was called the "Proceso de Reorganización Nacional," or the junta critics would call the "military process," or simply "the process."[33] Technocrats working for the military in the 1960s and 1970s concluded that Argentina needed to develop the economy first and then worry about political democracy, somewhat like Asia's economic horse *before* democratic cart. This shocked many North American academic observers.[34] The neighboring countries, Brazil and Chile, were also under military rule, but both were on an economic roll. In Brazil, the economic "miracle" between 1967 and 1973 made that country among the world's fastest growing economies. And Chile undertook a neoliberal economic reform that ruthlessly dismantled the statist-socialist economy that the Allende government had built between 1970 and 1973. Both Brazil and Chile were aggressively borrowing from international markets, which were awash with petrodollars. Videla, a firm believer in economic liberalism, was convinced that Argentina could do no less. The territorial disputes with Chile and Argentina's historic claim on the Falkland Islands required the junta to rebuild the military's preparedness. To some critics, Argentina was angling for wars on these two fronts. Videla remembered that, in Europe, preparations for war in Italy and Germany in the 1930s had reignited economic growth.[35]

Martínez de Hoz and the *plata dulce*

The junta appointed a market-friendly businessman and banker, José Alfredo Martínez de Hoz, to the all-powerful ministry of economy. In fact, Martínez de Hoz became the economic plenipotentiary of the junta to business, its architect, and its builder of a new economic order. One of the two civilian ministers in the all-military dominated government, Martínez de Hoz was the perfect choice. A scion of an important landholding family, he had solid credentials in both the agricultural and industrial federations. Briefly serving as the minister of finance in 1966, Martínez de Hoz was a chief executive of an important steel mill at the time of the appointment. Furthermore, he had worked for David Rockefeller and therefore his connections with the US business and global banking community were solid. The military had to focus on the urban "subversion" which could topple the regime, if an all-out containment strategy was not carried out. Martínez de Hoz needed to mind economic affairs, thus freeing the military from distraction. Soon the junta launched a "dirty war" which eventually jailed tens of thousands of opponents and killed ten thousand more in its six-year rule.[36] Civilian participation in junta decision making, though little publicized, was growing. David Pion-Berlin confirms that even at the height of the dictatorship, the military consulted "social interest groups" for key state decisions.[37]

There were extenuating external circumstances that assured the success of the economic reform in Argentina. International capital was once again flowing into Latin America, and it was of paramount importance for Argentina to get on board this investment momentum. The world economy was in upswing, having emerged from the first impact of the 1973 energy crisis. The Vietnam War ended in 1975, and, reeling from the defeat in Southeast Asia, US investors were gun shy about Asia Pacific and eager to head south. At the same time, Japanese and German companies began to discover Latin America. Their economies were fully recovered by the early 1960s: they began to invest in Latin America, often outbidding others, granting local partners better terms of technology transfer, and freely agreeing to joint ventures, which US corporations avoided with acuity. Most notorious in this regard were American auto manufacturers, chemical firms, and advanced technology-based firms. And there was a reason: Argentina's domestic content rule for the auto industry was up to 95 percent and domestic parts on the average cost 210 percent more than imports, the highest in Latin America.[38] Martínez de Hoz was determined to change the ambience for foreign investment. His policy was a direct response to emerging global capitalism.

Nothing short of massive economic restructuring could save the country.[39] The country could not take advantage of the availability of international capital (cheap money, *plata dulce*), unless it offered a competitive environment in investment. The junta's economic team defined the problem in a three-fold context: (1) the need to redefine the role of the state in the economy; (2) liberalizing and deregulating the economy; and (3) the need to restore monetary and fiscal stability. In order to implement these ambitious reform objectives, Martínez de Hoz and his team in April 1976 removed price controls, abolished the 40 percent agricultural export tax (permitting unrestricted export practices), and withdrew all restrictions on foreign investment. These were the kinds of radical measures that would have taken democracy decades to introduce, if at all. Multiple foreign exchange rates were abandoned in favor of a single unified rate. And the junta set wages downward. In the first year, real wages declined by a third.[40]

The initial effect was depressingly impressive. Agriculture boomed as its export soared. The 50 percent plus monthly inflation came down to 7 percent by the end of the first year of the junta. In the meantime, the government negotiated a price freeze, or "price truce," with Argentina's 700 major national and foreign firms for four months. It was crucial for the government to bring down inflation and keep it down. The government-controlled lending policy such as the interest rate ceiling and the lending quota was removed. Let the invisible hand guide. Banks could set their own rates and had to compete for clients. And Martínez de Hoz instituted insurance to guarantee the safety of bank deposits. High interest rates and liberalized banking rules enticed the entry of international capital. In fact, the boom was so intense that the era was called the "financial bicycles," an era of high speculation and free-for-all.[41] True to form, the financial community, national and international, became the staunchest ally of the junta.[42]

Economists versus generals

The junta imposed conditions on what the economic team could and could not do. Restructuring the state was acceptable, but unemployment was not. The economists patiently lectured the generals that one of the causes for the high deficits and high inflation was the runaway SOEs. If Martínez de Hoz could not privatize these money-guzzling monsters, his economic restructuring could do little good. But the junta was fearful of the potential repercussion from massive unemployment once privatization began to eliminate redundant labor. To win the subversive war, the junta leaders argued that the SOEs could not be allowed to go bankrupt. It was the extreme irony that the market-oriented junta became the staunch defender of SOEs and was willing to overlook their meandering populist habits. SOEs could not be privatized, ruled the junta. To add more fuel to the growing deficit, the military extracted an increase in their budget from Martínez de Hoz, seemingly in preparation for the wars against Chile and Britain. In 1975, the armed forces received 8 percent of the national budget; in 1977, the proportion went up to 11.8 percent, and by 1979 14 percent. Brazil was just emerging as Latin America's premier arms manufacturer and exporter. Under the embargo imposed by the Carter administration on the Pinochet regime, Chile too was gearing up its own arms industry to be self-sufficient. In view of these inter-American events, the Argentinian junta eminently justified the armed forces' demand for a greater portion of the national budget. This did not help the reform policy that the economic team put together.[43]

The economic collapse

The economy began to stagnate in the midst of high inflation and equally high interest rates. And strikes occurred more frequently. During this period the import policy was never fully liberalized and Argentinian industries had difficulty in acquiring inputs, thus forcing them to become less competitive in the semi-opened global market. In March 1980, the country's largest private bank (the Banco de Intercambio Regional) became illiquid and was seized by the Central Bank, thus setting off a series of bank failures. Capital flight, disinvestment, and withholding fresh credit followed. To get relief from the financial imbroglio, the junta printed more money, thus increasing inflation and pushing up the public deficit. In 1978, the peak of the economic reform, the deficit was less than 2 percent of the GDP; by 1979, it was 2.1 percent; in 1980, it reached 7 percent; and by 1981, it soared over 8 percent. Also Argentina's foreign debt began to soar, since the government borrowed money where and when it could, first to finance development projects and then to balance the books. When it was unable to borrow, the junta printed money. By the end of the junta's rule in 1983, the external debt reached more than $45 billion.[44] The peso was devalued massively overnight and the dual exchange rates were reinstituted, agricultural export taxes reintroduced, and high punitive import taxes were adopted to weaken the opposition from the workers.[45] The business community which had supported the return of the military to power in 1976 felt the deep "sense of betrayal ... "[46]

The junta at the end of the road

In November 1981, another coup brought in General Leopoldo Galtieri, the then army attaché at the Argentinian Embassy in Washington. There was precious little that Galtieri could do to save Argentina. To divert the nation's attention from the worsening domestic woes, early in April 1982 the Argentinian military invaded the Falkland Islands. This provoked Britain, a linchpin of NATO, to respond militarily. The United States and NATO supported Britain. Argentina was supported by Peru, Venezuela, and a few lesser Latin American countries. Brazil remained neutral, but secretly allowed the United Kingdom to use Rio Grande do Sul for refueling British aircraft en route to the Falklands. Chile allowed British helicopter squadrons to operate from its southern region. In two months, the war was over and Galtieri was on his way out.[47] When money ran out, so did the power of the junta. In 1979, the government deficit was equal to 42.1 percent of GDP. In 1983, it went up to 49.8 percent.[48] The collapse of the economy with the humiliating defeat in the South Atlantic war ingloriously ended the junta's rule.[49] In July, the military's musical chairs were once again in motion: Galtieri was replaced by another general who held a democratic election and turned the government over to the winner: Raúl Alfonsín.

A glimmer of hope

For the Radical senator, the advent to the presidency was a hollow personal and political triumph. The first democratically elected government in 20 years and the re-democratization of the country could not have happened at a worse time. The Third World debt crisis had just imploded. Argentina, like Mexico and Brazil before it, had been negotiating with the International Monetary Fund (IMF) and was forced to declare insolvency. The economy was prostrate, having suffered from a compounded state of alternatively taking the medication of austerity and that of growth for the past ten years. For two years, the economy actually shrank: over 6 percent for 1981 and 5 percent the following year, the year of the Falkland War.[50] Unlike other governments before his, the Alfonsín administration was confronted simultaneously with dealing with the external creditors and the multilateral financial agencies, while attempting to revive the recessive economy. It was no mean task.

Alfonsín's economic policy began on a wrong foot. Elected as the president of a center-left government with strong residual populism coming from the Radical (UCR) tradition, Alfonsín sought to introduce a liberal economic reform. His first economy minister, Bernardo Grinspun, defined the central purpose of the government to promote "growth for all." He promised to reduce the deficit (12 percent of the GDP in 1983), to increase real wages, to promote exports, to modernize industry, and to negotiate with foreign creditors.[51] Grinspun opposed all IMF stand-by agreements, a concession he deemed unpatriotic. He chose to apply an old-time Radical (populist) cure.[52]

Once in office, Alfonsín was confronted with choosing a difficult option, either to tackle inflation or to undertake a fundamental reform of the populist backlash. As it turned out, it was going to be neither. The best thing that can be said about Alfonsín's economic policy between 1983 and 1989 was that it provided a series of short-term stabilization programs but never ventured beyond that. Never a committed free marketer, Alfonsín yearned to build a government that consolidated political democracy with a mildly populist economy. The first of Grinspun's economic policies satisfied no one.

Turning to the IMF

By late September 1984, Argentina signed onto a 15-month IMF-supervised austerity (stabilization) program, a humiliating turnabout.[53] Globalization made Argentina realize that it had lost the power to legislate its own economic and financial future. In October 1984, the government had to raise utility rates (previously frozen) so that it could increase its own revenues; to keep workers happy, an 8 percent wage increase above the indexation rate was granted; the peso was devalued to please exporters; public spending was cut to please fiscal conservatives; and the IMF-imposed austerity program was implemented to allay the fear of foreign creditors. The curious result of this mixed bag of programs was to push down real wages and to push up inflation.

To make his economic policy work, Alfonsín was challenged with a task of dealing with a group of conglomerates, the new economic elite of Argentina. Typically, a conglomerate's holding company bought a bankrupt firm and lobbied the government to introduce a policy of promoting that company's sector, whether it was energy, informatics, auto parts, or infrastructure. New credit lines were opened and the government granted generous contracts and subsidies. Workers were happy and conglomerates made money. Some of Argentina's major financial conglomerates began their careers in the 1960s and had polished the art of living off the state. The business community was full of ideological diversity as well. Thus in the 1960s, the Onganía-led junta established an alliance with the national industrial group. In the 1970s, the Perón government did the same with the populist sector, and the Videla government tried the same with the liberal sector. These alliances were never permanent, but the corporatist relationship with each state remained intact and the ruling elites of the state and the corporatist entity benefitted from such collaboration. There were 24 such conglomerates, ranging from banks, oil and gas, automobile manufacturing, and construction, to agriculture and pastoral activities. Together, these 24 dominated Argentina's private sector.[54] They soon opposed the economic policy. Grinspun was out.[55]

The Austral Plan

Juan Sourrouille, a respected economist and businessman but not a Radical devotee, was named to succeed Grinspun. Sourrouille devised the Austral Plan, the first of the three reform plans which was unveiled in mid-June 1985, when Argentinian inflation hit 6500 percent per annum. To Alfonsín, it was "war economics." The plan was creative in that it combined features of the "monetary and fiscal policy of orthodox with heterodox shock treatment of inflation."[56] The country had already declared a moratorium on its $55 billion external debt. Squeezed by the IMF and external creditors and mounting domestic pressure from various corporatist entities, the government took a bold move, a combination of a short-term stabilization plan and a long-term state reform. The first phase of the plan included: (1) a price freeze, (2) a hefty 21 percent wage increase, (3) a 15 percent devaluation in exchange rate, (4) a 23.6 percent utility rate increase, and (5) an introduction of a new currency, the austral. One US dollar was set at 0.80 of one austral. In the meantime, the government swore that it could trim the deficit, while increasing revenues, ceasing to print money, increasing credit, and financing public works projects.[57] To organized labor, the plan was a typical IMF-styled bitter pill, putting all the sacrifice on the workers. The "captains of industry" bitterly complained about the price freeze. The agricultural sector opposed the increase in export taxes. And to further undermine the plan, the Central Bank, which Sourrouille could not control, continued to print money and extended generous credits to revenue-starved provinces. The Austral Plan lacked a moral backbone in a society where honest labor did not pay. Speculations, corruption, and political connections were the real capital and assets.

The second component of the plan was a long-term state reform program. In order to bring about fundamental changes to the national economy, Alfonsín had to restructure the state, redefine its role in the marketplace, and winnow the public sector's expansive appetite by divesting Argentina's some 800 SOEs. In this "reform of the state," Alfonsín ironically adopted the liberal reform plank: the liberalization of international trade, the deregulation of the domestic market, and the privatization of public-sector companies, the bedrock recipe of the Washington Consensus.

The initial brush with the political opposition to the "reform of the state" occurred when Alfonsín attempted to privatize the national airline, Aerolíneas Argentinas. When the bill was proposed in Congress, both Peronist legislators and those from Alfonsín's own party rallied to oppose the bill. The airline was a national icon, which had a monopoly on the domestic and international routes. The privatization plan never made it out of the key committees in both chambers.

The initial result of the Austral Plan was impressive, however: inflation was down from 348 percent to 20.2 percent in the second quarter of 1985 and the fiscal deficit also was down from 11.9 percent of GDP to a respectable 3 percent by the third quarter and to 2.2 percent by the fourth quarter. But at the same time, the international reserves were dwindling, the balance of payments worsened, and the debt service burden became unbearable. When a noted Argentinian analyst, Monica Peralta-Ramos, gave the prospect of the success of the plan a zero, she was not alone.[58]

Alfonsín's last tango

For Argentina, 1986 was the year that broke the economic camel's back. The public sector's spending in 1960 was equivalent to 30 percent of GDP, while in 1985 it was 50 percent. In 1960, the public sector's investment was equal to 7.5 percent of GDP, while in 1985 it more than doubled to 15.5 percent.[59] By these numbers the state continued to gain power and autonomy, but the economy failed to produce wealth to finance the populist projects. Within six months, the government introduced two more economic plans: Austral II of April 1986 and Austral III of August 1986. The second plan enforced a modest price adjustment, devaluing the peso again, and permitting the private sector to increase prices and the public sector to raise utility rates. The justification was that the state needed revenues. This time, the plan did not work. By August, the third plan had to be implemented, the "monetarist period," and focused on "deactivating" the state-heavy economy and tightening money supplies. Labor, industry, and agriculture were against the plan. By the end of 1988, the country entered the hyperinflation era, and once again the government caved in to public pressure and was forced to make concessions, allowing prices to rise and disindexing the economy. His own party's leaders began to distance themselves from the government. Alfonsín fired Juan Sourrouille.[60]

3
Brazil: Building a Capitalism without Risk

The liberals of 1964

The political and economic changes between 1964 and 1995 were superbly chronicled by Thomas Skidmore, Werner Baer, Alfred Stepan, Ronald Schneider, and many others.[1] And several important memoirs of the era were written by both military players and civilian technocrats.[2] Together they provide a good overview and an analysis of the period. For this reason, this chapter will focus on the specific dimensions of the B-A regime by looking at two case studies: creating an oil monopoly and an informatics monopoly policy. The military had been concerned with energy self-sufficiency, dating back to the 1930s, and some of the officers such as General Góis Monteiro, the army chief of staff in the 1940s and 1950s, and General Ernesto Geisel, president of Brazil in the 1970s, were proponents of strong nationalistic control of oil. Geisel was the president of the Brazilian national oil monopoly before he was made the chief of state. After he completed his term in the presidency, he returned to the oil company, heading a petrochemical subsidiary of Petrobrás.

Oil required the state to invest substantially to create, nurture, and manage Latin America's third largest oil company, Petróleo Brasileiro, S.A., or Petrobrás. The largest company in the country, including both public and private corporations, at its peak Petrobrás accounted for as much as 13 percent of the country's exports and consumed 66 percent of all SOE budgets. Furthermore, in its heyday, Petrobrás was the country's largest earner of foreign exchange and could buy dollars from the Central Bank at a one-third discount. Even to this day, supporters and detractors of the company do not agree if the SOE oil monopoly has helped or hurt the country during its 50 years in existence.

Computer technology, or *informática*, was the obsession with the young officers in the 1970s and 1980s, as the Brazilian economy was moving up the next notch of the global economic ladder. It required self-sufficiency in computer technologies. Many officers, led by General Golbery do Couto e Silva, firmly believed in the destiny of Brazil to emerge as the regional power in the South Atlantic.[3] By 1983, the government introduced the Lei Informática, reserving the manufacturing and marketing of computers to Brazilian companies.

The computer technology and marketing policy was introduced in 1983 to exclude foreign computer hardware and software makers from the Brazilian market. The state did not invest massive funds in creating an SOE, but instead adopted a national market regulatory policy that sought to establish independence in informatics by building up the private sector. The policy worked for awhile, but by the end of the 1980s, the nature of informatics technologies and the global market had changed. Then it became clear that the Brazilian nascent industry was good in copycatting, or cloning, as well as pirating technologies developed in the United States, Western Europe, and by the Asian Tigers, but failed to benefit from its own R & D capabilities.[4] The quality suffered and the price for a domestic copy cat remained outrageously high. Smuggling became so rampant that newspapers in metropolitan areas routinely advertized a foreign computer for sale, directly "imported" from Paraguay, an entrepôt for smuggled hardware and software. By 1993, the Informatics Law of 1983 was allowed to die in disgrace, thus opening the Brazilian market for newer and better machines and software from other countries. One glaring consequence of the Informatics was that the Brazilian auto industry was kept from importing computer components to be used for automobiles. As late as 1992, Brazilian automobiles lacked computer chips to monitor engine operations, braking systems, fuel injection flows, and even inbuilt CD players.

The state and the market

Brazil has had three types of "state enterprises," whose functions are well defined by Decree No. 84.128 of 19 October 1979. Article 2 defines the following three types: (1) public enterprises of mixed economy and their subsidiaries directly and indirectly controlled by the federal government, (2) autarkies and foundations created and maintained by the federal treasury, and (3) autonomously administered entities of the federal government. An earlier law, Decree-Law No. 200/67, also upheld such functional definitions. For cadastral purposes, however, the federal government divided its 485 SOEs into five categories:

Productive sector SOEs: monopolies or oligopolies that produced goods and services, such as Petrobrás, Telebrás, CVRD, Siderbrás, etc. In 1983, there were 246 such federal enterprises wholly and partly owned by the Union, the federal government.

Governmental subsidiaries: entities in education, public health, research, and archival activities, such as the "Ku of Brasília," the National Institute of Medical Assistance and Social Security (INAMPS); and Fundação Casa de Rui Barbosa, a research library and archives of the eminent Bahian politician, etc. There were 190 such entities directly administered by the federal government.

Social welfare group: all welfare agencies and programs reporting to the National System of Social Welfare and Assistance (SINAPAS), whose funds come from the contributions of employees and employers. There were seven in this category.

Official federal banks: working in the financial sector with the capital coming from the federal government; activities were defined by Lei No. 4.595/64. There were 14 such entities. The Bank of Brazil (BB) and the Federal Economic Bank (CEF) are the two best known.

Public enterprises on municipal and state levels: operating as federally designated concessionaires in energy, telecommunications, transportation, the two Metro systems in Rio and São Paulo, etc.; original investment in these projects came from the federal government and hence these SOEs depended on federal funding. There were 28 such entities.[5]

The year 1983 was the historical peak as far as the number of Brazil's SOEs went. The total (687) included federal, state, and municipal public enterprises, autarkies, foundations, governmental subsidiaries, and federal concessionaires to regional and local governments. The legal and political intent of SOEs has been to generate wealth (products, services, capital) and to redistribute it through various programs for universally accessible social welfare, educational services, public health, and public transportation. This statist developmentalist system was enormously successful throughout the 1960s and 1970s. Some SOEs consistently made profits.[6] Between 1973 and 1979–80, the two points of the global energy price hikes from $12.56 to $40.00 per barrel, the Brazilian economy grew 62 percent. In the early 1980s the country was producing and exporting more steel and automobiles than Great Britain, whose gross domestic product was nearly three times Brazil's.[7] By then, however, the system became much abused by the self-sustaining bureaucracy of SOEs, private contractors who lived off the public troughs, and the underclasses who considered SOEs national patrimony. As Brazil entered a deep financial crisis soon after the 1982 external debt crisis, the SOE system became frayed and for the first time in history became the target of public outcry and criticism.

The military-technocratic regimes built 500 (350 of which were federal) parastatal corporations during their 21-year rule. Many of these corporations were new subsidiaries, joint venture enterprises with private firms and international companies, and holding or "grupo" companies, as the Brazilian economy became bigger, more complex, internationalized, and then globalized. To meet these new challenges of the globalization era (from the 1970s onward), the SOEs either expanded or diversified their operations. CVRD's own merchant marine (Docenave), Petrobrás's international trading company (Interbrás), its overseas drilling company (Braspetro), and its petrochemical company (Petroquisa), the Banco do Brasil's BB Leasing Company and BB Tours-Voyages et Tourisme were the prime examples of SOEs' responses to the specialization and globalization of the world economy.

SOEs' borrowing schemes

By the late 1970s and the early 1980s, as the global economy expanded, diversified, and became borderless, so did the Brazilian economy in its own way. The military needed to make a key decision: either the state (SOEs) take the initiative of modifying, modernizing, and growing with the global economy, or better capitalized multinationals and their domestic partners be permitted to dominate the market. The nationalistic proclivities of the B-A regime leaned toward the former. Thus, the expansionist strategy pursued by the government soon after the two oil price hikes in 1973 and 1979–80 called for greater borrowing of external credit, while emphasizing technological self-sufficiency and the deepening of ISI.

The proliferation of estatais in the 1960s and 1970s had allowed the military to respond to the expanding export opportunities in the world economy on the one hand and on the other borrow international capital, first the Eurodollar and then the Petrodollar. As the operations of major estatais grew, the concept of a "holding company" was adopted as a way of centralizing operations, obtaining overseas borrowing, and encouraging exports. The economy of scale mattered. So did the quick integrated decision-making process. For these reasons, Siderbrás (Brazil's iron and steel holding company) was established by bringing together eight steel and iron mining SOEs, which in turn held a total of 14 subsidiaries. As of 1982, the holding company controlled directly and indirectly (in the latter case, typically, in partnerships) 22 subsidiaries, including one insurance company and a palm oil manufacturer. Instead of producing new technologies through R & D under the holding company, Siderbrás expanded activities of the conglomerate by entering the areas which had nothing to do with steel making. The SOEs burgeoned for the sake of growing. Brazil expanded for the sake of expansion. The state was willing, the military approved, organized labor and the left welcomed expansion, external credit was cheap and bountiful, and Brazil's borrowing soared. At one time, as much as 70 percent of the country's external debt was incurred by SOEs.[8] So was the state's takeover of the market.

Petrobrás also fathered more companies in the 1960s and 1970s: 6 direct subsidiaries, plus numerous firms partnered with other SOEs, domestic or foreign companies (especially Japanese and European), including its own tanker fleet company, a total of 41 subsidiaries.[9] Nuclebrás had 7 subsidiaries, Portobrás 10, CVRD 11, Eletrobrás 8, and Telebrás 29.[10] They were veritable parastatal conglomerates, and such parastatals as the Bank of Brazil, Petrobrás, and CVRD emerged as the Third World's transnationals. They competed against US, European, and Japanese transnationals in an increasingly entropic world of finite resources.

The creation of new estatais was fueled by the expanding overseas credit markets. Ironically, the globalization of financial markets opened up new opportunities for Brazil to build more SOEs, which either sought to replace or compete against multinationals, the foot soldiers of the global economy. Commercial bankers were more willing to grant credit to those companies with state guarantees, or *aval*. In 1967, the Brazilian federal government took two major steps toward parastatal expansion.

First, the government decreed an administrative reform (Decreto-Lei No. 200 of 27 February 1967) which decentralized the management of estatais by granting the companies more autonomy in financial decisions. Up to that time, it was the ministries of planning and finance, plus the "parent ministries" such as the Ministry of Mines and Energy in the case of Petrobrás and the Ministry of Communications in the case of Telebrás, that made decisions for the SOEs' offspring.

Second, Minister of Finance Antônio Delfim Netto won the military's support for a policy whereby the federal government would guarantee all loans SOEs contracted at home and with overseas financial markets. Known as Aviso GB-588 (26 July 1967), the federal government empowered the Bank of Brazil to meet the "obligations with the guarantee from the national treasury or from any other official financial institution" in the event that the estatal failed to honor debt payment.[11] The logic behind the Aviso was to make Brazil more credit worthy in the global financial market by ensuring the safety of loans to Brazilian SOEs, the policy wanted.

Allocation of and access to capital

These federally mandated guarantees had both positive and negative effects. The heated expansion in external financing was necessary to fuel the Brazilian economic growth machine, especially after 1973. By a conservative estimate, the years of 1967–74, or the "Brazilian Miracle" era, the GDP grew 10 percent annually, or higher, while the inflation rate was checked at about 20 percent. By 1974, the first year of the Geisel administration, the development strategy pursued by the Brazilian government was beginning to reshape and to redefine how the economy should be partitioned between the public and private sectors for the second decade in power.

João Paulo dos Reis Velloso, the planning minister, called for a "Statute of Public Enterprises" to define clearly the perimeters of the state and the market. He believed that the private sectors should prevail in the "transformation industry, construction industry, agriculture, pastoral activities, trade, insurance, banking, and other credit institutions." State banks, for instance, should play the role of "pioneers and stimulators" of the economy, but should not replace private sector banks.[12] The proper role of the government, therefore, was to provide incentives and subsidies to the private sector so that Brazil could be globally competitive. The minister realized that the defect of the "Brazilian Model" was found in placing too much emphasis on exports; he wanted to stress the continuation of import-substituting industrialization and expansion of the domestic market. Velloso wanted to please both the ideological left and the right. The chief instrument of such a development policy was the National Economic

Development Bank, which had US$1 billion in capital, but loaned out over $10 billion over its 20 years in operation. Eighty percent of the investment went to industrial projects and as much as 75 percent of the investment funds for the private sector came from the BNDES.[13] Velloso was a quintessential technocrat who spoke for the military in the economic area. In hindsight, the Brazilian state grew bigger than Velloso would have liked.[14]

Brazil's parastatals became the principal beneficiaries of the BNDE (now BNDES) capital, however. In each sector, over half of all credit went to SOEs. Industry in 1979–80 still consumed between 63 percent and 59 percent, and agriculture about 10 percent. The Southeast (the industrial heartland of Brazil) received between 57 percent and 54 percent respectively, followed by the Northeast (21 percent) and the South (18 percent).[15] Too many resources bred inefficiency. Some estatais began to abuse the international availability of capital, preferring to pay for personnel salaries and perks by borrowing from both the domestic and overseas sources. By the early 1980s, the abuses were so rampant that state-owned companies were falling behind on interest payments on overseas loans; many SOEs still diverted funds to cover the cost of personnel. The federal government took steps in vain to curb the abuse of funds by SOEs. Minister of Finance Ernâne Galvea simply classified all disclosure on the operation of GB-588 to be confidential and barred. Furthermore, the Bank of Brazil continued to extend credit to deficitary SOEs and to collect hefty fees on all such operations by charging interest and spread points for the parastatal debt service.[16]

"External savings and parallel dollars"

In a Byzantine way, parastatals became at once the prime beneficiaries and victims of the post-1973 petrodollar boom. Such major companies as Petrobrás, CVRD, Eletrobrás, Telebrás, and Nuclebrás borrowed money in dollars and in major Euro-currencies for their expansion programs. Under a disguised mechanism, the parastatal borrower would turn hard currency over to the Central Bank, for which it issued cruzeiros. The Central Bank then used hard currency to "balance the books," while estatais invested cruzeiros in development projects. Few foreign contractors could compete in the closed market. Brazilian legislation required the obligatory use of Brazilian products when and where possible (euphemistically known as the "nationalization" index), and hence the cruzeiro issued in exchange for hard currencies was quickly used as payment for goods and services from Brazilian industries. The Central Bank, however, reciprocated the favor by granting discounted dollars to SOE customers when needed. Petrobrás, the largest contributor to the dollar account, bought US currency at a discount, paying only 66 percent of the official rate.[17] In cruzeiro terms, Petrobrás inputs and capital goods bought with discounted dollars gave the SOE an undue competitive edge and a hefty margin of profit.

Borrowing overseas or tapping into "external savings" at times seemed redundant. Petrobrás, as early as 1964, was using upward of 86.8 percent of all equipment and supplies manufactured by Brazilian companies, presumably paid for in cruzeiros.[18] This high index of "nationalization" was not confined to the oil monopoly. The CVRD, the national monopoly of iron ores, boasted in 1985 that over 90 percent of the equipment, supplies, and engineering services used in the Carajás project were made by and bought from "national companies."[19] As foreign suppliers were locked out, some European countries began to impose conditions for granting bank loans to Brazil. European lenders, often SOE banks themselves, invented "parallel dollars" to pry open the closed Brazilian market. These dollars were unrestricted credit that came with the purchase of goods and services from the lending nation, often matched one on one. Brazil bought one dollar's worth of goods and received a second dollar as credit. To secure more hard currency, Brazil's parastatals bought equipment that could be found at home cheaper and was even unnecessary for their operations. It was an easy way to find foreign credit that otherwise was unavailable. Some state-owned companies even acquired sophisticated computers, equipment, and materials for which they had no use at the time of purchase. In the early 1980s, Brazil bought at least US$8 billion worth of redundant goods, all superfluous Planning ministry officials encouraged parastatal managers to "cook up" projects for the sake of securing more foreign credit. Between 1980 and 1983, a full 60 percent of all incoming foreign loans went to Brazil's estatais.[20] Abuses were abetted unchecked in the late 1970s and early 1980s.

None other than Mário Henrique Simonsen defended this practice of using estatais to raise overseas loans, which many technocrats considered cheaper than securing cruzeiro loans at home.[21] For one thing, overseas interest rates were consistently lower than those at home. For another, foreign lenders were eager to extend credit to SOEs, regardless of the merit of projects as long as the government guaranteed the safety of the investment. There was an overabundant credit in the world financial market and commercial banks were pressed to "sell money" for profits (fees and interest). Three-quarters of all bank debts in the world were held by 12 countries: 5 in Latin America, 5 in Asia, and 2 in the Middle East. These 12 also grew phenomenally: between 1967 and 1981, their combined GDPs expanded from $130 billion to $1 trillion.[22] Brazil, one of the 12, was a beneficiary of this global system of finances. Interestingly, Simonsen after retiring from the government went to work for Citibank as a director.

The global credit glut challenged the efficacy and even viability of the Brazilian Central Bank rates, often encouraging both SOEs and private companies to go overseas. The Brazilian sovereignty was eroding fast, as SOEs and private borrowers increasingly turned to overseas funds, instead of turning to the government banks. This was the first sign that the state was losing power and autonomy over its own finances. Brazil entered the age of globalization and took the bitter pill of all the negative consequences.

The money brought in added to the total stock of the money supply, thus undermining the antiinflationary measures that the government was undertaking. Before the first oil crisis in 1973, as much as 90 percent of the estatais investment came from Brazilian taxes.[23] Also the availability of cheap, plentiful credit (in fact, there was a credit glut in the global financial market) afforded the military regime the chance not to raise taxes at home and therefore to become politically tolerated or even popular in some quarters. In return, the military-technocratic officials borrowed heavily from "external savings" – some Brazilian policy makers thought that they were doing favors for overseas commercial banks by soaking up excess capital – first to finance pharaonic developmental projects such as Itaipú ($15 billion), Tucuruí ($6 billion), and Carajás ($60 billion), to name the best known.

These pharaonic projects had profound "geopolitical" implications in the South Atlantic. They were pathways to global power and the linchpin for national security. The Brazilian military envisioned the Rio–São Paulo industrial axis as ruling the region. To become the regional superpower in Latin America as well as in the South Atlantic, the B-A regimes promoted these megaprojects. To a lesser extent, Argentina was drawn into the silent race to neutralize Brazil's aspirations and began to build its own megadollar Yacyretá hydroelectric high dam on the Paraná River. The state patronage of big projects became an inevitable part of the political economy of all statist development strategies.[24] If the economic projects could enhance the geopolitical objectives of the military, so much the better. This dovetailing aspect was the quintessence of the B-A regime's political economy.

Soon, the Brazilian state was borrowing to cover the deficits in the current accounts and finally to pay for direct governmental operations, including personnel costs.[25] Latin America was borrowing heavily in general (Table 3.1). The consolidation of Brazilian state capitalism would not have been possible had it not been for the globalization – the "soft money," the petrodollars – and would have taken a different path had it not been for the basic changes wrought into the global economy by the two petroleum "shocks" in 1973 and 1979–80. By then, the autonomous borderless global systems of finance and resources were fulminating in operation.

State-owned enterprises vs. foreign direct investment

By restricting foreign direct investment (FDI), the Brazilian government had to encourage private companies to borrow from overseas sources. Foreign corporations already in Brazil opted for this venue, for it offered ways to exceed the 12 percent limit imposed on profit remittance. Typically, there was no limit on how much interest payments a corporation made. Soon more borrowing replaced FDIs in the financial transactions between the home office and its subsidiaries in Brazil. This

Table 3.1: Foreign Direct Investment Flows into Latin America, 1984–95 (US$mil)

	1984–89	1990	1991	1992	1993	1994	1995
Argentina	653	1,836	2,439	4,179	6,305	1,200	3,900
Brazil	1,416	989	1,103	2,061	1,292	3,072	4,959
Chile	614	590	523	699	841	2,518	3,021
Colombia	536	500	457	790	960	1,667	1,200
Ecuador	105	126	160	178	469	531	400
Mexico	2,436	2,549	4,742	4,393	4,389	7,978	6,984
Peru	9	41	–7	145	371	2,326	900
Venezuela	71	451	1,916	629	372	764	245
Others	1,872	1,818	4,029	4,457	5,246	5,051	n.a.
Latin America	7,739	8,900	15,362	17,698	19,456	25,302	26,560

Sources: *Latin Finance*, No. 84 (1996); UNCTAD, *World Investment Report 1997* (New York: UN, 1997).

allowed MNCs to expatriate more than the 12 percent of their profits. For SOEs, borrowing meant decision-making autonomy, as opposed to FDI which allowed SOEs' foreign and domestic partners to choose projects in which to invest. The military preferred joint ventures (foreign investors as minority partners) for reasons of nationalism. This meant that borrowing gave the Brazilian state the power to decide in which projects FDI could and could not enter, while FDI granted autonomy to international investors. Naturally, Brazil preferred the former.

The Médici administration (1969–73) set the all-time record for establishing estatais: 99 for a little over three years in power, or 3 per month. Castello Branco created 58 in three years; Costa e Silva, 55; Geisel, 50; and Figueiredo, 24.[26] Simonsen, Geisel's finance minister, justified the plethora of estatais as the state's filling the vacuum that private capital could not take up or that the multinationals should not be permitted to enter, and he believed that it was preferable for the state to fill the gap.[27] Velloso, planning minister under the Médici and Geisel administrations, insisted that the military's philosophy of the "Revolution" on the economy was still to promote "the alliance, the solidarity, the informal coexistence between the government (the state) and the private sector (the market)." And the minister declared that the state should be confined only to the infrastructure and social development areas, leaving the rest of the economy to the private sector.[28] To implement the political economy of Simonsen and Velloso, Brazil had to borrow and borrow heavily.

Antônio Delfim Netto, a quintessential technopol and the economic czar who made more impact than any other civilian minister during the 21 years of the bureaucratic-authoritarian partnership, also defended the practice of overseas borrowing by estatais, insisting that "it was absolutely correct to utilize the external savings to realize the internal development, because it is well invested and because we are confident that exports will increase and revenues from them will pay off the debt."[29] This might have been the official line of the Geisel administration, but the private sector suspected that the borrowing was used to encourage and sustain the statization, or worse, the supremacy of the state over the market. The expansion of the public sector was getting out of hand and reaching the point that not only did the unbridled expansion of the state stifle building market-oriented capitalism, but it also could suffocate the very survival of the existing private sector. Velloso's notion of a calibrated political economy of the state and the market never materialized. The state devoured the market. But proponents of this model such as Nelson Mortada, secretary general of the Secretariat for Budget and Control of Parastatals

(SEST) in the Figueiredo administration, could argue confidently that reductions in investments by the estatais would also hurt the private sector.[30] By the early 1980s, the private sector was living off the state largess and the trend, if allowed to continue, could perilously end the autonomy of the private-sector economy.

A success story gone bad: Petrobrás

Energy and water are two critical inputs which Third World countries need to develop their economy. About 86 percent of the world's energy was consumed by the geographic "north," falling in the band between 30 and 60 degrees latitudes north, when Brazil was midway through its two-decade long military rule.[31] To build a self-sufficient economy, then, would require a country to be equally self-sufficient in energy. It could be attained by a national monopoly of energy resources, as the Brazilian military and their technocrats advocated. As to water, Brazil did not suffer from a shortage, except for those drought-prone Polygon states in the Northeast. To differentiate from other Third World countries, Brazilian strategic thinkers and even politicians in the 1930s and 1940s called for independence in energy and other resources supplies.

A product of this strategic thinking, Petrobrás went through a turbulent era of growing pangs since its founding in 1953. In the first decade of operation, Petrobrás became the battle ground for civilian and military ideologues. It went through eight presidents in ten years. The company was plagued by chaotic labor troubles, which the conservatives considered a communist conspiracy; the left and radical nationalists complained that the parastatal oil monopoly was working for international capitalism.[32] Until the military coup in April 1964, Petrobrás was an unproductive economic behemoth that provided a political theater for the men of all ideological persuasions. While the right feared that the monopoly would be bad for private capitalism, the left applauded its statization as a pace setter for the rest of the parastatal sector to follow.[33]

After 1964, Petrobrás began to transform and became productive. The upper-echelon management was evenly divided between the civilian career people, most of them coming from geology, petroleum and chemical engineering, and accounting backgrounds, and the retired air force, army and navy officers.[34] The intense "depoliticization" of the company was the first order of the military government in 1964 that also infused more professionalism through graduate training at home and abroad, and that emphasized productivity by giving the better trained people attractive salaries and benefits. The military also used high-handed methods of dealing with the company's unions.

Between 1969 and 1973 when General Ernesto Geisel was the president of the company, the unions began to settle down to work. Many departmental chiefs were frequently turned over when Geisel's policies were not obeyed.[35] Geisel also gathered a group of very able civilian career people and military officers who introduced and implemented ambitious expansion policies. Investments grew; marketing strategies resulted in the expansion of distribution networks through a new subsidiary, BR (Petrobrás retail gas stations, and an SOE), and the marketing operations of foreign companies were first reduced and then restricted to those areas that Petrobrás was willing to give up. This forced expansion of BR at the expense of foreign oil firms was enormously popular. Practically all high visibility locations such as Copacabana and Ipanema beaches were dotted by BR stations. Once this "nationalization" was complete, Geisel's colleagues in the army rewarded him with the country's presidency.

By 1983, BR consolidated its place in the market as the largest gasoline retailer, controlling 22.3 percent of the domestic market. However, Shell, Esso (as Exxon is still known in Brazil), Atlantic, and Texaco together garnered 60.1 percent.[36] Economic nationalism, virulently xenophobic in hindsight, paid off with hefty dividends. The state succeeded in establishing a vertical and horizontal (upstream-downstream) linkage in the oil business, thus assuring the monopolist position of Petrobrás and also exerting the statist domination over the energy market.

Alberto Tamer, an economics editor of the *O Estado de S. Paulo*, was a persistent critic of the Petrobrás of the Geisel era, arguing cogently that the estatal squandered more capital and human resources in the commercialization of the imported oil than in discovering, exploring, and producing new domestic sources. Geisel, who had served for over three years at the helm of the company, believed that the mandate of Petrobrás was to provide an uninterrupted supply of energy to the nation at all cost, hence investing money in expanding transportation, refining, and distribution of oil became his priority, not exploration and production from the less viable and unpromising Brazilian fields.

However, as the president of the republic, Geisel reversed this position. In 1970, he had opposed, seconded by the armed forces, a risk contract scheme for foreign and Brazilian private firms to find oil. Five years later as the president of Brazil facing the adverse impact of the OPEC-provoked price gouging and an increasing domestic demand for energy to meet the growing economy, Geisel approved the risk contract scheme, thus turning around the historical policy of Petrobrás from the nation's leading marketer of oil to the aspiring monopoly producer of hydrocarbons. Third World economies as a whole increased their petroleum consumption by 20 percent, while Brazil's consumption through the 1970s increased a healthy average of 10 percent per annum. Strapped by a shortage of investment capital and prompted by an insatiable appetite for an endless list of developmental projects, Geisel had no choice but to open up the petroleum business to foreign and domestic private capital. This was entirely consistent with the national policy of resorting to relying heavily on the "external savings" to finance the domestic economic expansion.[37] While Brazil's economy was still closed, its technocrats learned how to tap the global financial markets at will. This did not last long.

After 1975, Petrobrás began to modify its policy from importing and marketing oil to exploration and production (E&P). The company had to borrow more from abroad to finance its E&P activities at home and abroad. In 1976, the company spent 56 percent more in exploration and developing production than the year before. Fully 66 percent of all parastatal budgets in 1984 went to Petrobrás. Between 1977 and 1981, the company drilled 2978 wells, of which 500 were offshore. Many were dry holes. In 1978, the height of the risk contract boom, Petrobrás chose 33 companies to explore. Only 7 were Brazilian.[38] The policy was controversial. The company's engineers opposed the policy, for they were not fully consulted. The old left going back to the early 1950s who opposed all forms of foreign participation in the Brazilian oil industry continued to cry foul. The intellectual left and radical nationalists also predicted the negative consequences of the risk contracts, which they saw as a harbinger for the takeover of the oil industry by international oil trusts. Opposition politicians in congress used the risk contracts as a pretext to attack the Geisel and Figueiredo governments.

Compounding the suspicion and fear among the opponents of the risk contracts was the belief that Brazil had gigantic oil reserves and that foreign firms wanted them. American oil companies especially were seen as villains in this affair.[39] By the early 1980s, the practice died a natural death, for the country offered many prospects, but few actual discoveries of commercial potential were made. No foreign or domestic firm ever made money from the exploration contracts. And all fears and predictions of the left and radical right never materialized. In hindsight, they were all political theaters.

This expanded policy in prospection, exploration, and production remained the official goal of the company until the 1990s, in spite of the increasing production of cane alcohol. The company also expanded its export of refined petroleum to Bolivia and Paraguay, which bought the Brazilian product at the world price and sold natural gas to Petrobrás cheap. For geopolitical reasons in the Southern Cone region, Brazil was eager to reduce the dependency of the two countries on Argentina by supplying gasoline to them. Although oil imports began to decline only after 1981, the import bill continued to climb: in 1975, Petrobrás imported 260 million barrels paying US$720 million. In 1978, Petrobrás imported 300 million barrels at $3.4 billion. A 15 percent increase in the crude imports led to a whopping 250 percent increase in cost. And in 1979, the year of the 'second petroleum price shock," Brazil spent $6.7 billion for 365 million barrels, a million barrels a day. After that, the imports began to decline, in part thanks to the increased alcohol production and in part because of the high price that discouraged consumption. In 1981, Brazil imported 308 million barrels at $10.5 billion. In the first ten months of 1983, the company bought 226 million barrels at $6.7 billion.[40] Brazil in the late 1970s and early 1980s was stabilizing its petroleum consumption, as passenger cars began to shift from petroleum to ethanol.

Energy self-sufficiency with ethanol

In 1975, the Pró-Alcool (Pro-Alcohol) Program was instituted and 10 years later Brazil was producing 15 billion liters,[41] thus reducing the consumption of petroleum-derived fuel. Upwards of 85 percent of all Brazilian passenger vehicles ran on sugarcane alcohol in 1985. Alcohol has been a supplementary source, not the replacement for gasoline, however. As Brazil began to emerge as a major world auto maker, the government financed the expansion of the cane alcohol industry. In São Paulo, it was public money that created more *usinas*, alcohol distilleries. The fatal error was committed: the price was tied to that of the world's oil, thus creating a policy nightmare that required a gargantuan state subsidy to *usineiros*, alcohol producers.

When Geisel left the presidency in 1979, Brazil was producing 170 000 barrels per day (bpd) of petroleum and by mid-1984 production surpassed 500 000 bpd. By the end of 1985, Petrobrás produced 600 000 bpd and since then it has been able to maintain the same level of productivity. Ten years later, Brazil was producing around 650 000 bpd.[42] Since 1989, the country used about 1 million bpd, still importing about half of the petroleum consumed. As the price of oil plummeted in the second half of the 1980s, the cane growers pressured the state to pay a higher price for alcohol than oil.[43] Cane growers and distillers refused to take the lower price, preferring to go out of business. This led to the collapse of the Pró-Alcool program.

Inefficiency of Petrobrás

To supporters in the Brazilian Congress and society at large, Petrobrás is considered a model parastatal, which turns a profit every year – in 1987, its sales reached US$20 billion – but to detractors it is an inefficient and unproductive machine by the present world standards. The mighty monopoly has become soft. The average daily production of international oil companies is 130 barrels per day, per employee. In the mid-1990s, the average for Latin American oil companies was 98 barrels per day, per employee. Petrobrás's was 33 barrels. Tax exempt, the Brazilian company contributed the least to the state revenues among companies. Great Britain charged its oil companies 12.5 percent in royalties, plus 67.5 percent in taxes. The United States levied 12.5 to 20 percent in royalties and 35 percent in taxes. Norway, the Congo, and Colombia all charged higher royalties and taxes than Brazil. Petrobrás paid 5 percent in royalties and no taxes. Petrobrás comes out the worst, measured by the conventional yardsticks by which the world's oil firms are judged. In the early 1990s, per employee revenue was also lower for Petrobrás. Idemitsu Kosan of Japan turned in $3130 per employee, Petrofina of Belgium $1160, and Exxon $1090, the most productive US oil firm. Petrobrás registered $260 per employee. Two other companies that performed worse than the Brazilian company were Indian Oil ($260) and Pemex ($170).[44]

In Latin America, only Mexico, Venezuela, and Brazil still retain the near 100-percent state monopoly in oil. Even in Mexico, the privatization of its petrochemical industry has gone further: private enterprises can enter the area. The general trend is to permit the private sector to compete against the SOEs. In this scale of comparison, Petrobrás is a dinosaur.[45] The company employs 50 000 people and produces a barrel of oil at $13, comparable to the cost of US oil production. In Latin America, the average cost is between $3 and $8. In the Middle East, the cheapest in the world, the oil production cost is 50 cents per barrel. In a world where private-SOE joint ventures in the oil business are the main trends, such as in Colombia, Russia, and even socialist China, Brazil is the sole holdout for the state monopoly. *Veja* pointed out that British Petroleum and Occidental Petroleum discovered a 3 billion-barrel reserve in Colombia, equivalent to what took Petrobrás 40 years to find in Brazil.

Interbrás boondoggle

One criticism that company officials are sensitive about is the company's rise as a veritable transnational corporation and its proclivity of expanding into businesses to which the state did not originally mandate the company to go. Its subsidiary Interbrás, founded in 1976 and abolished in 1990, was a subject of such intense criticism.[46] Interbrás, or Petrobrás Comércio Internacional, S.A., was a trading company. It was handling exports, ranging from Volkswagens to chicken, coffee, meat, as well as civil construction services. In fact it pioneered a countertrade with African, Middle Eastern, and Latin American countries. In 1976, Interbrás handled exports valued at $162 million, or 4.5 percent of the total Brazilian overseas sales. In 1980, its exports surpassed over $1 billion, and in 1983 the trading arm of Petrobrás exported $2.88 billion worth of goods and services, representing a full 13 percent of the Brazilian exports. It had international subsidiaries in the US (Internor in New York), Western Europe, and two in the Cayman Islands, in addition to overseas representatives scattered in 16 countries, plus Hong Kong.[47] It was alleged that mismanagement, corruption, and often sweetheart deals with Brazilian suppliers guided the Interbrás operations. Officials hotly disputed this allegation.

One typical case gone bad was the Tama project in Nigeria in the mid-1970s, involving no less than the international soccer player, Pelé, as the chief public relations man, and a pool of Brazilian home appliance suppliers. Awash with petrodollars, oil-rich Nigeria offered a solid market potential. A local tribal "chief" and owner of a business firm, Joas, was persuaded to establish a joint venture, Jobrás, with a 60 percent stake for the Nigerian and a 40 percent share for Interbrás. Nigeria was to be a proving ground for Brazil's ambitious plan of exporting to Africa. From the outset, the joint venture encountered a strong headwind. It was unable to overcome the local inertia from the Nigerian partner; the project failed, forcing Interbrás to assume over $2 million in losses.[48] Interbrás blamed the sudden turns of political and economic events in coup-prone Nigeria in 1977–78 for the failure of the project. The Brazilians sold $6.7 million worth of home appliances, but at a loss. But the trading company pointed out that in April 1984, Interbrás sold more than $32 million worth of products, including refrigerators, cooking stoves, and so forth. It considered the Nigerian experience indispensable for the future success of home appliance exports to Third World countries.[49] It is difficult to provide a balanced picture of Petrobrás domestic and overseas operations, for many of the records are not available for outside scrutiny.

Bureaucratic patrimony

The presidents of the company always came from the ranks of military and political leaders during the military years. It was only during the last year of the Sarney government that the presidents came from the ranks of the company's career administrators. According to one study, all the chief executives represented their particular corporatist sector interests whether they were military or civilian. The height of such a politically charged environment was under the tutelage of Marshal Osvino F. Alves, former commander of the Brazilian First Army and often an ardent populist. Known as the "Red Marshal," Alves was one of President João Goulart's favorite generals and was placed in the presidency to tilt the company to a further nationalistic stance, with an objective of turning the company into a worker's haven.[50] This was consistent with a socialist ideal of making a parastatal a worker-managed entity. Petrobrás was also managed by Geisel's political confidants, none of whom had formal training or job experience in the oil business. And finally, the navy and the air force had their share of running the oil company in the 1970s and 1980s, as the army had dominated it in its formative phase.

The end of the monopoly

In 1994, while congress was working through the constitutional amendments, the company hired an expensive publicity team of actors, political pundits, athletes with household names, and other well-known citizens to head off all talk of privatization and deregulation of the oil monopoly. The Cardoso government in early 1995 was earnestly considering ways to pry open the oil monopoly still in the hands of Petrobrás. Indeed, the SOE's power was formidable. In late May 1995, the strike of petroleum workers threatened to undo Cardoso's economic reform plan, although the hemisphere's trend was to go private.[51] Cardoso sent in army units to occupy refineries, and the workers returned to work.

By late 1996, the oil monopoly ended. The Brazilian congress passed a bill that effectively deregulated the oil market, thus allowing in foreign competition, a classic compromise for the conflict between the privatization and statization that Brazilian society could not resolve. In January 1998, the Cardoso government created the National Petroleum Agency (ANP in Portuguese) to manage the energy policy – from granting exploration concessions to choosing international companies to compete in the Brazilian hydrocarbon market. The transfer of power from the Ministry of Mines and Energy to the ANP was the first step toward depoliticizing and eventually privatizating Petrobrás, that might take place soon after the October 1998 presidential election. After the election, instead, Cardoso put his son-in-law to run the ANP. The full privatization of Petrobrás is still years away, but now it has to compete in exploration, production, and marketing along with domestic and multinational oil companies.

National informatics policy

The Brazilian computer market reserve was based on two considerations. First, by the early 1970s, Brazil was becoming an important computer market. Its big and small businesses, especially banks, began to computerize their operations. Such major multinationals as IBM, Olivetti, Hewlett-Packard, DEC, Burroughs, and Texas Instruments became the major players in the domestic market. The idea that computer technology would be critical for the modernization of the economy was widely accepted. Those in the scientific community, including universities, the armed forces, and business came to realize that Brazil must seize whatever opportunities that were at hand to develop its home-grown computer industry. It must gain informatics independence. MNCs traditionally did not carry out basic research and development of hardware and software in Brazil, except those relating to customer services such as installation, repairs, and networking. Hence, officials in the Brazilian Ministry of Foreign Affairs (Itamaraty), the armed forces, the nascent computer sector, and the scientific establishment advocated a policy that would give Brazil opportunities to engage in R & D and eventually informatics independence.[52]

In 1971, the Brazilian Navy and the then National Economic Development Bank jointly funded $2 million for two universities to begin basic research and development of a microcomputer model, known as G-10. The following year, the armed forces established CAPRE (Coordenação das Atividades de Processamento Eletrônico) charged with the development of domestic computer technology by assisting existing companies and establishing new informatics SOEs. As in the past, when there was a vacuum in the market, the state moved in to seize the opportunity to develop new industry.

National security-driven economic nationalism

By 1979, the National Intelligence Service (SNI), Itamaraty, and the National Council on Scientific Research (CNPq) formed a joint screening agency which had complete authority over all encompassing aspects of computer technology development, import, and marketing. In fact, the trio along with the Central Bank and the patent office (INPI – National Institute of Industrial Properties) vetoed all product development proposals made by IBM and other international companies on the grounds that the plans did not include the transfer of technology to Brazil, acceptable overseas marketing strategies, and lack of Brazilian capital participation. Instead, CAPRE actively encouraged Brazilian companies and SOEs to develop domestic technologies and granted liberal credit to redouble R & D efforts.[53]

Second, given the enormous size of the Brazilian computer market, the notion of the "dependency theory," or an anti-dependent objective of acquiring self-sufficiency in "supermini" computer technology, played a decisive role in forming the market reserve policy. In 1978, two multinational companies imported 77 percent of all microcomputers. The domestic market was growing so fast that the Brazilian computer industry feared that MNCs would monopolize the market, leaving little or no room for it. Such dependency would condemn Brazil to a permanent status of informatics underdevelopment. Exhorting economic nationalism of self-sufficiency in informatics technology and supporting excessive protection for the domestic industry from foreign competition, the armed forces, especially those in the National Security Council and the SNI, began to institute restrictive decrees against multinationals. In 1983, the computer market stood at $1.5 billion in sales and the country imported over $400 million worth of hardware and peripherals.[54] It was the economic potential of the computer market that justified the military rationale of restricting MNC access to Brazil. As it turned out, countries without computer market reserves such as Taiwan, Korea, and Singapore did better in gaining informatics self-sufficiency.

In 1979, the military wing of the National Security Council and SNI adopted the next logical step in computer policy: the introduction of the Informatics Law. To enforce this law efficiently, a strong agency had to be created. CAPRE reported to the ministry of planning, whose head was always a civilian technocrat and who had no direct access to the armed forces high command. A new proposed enforcement organization was the Special Secretariat for Informatics (SEI) that would report directly to the president through the National Security Council. The law also expanded the power of SEI substantially, making it the absolute czar in the matter of computer policy making and enforcement.

Those who favored this domestic market reserve claimed that Brazil was emulating Japan, although there were fundamental differences. In the early years of its computer industry, the Japanese government deliberately dragged its feet on granting patent rights and permission to American companies to operate in Japan. This delay (which was perfectly legal in Japan) gave Japanese competitors time to develop their own products with governmental subsidies and support, typically from the Ministry of International Trade and Industry (MITI). Texas Instruments, the pioneer in semiconductor making, secured a Japanese patent 20 years after it filed. By then MITI had made sure that Japanese companies had established their foothold in the domestic and world markets.[55] Those who pushed for this Japanese model as Brazil's policy foundation came from all sectors of society: SEI (which means "I know" in Portuguese), the left, organized labor, universities, the armed forces, the scientific community, the small but growing domestic computer industry, and even a large segment of the media. The die was cast: Brazil would do whatever it took to keep international competition out while the domestic manufacturers illegally copied American computers and software. SEI even vetoed IBM's request to continue to produce an existing personal computer known as Model 36, although production had begun well before the market reserve practice was in place. The agency also rejected Apple and Hewlett-Packard proposals to establish plants in Brazil to build personal computers and export them.[56]

SEI dictatorship

It bears repeating that the market reserve policy, or the informatics ISI, was established in a series of SEI-issued decrees and regulations, not by legislation. The process was not reviewed by congress; rather it was done by an executive fiat. In September 1980, SEI decreed that the domestic market for hardware and software would be "guaranteed" to domestic private companies and encouraged SOEs and other government organs to use Brazilian computers and programs. This policy was followed by another regulation in 1982 that SEI would have complete authority to grant or deny permission to import computer systems into the domestic market. Many Brazilian SOEs and private companies became victims of this regulation, which routinely barred them from importing cutting edge technologies. And in 1983, SEI was granted more sweeping power to oversee the introduction of all computerized instrumentation and parts into the country. No fewer than 30 organizations expressed their enthusiastic support of the overarching jurisdiction, including the Brazilian Society for Scientific Progress (SBPC), the nation's main congregation of university scientists which carried political clout and prestige as a chronic critique of the military regime.

This time the SBPC endorsed strongly the SEI market reserve policy, a self-serving act.[57] The supreme irony was that Brazil had no computers of its own design and even fewer software programs that could compete against American and Asian products. This market closure was supposed to encourage domestic R & D in hardware and software. This never happened. What followed was wanton piracy and copycatting, complete disregard of the internationally accepted intellectual and trade mark regimes.

The United States vigorously protested this informatics authoritarianism. The US Congress considered retaliatory legislation against Brazil. SEI operated as an arm of the military but with strong support from the traditional opponents of the regime. This made the market reserve policy viable and SEI became emboldened. An unlikely political alliance formed: the ideological left of the country found one policy that they could support coming from the rightwing military. The business community was split. The São Paulo Industrial Federation (FIESP), the nation's largest organization of such a type, publicly denounced the market reserve policy, fearing sweeping denial of Brazilian access to cutting-edge technologies of non-informatic kinds. But many rightwing businessmen saw an opportunity to profit from the protectionist policy and rushed into the computer business.[58] As in similar industrial policy elsewhere, the state chose the winners. In the Brazilian case, the policy chose those who stood to profit from the closed market policy, not those likely to invest in researching and developing new informatic technology. This was the difference between Japan and Korea on the one hand and Brazil on the other.

Furthermore, in the late 1970s and early 1980s, the military pumped a generous amount of money into higher education and as a result university professors were making as much, if not more than, their counterparts in the First World. This had a tremendous impact on the morale of the intellectuals. The co-opted university scientists enjoyed generous research grants from the CNPq and other similar funding agencies, and enthusiastically supported an independent computer development policy. They justified this as patriotism for Brazil, not necessarily as political support for the regime. No longer were MNCs seen as useful adjuncts to the Brazilian development; on the contrary, they were competitors to be dealt with and even detractors of national economic independence. The informatics independence would be the final stop en route to global power. So thought the military and their newly found digital allies.

The Shi'ites of informatic nationalism

US protests fell on deaf ears. Those criticizing the SEI's informatics policy were branded as unpatriotic, favoring MNC interests, and, worse, condemning Brazil to eternal underdevelopment. Much like the McCarthy era in the United States, the Xi'itas or Shi'ites, as the ultra-nationalists of both the extreme left and right were called, went on massive witch hunts. Roberto Campos, the most articulate and out-spoken opponent of the informatics policy, was ridiculed as a sellout to foreign interests. Campos, like other critics, deplored the extremes of the reserve policy, but not always the "Buy Brazilian" aspect of it. No foreign participation was allowed in the personal computer busi-ness – importing, manufacturing, distribution, or marketing. The critics saw such a comprehensive policy as equally unpatriotic.[59]

The irony of all this was that the Informatics Law (Lei No. 7232 of 20 October 1984) did not call for closing the market. The purpose of the law was to promote and develop domestic technological capabilities while empowering SEI to control the import of hardware and software for eight years, until 1992 (Art. 4, VIII). As the US ambassador judi-ciously pointed out, it was extremely confusing to have the law read in one way and see the enforcement of it in another.[60] Periodically, the United States refused to sell computer technology to Brazil. Other coun-tries followed suit. As of late 1990, SEI still prohibited the import of some 300 computer components and peripherals. In June and July 1991, after emotional debates in the congress, the Collor government signed a bill into law which would end the market reserve by late 1992. The 1991 law allowed foreign computer firms to enter Brazil and manu-facture hardware and software, but only under the condition that they would be a minority partner to a joint venture, guarantee the transfer of technology to Brazilian partners, and pay a surtax which would go into the country's R & D funds. Domestic companies were exempt.[61] As it turned out, this law proved to be impractical.

The collapse of the policy

Why did Brazil acquiesce to the pressure and abandon the market reserve? First, it was not voluntary. Brazil was isolated by international computer makers who denied it access to new and advanced technolo-gies. This boycott was effective. The market reserve policy made half a dozen Brazilian companies rich, but they spent precious little on R & D. Second, copycatting or piracy of trade marks, computers, and software was fought by US and European firms in Brazilian courts and at times they won. It became untenable. Third, by the end of the 1980s, Brazilian computer technology fell so far behind international standards that exports never materialized, to the chagrin of the ultra-nationalists and the government. When SEI even denied Embraer, Petrobrás, Telebrás, and other major SOEs the permission to import advanced computer technologies, it made powerful enemies within the government.[62] By the time the Collor government came into office in early April 1990, a national consensus developed: the excessive market reserve hurt Brazil more than it helped.

Brazil's strategy was to build a capitalism without risk and a capitalism with closed markets. Even if it had been achievable, this objective could never become a lasting reality. First, Brazil's ISI, which made Brazil industrialized and competitive by the end of the 1970s, began to falter, because it lacked fresh home-made technologies to compete successfully in the global market. True, Brazil produced more steel and automobiles than Great Britain, an astounding accomplishment in itself. But computers were another matter. They required a massive investment. Brazil sought to make a flawed policy work. Heavy external borrowing during the time of high energy costs and continued investment in b.g development projects took their toll. As the global economy diversified but shrank at once during the early 1980s, Brazil was unable to keep tapping the external source of credit forever.

Second, the political opening, or *abertura*, in the late 1970s and early 1980s prompted public debate on the developmental policies of the B-A regime, and the opposition flourished faster than anticipated. The regime was caught in the crosscurrents of the leftist-nationalist demand of expanding the populist economic policy of a closed market, protected SOEs, and highly regulated trade and investment practices, and the global pressure of deregulation, liberalization, and privatization. Both the Figueiredo and Sarney governments introduced reform measures, but were unable to muster sufficient domestic support to implement them. Toward the end of his government, Figueiredo had no credibility to forge ahead with viable reform plans. Sarney was seen as a perfect stand-in for transition from the military to civilian rule, and hence was not expected to do anything serious And the man lacked political courage to implement bold reforms. Slowly, time ran out. The global economic train left the station, leaving Brazil behind, as the performance of Petrobrás and the ill-fated Informatics Law so eloquently demonstrated.

Third, none of the informatics-related agencies from CAPRE to SEI and the Ministry of Science and Technology were themselves big users of domestic computers. In Korea, the computer policy was made and enforced by the Ministry of Telecommunications, the country's biggest consumer of computers, peripherals, digital equipment, and software. In Brazil, the purchasing power was in the hands of SOEs and other ministries, but none was directly involved in computer technology development and marketing processes. The curious consequence was that Brazil's SEI prevented sister SOEs and ministries from using the latest foreign computer technologies to improve their efficiency. In brief, the policy breakdown between the informatics policy advocates and those with the consumption power provoked a market failure.

And finally, the transition to democracy after 1985 has placed Brazilian politics in a catatonic state. Accustomed to bureaucratic-authoritarian regimes and their decision-making style, the old civilian politicians, who had learned to cohabit with the military in the 1960s through 1980s, and the new crop of politicians, most of them born after 1964, frequently collided in the political arena. The making of the Constitution of 1988 was a national theater of the polymastic state trying to be a good cow to 155 million Brazilians. A peculiar democracy flourished to maximize the individual gains of politicians, ignoring the general well-being of society. This distorted democracy inevitably begat a series of corrupt acts in high places, ranging from the president of the republic to senators, deputies, cabinet ministers, and mayors of small towns. The impeachment of President Collor in December 1993 and the expulsion of a dozen federal deputies in May and June 1994 was the high point of this peculiar democracy. Brazil closed its chapter on the final phase of the statist economic development model and produced a new volatile mix of economic reform and free-wheeling political system, as it embraced its third elected civilian presidency in five years since 1985, that of Fernando Henrique Cardoso.

As it turned out, it would fall on Cardoso, a former socialist (to some, a Marxist) to dismantle the seven-decade long populist closed-market policy that Vargas had initiated in the 1930s, that his heirs built up, and that the military expanded. Once in office, Cardoso began to move the country closer to an open-market economy. Ironically, the loss of state power and autonomy was accelerating under the social democrat president who once believed in the invincibility and virtues of the state.

4
Chile: the Revolution That No One Desired

The end of the calm

The 1960s were turbulent but exciting times for Latin America. Change was in the air. Chile, between the election of Eduardo Frei Montalva in 1964 as president and the violent overthrow of Latin America's first elected Marxist government in 1973, was facing a crucial decision of how to restructure its democratic but populist state system. Chile was at the last phase of becoming autonomous and acquiring power to determine its own destiny. The slow process of the statist intervention in the market since the early 1930s ran into setbacks first under General Carlos Ibáñez, who came to office by coup and then by election and then under the rule of the Alessandri father-and-son team of the conservative nationalist tradition. The decade between 1964 and 1973 was going to be a decisive period for Chile to finalize its quest for power and autonomy.

The country had a long tradition of democratic participation. In the early 1930s, Chile already had strong socialist movements and for a brief period a socialist government was in power. During the 1930s, as in Brazil and Mexico, Chile was establishing state-owned enterprises (SOEs) to develop the economy and to marshal state resources. The best known of the SOEs was, and still is, the state development bank, the Corporación de Fomento de la Producción, or CORFO. The economic power was firmly in the hands of the country's key landholding oligarchy, international mining companies, small domestic but vociferous industrialists, and the financial sector which was completely dominated by outsiders. The class delineation in Chile was more graphic and the politicization was far more pronounced than earlier in Argentina or Brazil. Chile derived as much as 80 percent of its revenue from exporting copper, and the copper industry in Chile was in the hands of three US mining firms. No other country in South America schematically fitted the dependency model so well.[1]

Compared to the experiences of Argentina and Brazil, the Chilean political universe and the economic universe between 1964 and 1973 were mutually antagonistic and even in a life–death struggle. The state, regardless of who was in power, sought to expand its autonomy and power, while the market resisted. The political economy was not calibrated in a manner whereby either could control the other. In Argentina, the dependency of the market on the state was absolute, while, in Brazil, the market was willing to be co-opted by the state for its own benefits. In Chile, the power of the state and the market's ability to resist the state's whims were about on par during the period under study, hence generating an intense conflict. Manuel Antonio Garretón observed that, unlike other countries, the import-substituting industrialization in Chile took place under a democratic state, not authoritarian, and hence the incorporation of the underclass into the political system occurred simultaneously.[2] This is an important distinction to note.

Chile, unlike Argentina and Brazil, has also had a longer tradition of a democratic political system.[3] Hence, as the state encroached on the market and invested in infrastructure and import-substituting industrialization (ISI) projects, the political power of the incorporated class (the middle and lower classes) also expanded and these newly integrated sectors often confronted successfully in the democratic arena the upper class, the bourgeoisie, the agrarian oligarchy, and the commercial and financial elites. This had a greater propensity for creating a crisis and resulting in a political stalemate. Chile's experience was one of confrontation between the state dominated by the middle classes and underclass and the market then dominated by the traditional oligarchy and foreign capital. After 1970, as the state forcibly took over the market, the international capitalist core countries successfully isolated the socialist-Marxist Chile. The failure to establish a mutually acceptable condominium among various internal groups and with the world capitalist core resulted in the military coup of September 1973 and the adoption of an antipopulist, neoliberal market-oriented economy. The rise of the state as the dominant player in Chile began in 1925, not in 1970 after Allende's election.

Early statization

A group of young officers overthrew the government in 1925. They introduced the 1925 constitution de-enshrining the firm guarantee of rights to property as the primacy of political power. Although "the inviolability of property" was mentioned in the constitution, individual rights were superseded by the larger societal goals. The document also highlighted the duties of the state in the areas of health, education, and the well-being of workers.[4] In brief, the state could seize the properties and could intervene in the market as the ultimate arbitrator, when such action could justify the country's collective interests. The constitution did not give political hegemony to the Conservatives but the fractious parliamentary system permitted them to thrive as the nation's political and economic elites. After two years of internal power struggle and purges of opponents, Colonel Carlos Ibáñez emerged as the strong man of Chile by 1927. In an election in which less than 10 percent of the population was qualified to vote and fewer than half the eligible voted, Ibáñez won 98 percent of the votes cast.[5]

The government promoted the first phase of Chile's industrialization and trade expansion. Comparing the per capita steel consumption figure, at the height of Ibáñez's rule (1930), the average per capita consumption reached 126 pounds, while that for 1925–29 was 83 pounds and for 1947–51, a scant of 64.5 pounds.[6] The steel consumption was prima facie evidence that Chile was being industrialized. Fred Nunn argued that the Ibáñez government was not a military dictatorship, rather a military-civilian coalition government in which military and civilian supporters of Ibáñez shared the power.[7] Both groups promoted industrialization and a strong activist state. But unlike Pinochet's regime, the Ibáñez government was partial to big business.

The dominant classes from the 1930s to the 1950s came from the same bolt of cloth, with a new influx from the professions, or the middle classes. In the 1938 election, Chile chose a government which promoted industrialization through state patronage. The founding of CORFO was the turning point, when the country seriously sought to acquire autonomy and power over its economic decision making. As in so many cases in history like the IRI – Institute of Industrial Reconstruction – of Italy (the massive corporate bankruptcy following the First World War) and SUDENE – the Northeastern Superintendency of Development – of Brazil (the chronic droughts of the Northeast), the 1939 earthquake at Chillán provided the government with an opportunity to link the post-quake restoration projects to more long-term development objectives by creating a development bank.[8] Steel, energy, and petroleum became the bailiwicks of CORFO and the government also offered social programs for the working class.[9]

By 1970, CORFO emerged as the holding company of all Chilean state-owned enterprises and more. Succeeding governments in the late 1930s until 1970 followed the variegated form of the statist development approaches. But families remained organizing units in economic activities, whether in landholding, commerce, banking, or industry. They in turn had access to state credit to modernize and expand their operations. The interlocking system of elite networking was prevalent. Business mergers and marriages among prominent elite families also cemented new political alliances. The Edwards clan was connected to 290 of the nation's 1300 firms in the 1950s, representing 70.6 percent of all capital assets in banks, insurance companies, shipping, commercial agriculture, mining, and manufacturing. Also men of letters and of political prominence came from the family.[10] By the 1950s, the traditional political parties began to lose their popular appeal and a new vibrant political movement was emerging. Various historians estimated that one hundred families ruled the country in an iron grip.

The rise of Christian Democrats

The Christian Democratic movement in Chile dates back to the 1930s. But it was not until after the Second World War that the movement gained currency. Originally a small and elitist movement of intellectuals closely identified with the Catholic Church and Europe's *falangista* thinking, the Chilean movement became a political party in 1957. The Christian Democratic Party (PDC) was often personified by its leader, Eduardo Frei. His association with the *falangistas* in Europe and Latin America was deep and strong.[11] In fact, the Falange Nacional was the first political institution Frei was associated with. But other founders of the party such as Romodiro Tomic and Rafael Agustín Gumucio had equally strong ties with the international and Latin American leftist movements. All were acutely aware of the fragmented nature of Chilean society and thought that ideology could unify the country. As a viable alternative to Marxism and the radical left, the PDC leaders were also acutely aware of their historical mission against the rising tides of the leftist movements around the world and in Latin America. On the continent alone, the Guatemalan Revolution of 1952–54, the Bolivian Revolution of 1952, and the Cuban Revolution of 1959 left a strong imprint on their thinking. As the ideals of the democratic alternative to Latin America's left began to catch on, the PDC drew its supporters and members from a wide-ranging circle: Liberals, Conservatives, Radicals, and even followers of the Carlos Ibáñez regime of the 1950s. Together, they forged a new party, which decidedly lost the elitist flavor and began to reach out to the working class, those unionists who preferred Christian communitarianism to revolutionary Marxism.

The economic situation in the mid-1950s was dismal. One observer described it as an economy infected by "an inflation with recession." The inflation in 1954 reached 60 percent and the following year rose to 84 percent. Both foreign trade and domestic manufacturing were in recession. Unemployment was soaring from 6.5 percent in 1955 to 9.5 percent a year later.[12] Frei and his PDC collaborators were under strong pressure to find solutions. By the late 1950s, the PDC under Frei's leadership carved out its niche. The party embodied Christian values and democratic reformist alternatives to the Chilean and Latin American political left.[13] The democratic convergence since then has remained the core of Christian Democrat ideology, as we will see later.

The 1958 presidential election was the first major contest among ideologically well-defined candidates. Jorge Alessandri, following in his father's footsteps, occupied the right of the spectrum. His supporters were among the country's major bourgeoisie. The left was represented by Salvador Allende, a physician and a socialist, whom the country's leftist parties and communist-Marxist controlled unions supported. The standard bearer of the center or more precisely, center-left, was Eduardo Frei, carving out the growing middle sector and antioligarchical and antileftist labor and business organizations. It was a bitter election, splitting the country as never before. The rightwing candidate won with Allende and Frei coming in second and third place, respectively.[14] These three, Alessandri, Allende, and Frei, would remain the principal actors who would redefine the Chilean political matrix for the next two decades.

Two critical issues confronted Chile in the two decades after the Second World War: the transfer of the foreign ownership of copper mines to Chile and the need for sweeping agrarian reform. By the time the election of 1964 rolled around, the PDC emerged as the nation's largest political party. The Popular Action Front (FRAP in Spanish) was a coalition of Chile's two major leftist parties, communist and socialist. On the right were the Liberal and Conservative parties, with the centrist Radicals now moving toward the right. In 1962, the three parties formed the Democratic Front and four years later they became the Nationalist Party, Chile's rightwing bedrock. The Chilean center and rightwing groups were generously supported by the United States – the CIA, US Agency for International Development (USAID), and United States businesses such as David Rockefeller's Business Group for Latin America, later to become the Council of the Americas in 1970. Besides Rockefeller, who was then chairman of the Chase Manhattan Bank, the chief executive officer of Anaconda, C. Jay Parkinson, chief executive of Pepsi Cola, Donald M. Kendall, a personal friend of US president Richard Nixon, and the chairman of ITT, Harold S. Geneen, were key contributors. All four had strong business interests in Latin America, and in Chile, Chase, ITT, Anaconda, and Pepsi were extraordinarily strong.

At least $20 million was pumped into the Frei candidacy in the 1964 campaign. Also benefiting from such ties was *El Mercurio*, the family newspaper of Agustín Edwards, the scion of the country's major economic elite, which led the indomitable struggle against the left in general and Allende in particular. Seymour Hersch of the *New York Times* claimed that *El Mercurio* and the Edwards group were recipients of CIA largesse as well as the Council of the Americas' generous financial contributions.[15] Globalization came to Chile through political contributions; Chile did not seek to embrace globalization.

The PDC was the only party with the broad spectrum of ideological representation of the right, the center, and the left. This was the decidedly advantageous feature of the party. Frei throughout his career remained a centrist; however, Rodomiro Tomic led the leftwing of the party; and on the right were the followers of the old falangistas. The ideological linchpin was the 1931 papal encyclical *Quadragesimo Anno* of Pius XI, which rejected both extremes of the left and the right and sought to build a Christian middle, the "communitarian" solutions.[16]

In fact, the election of 1964 was a contest between the FRAP candidate (Allende) and the PDC standard bearer (Frei). The rightist candidate was a minor factor. Frei handily won, although in the congressional election leftist candidates fared better, building a hefty power bloc in the legislature and an intractable nemesis to the Frei government.

Frei's reforms

There were several outstanding social and economic issues that the Frei government inherited: agrarian reform, the role of international capital, and the future of the mining sector.

The agrarian question and the quasi-monopoly of foreign mining companies occupied the center of the political debate. Only 7 percent of Chile's land barons owned two-thirds of all lands and 78 percent of the arable and irrigated land. A large estate, *fundo* or *latifundio*, was a maddeningly inefficient social symbol of wealth. Also, *minifundios*, plots too small to be economically viable, were proliferating. Compounding this was the onset of the forced rural-to-urban migration, the result of the decades-long population growth. By one estimate, as much as 10 percent of the population was on the move, thus radicalizing the rural problem as a national issue and gradually securing urban supporters.[17]

In the early 1960s, the country was spending $100 million annually on importing grains. All three parties fundamentally viewed the land question as one of economic inefficiency and social injustice. The Alessandri government adopted an agrarian reform law and established two implementation agencies: the Agrarian Reform Corporation (CORA) and the Institute of Agrarian Development (INDAP). The Alessandri law called for the expropriation of inefficiently used land above 80 *irrigated* hectares with a payment combination of 10 percent in cash and the remainder with state bonds. The basic irrigated hectare in the Central Valley came to be 500 hectares or about 2000 acres. Although the law called for the annual redistribution of 5000 farms, the Alessandri administration distributed lands to a little more than 1000 new owners by 1964, when Eduardo Frei took over power. The land distribution was no showcase success; the one area of social programs in which the Alessandri government did make a significant contribution was the public housing project. The president claimed that over 100 000 "real houses" were built and distributed to the needy.[18] In spite of all the fanfare and national tumult that surrounded the issue, however, the Frei government during the five years 1965–70 was able to redistribute only 12 percent of the arable land.[19]

During the 1960s and 1970s, the state revenues from copper exports fluctuated between 70 and 80 percent a year. Copper until 1970 was a foreign-dominated business in Chile. International copper pricing efforts often ignored the concerns of the Chilean government, while the US companies set the pace and tone in the international copper market. As in so many other raw materials, it was the consumer, not the producer, who controlled the market. It was not until 1973, when the 13 petroleum producing countries imposed the first OPEC price hike on the consumer countries, that major raw material producers like Chile, Brazil, Zaire, and South Africa had any impact on the international metals market.

Often, domestic legislation to forge the development of raw materials failed to produce the intended result. The 1955 legislation seeking to encourage foreign investment in copper ironically permitted the de-escalating tax schedule, as the production went up. Anaconda operated the world's largest open pit mine, Chuquicamata. With Kennecott, the other US mining behemoth, the two companies held a stranglehold on the national economy. During the 1960s, Anaconda earned over $500 million in profit from its Chilean operation, although the company placed the profit at a lower figure.[20]

The manipulation of reporting profits by foreign corporations throughout Latin America to the host government was rampant in the mining economies of Bolivia, Peru, Chile, and Ecuador during the 1960s and 1970s. It was commonplace for US multinationals to under-report their profits in overseas operations (to reduce taxes) but, to keep the value of their stocks up in the US market, to report the higher but more realistic figure to the Securities and Exchange Commission. In order to correct this glaring discrepancy, the Andean Pact countries established a common rule of using 14 percent profit as the base reference for taxing MNCs in the region. Bolivia, Peru, Ecuador, Colombia, and Venezuela, the other members of the pact adhered to the rule, while in 1976 Chile left the pact.[21]

Chileanization

From the left, the FRAP called for the state takeover of key economic sectors, including mining. Squeezed by the rising nationalist sentiment against foreign ownership, low taxes, and tax avoidance, the PDC began to stake out a tough position – the state's ownership of a majority equity. In the first phase of the Chileanization of 1967, Kennecott agreed to sell 51 percent of its shares to the government of Chile, while Anaconda sold 25 percent. In fact, Chile paid $80 million for Anaconda's operation, although the book value was priced at $67 million. This was because the companies were allowed to under-value their properties to lower the tax burdens on Chile. Furthermore, the futures contract guaranteed that both companies would continue to market copper throughout the world and would retain the management responsibility.[22] This in fact was no nationalization. This "Chileanization" plan was, however, a palatable alternative to a complete nationalization.

More importantly, Chile lacked resources and trained personnel to succeed in the globalized and almost cartelized copper market. Allowing the US firms to remain in Chile as partners to the government was a prudent mid-step alternative. Frei's strategy was to take over the mining sector by stages. Chile needed time to develop its own technical expertise, managerial staff, and capital to expand. Within the ranks of the PDC, however, there was growing support for the complete nationalization of mines, especially strong among Tomic's leftwing.[23]

Politically both in the agrarian reform and the Chileanization of mines, the Frei government came up short. To the agrarian radicals in the party, the Alessandri law did not go far enough. Thus, the Christian Democratic government passed the second law in November 1965, guaranteeing the establishment of *asentamientos*, or settlement, midway between the collective farm and private ownership, for three to five years. This compromise satisfied no one. By then, the Cuban Revolution had an explosive impact on Latin America; and both the Chilean agrarians and FRAP had strong ties to Cuba, which introduced a collective farm system. Some like Jacques Chonchol favored a Yugoslavian model, a mixed land tenure of private and collectivist farms. The Frei government could not forge a consensus, as the PDC split into three ideological factions: the followers of the government, or *oficialistas*; those who opposed many of the Frei programs, or *rebeldes*; and those who fell between the first two groups but often supported the former.[24] Also, the policies of reform could be categorized into three types: incrementalist, populist, and oppositior (*ruptura*). The "rebel" faction even called for the need to adopt a "noncapitalist way to development" (*via no capitalista de desarrollo*).[25] It is clear that the ideological division became untenable and Frei's willingness to move to the left crippled his program, as the right and the center hammered him with incessant criticism.

More disturbingly, Frei's power base in the PDC was eroding. In 1965, the government increased its housing spending by 95 percent over 1964. By 1968, the spending was up by 237.4 percent.[26] The business recession of 1967 and the PDC's weak showing (35.6 percent) in municipal and local elections aggravated the situation further; the stubborn inflation (27 percent per annum), labor unrest, and growing peasant militancy compounded Frei's woes; and the military revolt for higher salaries in 1969 tattered Frei's relations with the armed forces. It was said that the real purpose of the revolt was to register the armed forces' concern for the power gain made by the followers of the pro-Cuban and pro-Czech factions of the Chilean left.[27] Like others in civilian politics, military officers were convinced that the victor in the 1970 election would be a socialist or a communist. General Roberto Viaux made it clear that the armed forces, the disgruntled segment of the PDC, and the right feared the election of Allende or Tomic. Some suspected that Frei was duped into bringing "communism without communists" to Chile. The US Embassy and the CIA station in Santiago were convinced that Frei had moved too far to the left. Embassy officials in Chile pressed for a change in the US foreign policy: disown the PDC, Frei, and Tomic and support archconservative Jorge Alessandri.[28] Like it or not, Chile was drawn into the global tug of the Cold War.

The presidential election of 1970

The three leading contenders for the presidency were Salvador Allende from the leftist coalition of the Popular Unity (UP), Rodomiro Tomic, chief of the leftwing group of the Christian Democrats, and the insatiable Jorge Alessandri, running for the third time in two decades. The issues and solutions proposed by the three candidates were clearly enunciated but philosophically divergent. Two particular issues predominated in the electoral rhetoric: nationalization of the American copper mining companies and radical agrarian reform.

Chile was one of a few Latin American countries where the Central Intelligence Agency successfully penetrated all levels of government and society. It was viewed as the country that the US knew. However, Allende's election with 36.6 percent of the votes came as a big surprise to Washington. In fact, it "astounded the Central Intelligence Agency and the White House,"[29] according to one observer. The United States government and big business had channeled money into Alessandri's campaign through the Edwards organization, as the Johnson administration had financed the election of Frei some six years earlier. Deceptively, the polls taken by the Edwards organization showed that Alessandri was ahead of the other two candidates.

From the Chilean perspective, the election of 1970 was preordained as a final showdown between the left and the right. The centrist approach that the Frei administration wanted but failed to pursue did produce growth but no reforms. The leftwing of the PDC by the end of the 1960s was convinced that the party should carve out a clearly delineated center-leftist position. It called for the nationalization of key industries, including foreign-owned mining, utilities, and manufacturing companies, thus going beyond Frei's Chileanization. The major difference between the Popular Front and the PDC leftwing was one of approach. The PDC behaved like a European social democratic party: pushing a fundamental structural change in the economy, society, and politics, but *by constitutional means*. No violent revolutionary approach was to be advocated. Frei successfully negotiated the purchase of telephone, power, and other utilities companies from the foreign owners during the last years of his government. The public sector was becoming an overwhelming economic force. Toward the end of Frei's term, 70 and 75 percent of all investment came from the government.[30]

United States President Nixon never liked the Christian Democrats, the darlings of the Kennedys and the Georgetown crowd, but thought Allende was worse. Something had to be done. By a National Security Council directive, Nixon set up a special task force. Known as the 40 Committee,[31] it was placed under Kissinger's personal direction. A White House task force was known as the Special Group under Kennedy, then the 303 Committee during the Johnson years, and by 1970 the 40 Committee. The reconstructed committee had the responsibility of overseeing CIA covert operations. State, Justice, and Defense, the Joint Chiefs, and the National Security Council ran the committee.[32] At a meeting with Nixon and his top aides, Kendall and Edwards sought White House support for an anti-Allende campaign that would become one of the biggest US corporate involvements in a foreign election. Without consulting anyone, Nixon ordered Kissinger, CIA director Richard Helms, and Attorney General John Mitchell to "move against Allende."[33]

Track I, Track II

The role of the 40 Committee and the CIA in overthrowing the Allende government was under scrutiny by journalists, scholars, and US Senate and House committees, most notably by Senator Frank Church's committee. The records and testimonies of the officials involved from the White House to the CIA indicate that the Nixon policy was comprised of two tracks. Track I was *to stop Allende from being elected in the Chilean legislature*. Failing that, the second option would be launched. Track II was a supersecret plot, not even known to the committee, but was based on a direct order from Nixon to the CIA – *a military coup to prevent Allende from taking office*. The second tract would cost US taxpayers $10 million.

The first track failed, as predicted by the US Embassy, once the PDC threw its support to the socialist candidate rather than the rightwing politician. Even before it could be launched in full force, Track II suffered its fatal blow. The United States was covertly cultivating the support of General René Schneider, the army commander in chief and a staunch constitutionalist for the anti-Allende cause. When the general was assassinated, the plan suffered a sudden setback. The CIA station in Santiago had espoused the encouraging assessment that the army would rally around Schneider's cause of defending the constitutional government. The only other general who could possibly stop Allende was Roberto Viaux, now retired, whom Kissinger deridingly called "the general without [an] army." As it turned out, Viaux was the mastermind of Schneider's assassination. The general was convicted of the crime and became a non-option. This episode ended Track II. Later Kissinger, Alexander Haig (then Kissinger's assistant at the White House), and others testified in public that a plot to remove Allende from power was no longer in force.[34]

However, the Nixon White House did not stop there. The National Security Council Decision Memorandum, or NSDM, No. 93 entitled "Policy toward Chile" of November 1970 clearly outlined the economic sanctions that the US would impose on Allende's Chile. Allende became such an obsession of the president and his National Security adviser that a senior State Department official said "Kissinger, in effect, became a Chilean desk officer." The White House, not the State Department nor the CIA, was managing US policy toward Chile. Hence, the covert objective of Track II survived, although officially it did not exist. Between November 1970 and September 1973, the United States spent $8 million in the CIA's economic sabotage activities that also encouraged directly or indirectly "the military coup groups into a strong unified move against the government," according to the Senate Intelligence Committee.[35]

Chile and the cold war detente

The war against Chile became the personal crusade of Nixon and Kissinger for different reasons. Nixon wanted to protect the interests of his corporate patrons; Kissinger, more sophisticated than Nixon in the international balance of power politics, saw Allende's victory as a dangerous harbinger that could lead to the rise of Soviet naval preeminence in South America. The Soviet navy already countered the US naval movements in the Atlantic from their Cuban base in Cienfuegos. To have Chile fall into the hands of the Soviets would mean the fall of the South Pacific, a potential danger to Hawaii, the seat of the Commander in Chief Pacific (CINCPAC) that watched over Asia Pacific. The United States maintained two top-secret military listening posts in Chile: the missile tracking station on Easter Island, where National Security Agency men and their supercomputers monitored Soviet missiles in flight and French nuclear tests in the Pacific; and, high in the

Chilean Andean mountains, NSA maintained a monitoring station that kept track of Soviet submarine movements in the South Pacific. Immediately after Allende's election, these posts were dismantled and the equipment flown to Panama. To Kissinger, Allende's election was not a localized Marxist electoral victory owed "due to the irresponsibility of its own [Chile's] people"[36] but had tremendous consequences for the future of the superpower confrontations in the Pacific that the people "without history" [read Chileans] had no right to influence. For the pro-Atlantic Kissinger, history occurred in Europe, not in the Pacific and least of all in Chile.

Allende and Chile became the first victim of superpower politics in the early days of a thaw in Cold War diplomacy (or the Nixon–Brezhnev détente) that Henry Kissinger masterminded first as Nixon's national security adviser and later as one of the most prolific secretaries of state of the United States. The timing of the advent of the Popular Unity could not have been worse. The world in the 1970s was no longer one of inching toward Cold War confrontations, but rather one of managed détente between the two superpowers. Clearly, Soviets were not interested in Chile; the Soviets were more interested in the détente arrangements with the Nixon administration. The Soviets wanted to expand their geopolitical and economic presence in the Middle East (Iraq, Syria, and Libya), Africa (Angola, Mozambique, and Namibia), South Asia (India and Afghanistan), and Southeast Asia (Vietnam, Cambodia, and Laos). The tacit exchange of the mutual recognition of "Your Poland for My Poland" worked well in the Western Hemisphere to the likings of Kissinger and Brezhnev. The Soviet military felt secure with the bases in Cuba and Vietnam, new military gains in their global strategy in the 1960s and 1970s. Furthermore, the Soviet Union in the 1970s was experiencing a series of internal economic difficulties for the first time since the revolution. Agricultural production was down, industrial infrastructure was aging, social dissent on the rise, and its political system was beginning to show wear and tear. The Soviet resources were overtaxed to cover both the domestic needs and overseas geopolitical expansion. The Soviets were hard pressed to prop up Eastern and Central Europe and to revise the downsizing of their expensive strategy of global reach. Chile was expendable. And Kissinger knew it.

A reluctant revolutionary

Salvador Allende Gossens was a well-known and even well-liked socialist senator, when he ran for president for the third time in 1970. In the late 1940s, when communists and socialists were discussing unity, Allende, the secretary general of the Chilean Socialist Party, was against such a merger for the fear of a communist takeover as happened in Eastern Europe after the War. The socialists favored a constitutional and peaceful means of change, while the communists pushed for a Russian-style and Cuban-style violent revolution.[37] Through the 1950s and 1960s, Allende resisted the temptation of adopting a more militant revolutionary approach for his party, but consented to a series of electoral and political collaborations with the communists. At the outset Allende's Popular Unity was a government of several leftist factions and participation from the PDC. Allende never forgot that had it not been for the 75 PDC votes in the congress, he would never have been president of Chile. Violent solutions to the reform, however urgent, were not his first choice. But once in power, the government acceded to the demands of the communists and the revolutionary wing of the coalition such as the Movement of the Revolutionary Left (MIR). In time, the Marxist revolutionaries in the coalition overwhelmed Allende, succeeded in taking over the daily administration of the government, and pushed a small number of PDC and Nationalist collaborators out of government. The rightist politicians said that they had known all along Allende could not control Marxists and would become a pawn of communists.[38]

Seizure of copper mines

The Allende government had to deal with two crucial unresolved issues: American mining companies and agrarian reform. Well before 1970, Allende's advisers convinced him that nothing short of the complete nationalization and statization of the mining sector would do. In 1968, Richard M. Nixon was elected president of the United States. Considerably less sympathetic toward social reforms in Latin America where he had been viciously attacked in his 1958 trip as vice-president for the Eisenhower administration, Nixon was not amused by the election of the first Marxist president in the Western Hemisphere. Neither was he amused by the events leading to 1970.

The Allende government nationalized foreign-owned mines. It offered to compensate the American mining companies with a convoluted formula: the compensation would be based on the value of the original investment, after deducting the depreciation, amortization, and excess profits that the companies had taken out of the country after the 1955 law was passed. Furthermore, the president by law had the power to define what constituted excess profits and could not be overruled by the court. Under this formula, the US firms had to reimburse Chile the difference between the excess profits expatriated for decades and the current value of the mines.

Chile invited two outside consulting teams, one from the Soviet Union and the second from France, to assess the value of the mines, especially Chuquicamata, El Teniente, and El Salvador, the three major mines of the country. Before the foreign consultants could complete ,the study, Allende accused Anaconda and Kennecott of having removed the excess profits of $774 million out of Chile. When the value of the mines was deducted from the profit in flight, these companies ended up owing Chile. Hence, there would be no compensation. The United States government proposed a fair compensation formula and offered to pay the affected companies with US Treasury bonds which Chile would buy and would pay back for over 20 to 25 years. The Socialist Party dismissed the offer and Allende never bothered to respond to Nixon's plan.[39] The Chilean congress "unanimously" approved the UP's proposal to nationalize and statize the mining (*gran minería*) operated by foreign companies. A scant four days after the law was passed, Allende seized the mines.[40]

The nationalization of the foreign-owned mines was popular and had support from all sectors. However, the seizure of other private properties was another matter. The Central Bank was ordered to buy up private banks. Up to that time, Santiago consumed as much as two-thirds of all private credit available and banks granted credits to major companies, seldom extending credit to small businesses and individuals beyond the capital. The bank owned by the Edwards family was accused of exceeding the credit limit set up by the Central Bank and was promptly seized. Also, two US banks were affected in the nationalization.[41] Allende wanted credit to be available to the countryside.

The government also forced other industries to sell majority equity to the state or be forcibly seized. The automobile assemblers were told that they would be participating in the production of single standardized cars, trucks, and buses. The state development bank (CORFO) ordered all auto manufacturers to sell 51 percent of their shares to the government and opened a bid for future models to be produced. Ford, having refused to participate, was taken over by the state in May 1971. GM voluntarily closed down its operations. Nine European and one Japanese car makers submitted bids, and the government chose one

Japanese, two French, and one Spanish manufacturers. In addition, the government also nationalized the fisheries and textile industries.[42]

Peasants empowering themselves

The agrarian reform presented a multifaceted problem for Allende. Like the Alessandri government, the Frei government had failed to meet its own target of creating 100 000 peasant proprietors. By 1970, only 20 000 new landholders were created. Frustrated and impatient peasants began to organize under several leftist groups, most notably the MIR and the Communist Party. Before 1970, MIR-and-Communist-led peasant groups had taken over fundos in the south. Between November 1970 and December 1971, some 1500 illegal seizures took place. The Mapuche Indians reclaimed their ancestral land.

Allende's first minister of agriculture, Jacques Chonchol, proposed relocating the ministry of agriculture to the south so that he could assist in the "accelerated agricultural reform." The Popular Unity groups established peasant councils throughout the country. The Communists wanted the councils to serve as mediators among the state agricultural bureaucracy, leftist parties, and peasants. MIR, the more militant of the two, advocated that the councils themselves should actively become producers, thus becoming a new power group at the local level. Further undermining the leftist-led agrarian reform process were the political and ideological sectarian disputes. No one seemed to come up with a solution as to how to reconcile peasant councils and peasant unions, which were sprouting up throughout the country under the myriad leftist organizations, all claiming to support the Allende government.

By the end of Allende's first year in office, Chile had 181 councils and, by 1973, every province in the country had more than 1 council operating. Although the level of their power differed from region to region, the councils openly dictated their terms to the agrarian reform agency and participated in the expropriation process. What compounded the reform and eventually caused it to fail was that the UP government did not have the power to control the leftist groups instigating and directing takeovers and de facto expropriation.[43] All this was happening in Chile, while the world economy was globalizing and the Soviet economy was stalling.

The negative impact of ill-managed agrarian reform, or, better yet, out of control seizures, began to show in food production. For 1971, Chile's agricultural productivity went up by 5 percent. For 1972, the first year of Allende's land reform, the production fell by 3.6 percent and the following year by a whopping 16 percent. Chile was already a net importer of grains. For 1971, the country imported $260 million worth of grain; for 1972 and 1973, the imports reached $383 million and $700 million respectively. The Central Bank reported that the area sown for wheat during 1973–74 decreased by 5 percent.[44] During the Allende years, the United States did not embargo the exports of foodstuff; in fact, the United States continued to sell the goods.

Nixon's retaliation

The Nixon administration had to select its retaliatory steps. Unlike Cuba, however, Chile could not be cordoned off. Also unlike Cuba and to the credit of the Popular Unity government, Chile allowed a vigorous political opposition throughout the socialist years. Chile had an elected socialist-Marxist regime – the socialist president and his Marxist-Communist collaborators in congress – while Cuba's Castro came to power through a revolution and remained in power by force. Hence, the Nixon government conceived a different policy directed at Chile. In the administration, Treasury Secretary John Connally and National Security Adviser Kissinger were the least sympathetic voices and were openly hostile to Allende. Other cabinet members had no stated position. Thus the 40 Committee, unopposed in the government, crafted the fundamentals of the Nixon administration's economic retaliation toward Chile.

Most concretely, the administration took several steps. First, the United States government withdrew all Ex-Im Bank credit to Chile. When Lan-Chile, the country's air carrier, wanted to buy Boeing jetliners, the credit approval was "postponed." Second, the administration encouraged US banks to reduce and then withdraw all commercial credit to Chile. Short-term credit is the lifeblood of trade. Before Allende came to power, the US banks extended Chile $220 million per year to finance foreign trade. But during Allende's first year in office, the credit shrank to $35 million.[45] Third, the government assisted Kennecott in embargoing Chilean copper. Chile's copper exported to Western Europe was impounded, as the American mining company sought a court injunction. In France and Holland, Chile went to court to secure the release of the impounded copper, claiming that the French and Dutch courts had no jurisdiction over the Chilean nationalization decision. The French court ruled that the copper could be sold, but the money should be held in a special escrow account until a court-appointed referee could decide the legality of the nationalization and statization. As Chile rejected the extraterritorial jurisdiction, the litigation dragged on.

And finally, the United States pressured the World Bank (WB), the International Monetary Fund (IMF), and the Inter-American Development Bank (IDB) to reject Chile's loan applications. The last loan from the IDB was July 1971 and, after mid-1972, no credit was made available from the World Bank and the IMF, which classified Allende's Chile as "not credit worthy." In a 1972 visit to Chile, Robert McNamara, the then president of the World Bank, informed Allende's men that Bank credit was still available for Chile and that the Allende government needed to submit applications. But McNamara said that Chile chose not to apply after his visit, which contradicted the leftist assertion that the United States had put heavy pressure on the World Bank not to grant further loans.[46]

Allende's global reach

Having failed to convince the European courts to release his copper, Allende turned to the socialist East to solve his economic and financial woes. Allende was now turning to the socialist world for assistance as had Castro before him. He also needed to present his side in a world forum. The United Nations was gearing up to push the New International Economic Order, rallying the raw-material-producing Third World. The timing seemed perfect. He defended his nationalization of the American copper companies in the United Nations' opening session of 1972. He said that all sovereign countries must have the right to dispose of their natural resources as they saw fit. The two US mining companies, Allende thundered before the world forum, extracted over $4 billion during their four decade-long exploitation of Chile. Then he traveled to Cuba, Venezuela, Peru, Mexico, Algeria, and the Soviet Union to drum up financial support. Moscow granted trade credit, offered to buy Chilean copper and copper products, volunteered to sell arms to the Chilean military, but offered no development funds, or long-term, interest-free credit for an economic bailout.[47] In the end, the much touted foreign aid and investment from the Socialist East never materialized.

Marxism-socialism *with* opposition

Allende's advisers had all along preferred socialist autarky, and the events during the first year of the UP government convincingly demonstrated that Chile should play an autonomy card. By May 1972, when mid-term congressional and local elections were held, the Chilean economy was already in a deep recession. The inflation was raging at 160 percent a year and industrial, mineral, and agricultural production declined steeply. By 1972, Allende was increasingly bypassing congress and resorted to ruling the country by decrees. Furthermore, he lost control over the UP's leftwing-dominated bureaucracy, which pushed for a frontal attack on Chilean capitalism as the government's priority.[48] The government created over 1200 state-owned enterprises by nationalization and outright seizures of private agricultural properties. The SOEs were running deficits that the government could not sustain. For 1972, the SOE operational deficits reached 50 billion escudos and by 1973 a mind boggling half a trillion escudos. The president visited one nationalized textile mill where the production had declined, that suffered from high absenteeism, and that was run by workers. Allende was appalled to learn that in that time of crisis, the workers gave themselves a 400 percent wage increase.[49] As Allende learned later, this was not unique to the textile factory, but rampant among Chile's state-owned enterprises.

In October 1972, Chile was crippled by a massive strike, which the government termed an "employers' lockout." In fact, the Chilean minister of economy admitted that the participants came from all walks of life. The country's economic condition moved from bad to worse, and by January 1973 the government was forced to institute a food rationing program, in part to distribute foods equitably and in part to stamp out hoarding and black marketing. Government inspectors fanned out to check cheating, and the distribution of food was implemented through neighborhood organizations, which the opposition paper, *El Mercurio*, promptly declared politically motivated. For each crisis, Allende responded by reshuffling the cabinet. There was little else he could do.

By mid-1973, the government was confronted with hard choices. Inflation was running at 1 percent a day. The economy exhibited all the signs of stagnation. Speculation and black market activities mushroomed.[50] In the mid-term election, Eduardo Frei, running for senate from Santiago, collected the largest number of votes in history. The socialist and communist candidates were elected coming in second and third. Frei considered his landslide victory as a negative referendum on the performance of the government, while Allende considered the election of two UP senators from the capital a resounding approval of his government. The election sent a mixed signal. Allende organized a new cabinet: socialists picked up the portfolios of agriculture and the interior, while communists held on to economy, labor, and justice. Military officers, except for General Carlos Prats, the army chief, were having second thoughts about joining the government.

Anti-Allendista movements

In Santa Cruz and elsewhere in Bolivia, anti-Allende guerrillas were trained by operatives from Brazil, Bolivia, and the United States. The saboteurs of Patria y Libertad initiated bombing attacks on power lines, roads, and other infrastructures throughout Chile, "reaching a level of one attack during every hour the last months of Allende's government."[51] But it was the truck drivers' strikes in mid-1973 that forced the first major showdown between the government and the workers. For months, nothing moved. Heating fuel, bread, oil, wine, and other daily comestibles were becoming scarce. The government's attempt to seize trucks resulted in violent confrontation between the police and drivers. The government backed off and sought a political solution.

Allende had to reshuffle the ministry, and by August 1973 succeeded in appointing military officers to his "national security cabinet": a navy admiral was named minister of finance; a national police general was appointed to head the ministry of land and colonization; and an air force general was entrusted to run the public works and transportation ministry. These appointments were superbly political. Allende's appointments failed to instill a consensus among the disparate Popular Unity followers and rally the nation. Sectarian differences continued to rage. By late August, the truckers' strike went on for the fifth week, and according to one estimate the loss to the national economy surpassed $100 million. The country's inflation was running over 300 percent annually and its foreign trade deficit ran an incredible $1.75 million per day, far surpassing the one million dollar upkeep that the USSR was giving Cuba.[52] Strange as it might have seemed to Allende's Chile, the Soviets failed to come to the rescue.

Retreat of the generals

In June 1973, military intelligence discovered a plot to overthrow the government. Six tanks from a Santiago regiment attacked the presidential palace, supposedly inspired by Patria y Libertad. Fortunately for Allende and the UP, the "Tancazo" was a sole incident that no other military units joined in. Some 30 people were killed, however, including a Swedish journalist.[53] Soon after that, there were more ensuing crises and confrontations between the government and the armed forces.

The Council of Generals (the army) in June voted against any participation in the government as cabinet officers. The leftist labor union called for a workers' takeover of factories, stores, farms, and ranches. In one month, over 500 companies and establishments were taken over. In August, the air force officer serving as minister of public works and transportation tendered his resignation. An infuriated Allende demanded that the general resign his commission as well. The general refused. Wives of army officers marched to the residence of General Carlos Prats, who was still serving as Allende's minister of defense and army chief, demanding that he resign. The general was outvoted the following day in the Council of Generals and promptly resigned, thus provoking another crisis or, more precisely, a confrontation between the government and the military corporation.

The Short Coup

Everyone knew a coup was coming. In an anticipation of an upcoming coup, the UP supporters, the rightwing groups, workers, peasants, and even the middle classes were arming themselves. One foreign diplomat observed that Chile was one giant armed camp, ready to explode.[54] After the 29 June Tancazo, the role of the military remained undefined and whatever support that Allende enjoyed began to evaporate.[55] Brian Loveman stated that the coup makers were rapidly purging high-ranking officers who might be resisting the overthrow of the Allende government.[56]

At 6:20 in the morning of 11 September 1973, Allende was told that the navy had taken over Valparaiso and disarmed UP supporters in that city. The army had been on alert since 4 a.m. and by 7 a.m. was on the move. By 8:15 a.m., the city of Concepción, one of the hardcore bastions of the Chilean left, was under the control of the army. The air force chief offered Allende a plane and safe conduct out of the country. The president refused. By 11:55 a.m., the air force began to bomb the presidential palace. Mrs. Allende was safely in the Mexican Embassy, while her husband put up a valiant fight. By 1:30 in the afternoon, the whole thing was over. Groups of officials and aides with white flags came out of the Moneda Palace, the presidential office. One physician told the military that the president was dead. The junta, made up of the chiefs of the army, navy, air force, and national police, swiftly took over the country.

Paradise lost

Celso Furtado, who lived in Santiago for years when the United Nations was establishing its ECLA (Economic Commission for Latin

America, or CEPAL in Spanish, now ECLAC, C for the Caribbean), had a wide circle of friends in Chile. In fact, Pedro Vuscovic, the minister of economy of the Allende government, was on Furtado's staff in CEPAL. Furtado was the founder and first superintendent of the Northeast Development Agency (SUDENE) and minister of planning in the Goulart government. As such, he was among the world's top specialists on economic development. Visiting Chile in 1972, Furtado was appalled by Vuscovic's adamant defense of the radicalization of agrarian reform, the nationalization and statization of the copper industry, and the expansion of the state takeover of the economy. The minister was more interested in explaining how the radicalization and speed of economic transformation could prevent a reversal of Chile's socialist transformation than how the government should deal with the declining productivity of the economy. Also, imports were low and insufficient to stimulate growth. Although Vuscovic said Chile welcomed foreign capital and assistance, it was clear that he meant such assistance and investment to come from the socialist bloc, not from the West.[57]

The planning ministry reported that for 1972, the most serious economic problem would be the fall in agricultural productivity. Because of the deteriorating terms of foreign trade, the planning ministry anticipated a decline in living standards for the workers as well as shortages in comestibles of all kinds, except for certain industrial products.[58] To Furtado, who wanted to see the Chilean socialist revolution succeed, it was an opportunity lost. Politics, not economics, was the chief preoccupation of the Allende regime. And Furtado sadly concluded that Allende's men never had a sense of history.[59] Chile could have been the first successful Latin American socialist country. At last, Furtado and Kissinger had something to agree on.

In retrospect

The rise and fall of the Allende government and his revolution must be seen in the context of both the domestic political economy of agrarian reform and the international political economy of the nationalization and statization of copper mines. In both fields, Allende was overwhelmed by the swelling tides of global events, an impossible political geometry of the Chilean left, and inaccessible global systems of markets and finances. Further compounding these situations were the growing trends toward the superpower political accommodations, not conflicts, in the penultimate decade of the Cold War. The success of the revolution would have been possible had Chile been fully integrated into the capitalist world systems of resources transfer, finances, trade, and politics, because global socialism was already in decline. By disengaging Chile from the capitalist world system, Allende reduced the chances for the success of his revolution that much more. His had been the style of the era's Marxist and communist revolutionary thinking, one of destroying the predatory capitalist world system and building a new socialist economic order. But the realities called for a different approach. Neither Soviets nor Americans were eager to sacrifice their interests to support pro- or anti-communist revolutions everywhere. The world was becoming more integrated and less ideological. To consolidate the state power and autonomy, Allende could have built a solid social democracy by choosing a different path. The reality called for the revolution either to be Marxist and autarkic or to forge an accommodation with the global capitalist economy. The former would have transformed Chile into an Albania of Latin America, and the latter would have rendered the Allende regime into a social democratic Costa Rica. The former required the unfailing support of the Soviet Union, China, and Cuba. The latter required the placating of Nixon and his hardliners. It was the oleaginous mixture of domestic dissenting voices, especially within the UP coalition, with superpower accommodation that limited Allende to either option. Perhaps, Kissinger was right. History did unfold in the North, not in the South. And Furtado was right. Chile failed to think of the impact of the election of Allende beyond its borders. The president and his men suffered from an illusion of power by challenging the United States.

Part III

Transition and Consolidation of Democracy and Market

5
Argentina's Travails of Democracy and Market Economy

Populism's last tango

Between 1980 and 1991, the growth rate of Argentina was –3.2 percent. The only other country in the Western Hemisphere which outstripped Argentina's negative growth rate was Guyana which recorded –3.3 percent during the same period.[1] The dismal economic decline did not begin in the 1980s, however. Rather, it was in the offing by the early 1960s, after the decades of Argentina's second phase of populism, or the "classic" phase under General Juan Domingo Perón. The governments, both civilian and military in between, had sought to unravel the Peronist structure with little success. In fact, the tradition of the statist economic and social welfare policies thrived until the mid-1980s, and Argentina was among the world's most closed economies. Of the 126 countries studied by the World Bank, Argentina was 117th in the trade/GDP ratio, or the country openness index. Only the USSR, Burma, Bangladesh, Iran, and Iraq ranked lower. In the Western Hemisphere, however, Argentina was ahead of Brazil and the Dominican Republic.[2]

The transformation of the world economy, its financial markets and trade practices was in a full swing and the *market* was emerging as the driving force everywhere, while the *state* was retreating. In Argentina the public sector was the problem, and an unlikely political odd couple of President Carlos Menem and Economy Minister Domingo Cavallo would successfully tackle the intractable problem of the state-*heavy* economy.

In October 1983, when Raúl Alfonsín, a Radical, was elected president, the country had 707 state-owned enterprises. As much as 85 percent of the national government's deficit came from the mismanagement of SOEs. In 1982, YPF, the Argentinian state oil monopoly, became the only money loser among the world's major public and private oil companies, chalking up $4.6 billion in the red. The Peronist legacy resulted in redistributing national wealth and income, but bequeathed to the nation a stagnant and near moribund economy that consumed more than it produced. Compounding this legacy was the external indebtedness incurred during the years of military rule in the 1970s and early 1980s that reached a whopping $46 billion, or the equivalent of 80 percent of the country's GDP.[3]

Al-Mukhalis from La Rioja

Carlos Saúl Menem, a son of Syrian immigrants, was born in one of the country's poorest provinces, La Rioja. Although he was born in the capital city of La Rioja at the house which doubled as his family's dry goods store and residence, his biographers have often promoted the image of Menem as a magical, mysterious, and charismatic man from Anillaco, an Andean hill town, far removed from the capital. The name means "a drop from the sky" (*la gota del cielo*) in Quechua. For all his career, Menem has cultivated the image of the man fallen from the sky to do God's work of saving Argentina.[4] During the campaign, Menem dressed in white with long and wide sideburns. In fact, he looked the part of the mysterious and magical savior from La Rioja. Like an American country singer, Menem traveled in a bus, specially equipped with phones, a TV, a bar, telexes, and a meeting room. At each stop, the candidate would speak from the roof of his "Menemobile" to the people. One popular saying went:

> Perón descended to power from the army and the state, while Menem ascended to power from the university and the people. Perón boasted the power of knowledge, while Menem boasted the force of common sense. Perón read a lot and thought a lot, while Menem is hyperactive and a man of action.[5]

True to his image, Menem never revealed his real political and economic objectives before he was elected. In fact, during the campaign, he criticized corruption, doubted the success of privatization, and stressed the need to expand the domestic market as the engine for economic recovery and growth. Furthermore, he criticized Alfonsín's debt negotiation as one of transferring an enormous amount of financial resources to foreign bankers, resources which Argentina sorely needed to rebuild the economy. Menem condemned Alfonsín's economic team for consulting the IMF too much, which he portrayed as the overlord of the national economic policy.[6] Menem proposed that he would govern the country by four principles: (1) reduce interest rates and subsidies; (2) encourage real savings and discourage speculation; (3) clean up the financial market by ending all behind-the-scenes transactions; and (4) reinsert Argentina into the global economy. The candidate added that "there will be no islands in the Productive Revolution." He repeated this vaguely populist position throughout the campaign.[7]

Taming historic Peronism

But the real Menem was going in the opposite direction. The state-centric model had to be abandoned in favor of a market-centric economy. The candidate knew better than any one that forging a working relationship with the private sector was vital for the success of his government. During the campaign, the industrialists, financial elites, and agricultural producers came to a similar conclusion. This grand compromise between statist labor and profit-driven business was to transform Argentina in the 1990s.

The Radicals, who put up Eduardo Angeloz, governor of Córdoba province as their candidate, had no more credibility. Unbeknown to the public during the election Argentina's leading industrial and conglomerate firms, led by the venerable Bunge y Born, were quietly forging an alliance with the Menem camp. The industrial and agricultural conglomerates were historical enemies of Peronist populism but had little choice. Big business wanted Menem to bring labor under control by working with them, implementing privatization, taming the runaway inflation, and restraining wage increases. A military option was out, for Washington was vigorously opposed to it. And Alfonsín's, and by extension Angeloz's, economic policies would wreak more havoc and would create an uneasy climate for domestic and international business. There was no other option but Peronism.

A group of Argentina's business leaders trekked to La Rioja to meet with Menem. The meeting convinced the business leaders that Menem was no old-line Peronist. The unions were equally convinced of the need for change. The transfer of the national income to the workers shrank from 50 percent in the early 1980s to 28 percent of the GDP by 1989. Menemism became the harbinger of the neoliberal economic model, as it turned out. The government would continue to dismantle the statist economy that the military had begun in the late 1970s. The unions and big business, for the first time in history, rallied around the same candidate.[8]

Cornerstone for Menem's reform

To the consternation of Argentinians, Menem chose his key economic team from the Bunge y Born firm,[9] the country's most conservative conglomerate, and announced that his economic policy would be anchored in anti-populist and neoconservative foundations. The three-pronged policy would emphasize the massive privatization of SOEs to reduce the never-ending transfer of public funds to money-losing state and provincial enterprises; it would open the domestic market to imports, thus allowing the flow of fresh technologies and capital and at the same time subjecting the inefficient private and public firms to international competition; and finally, it would deregulate the domestic market (financial institutions, pricing, wage negotiations, pensions, and insurance) by exposing staid Argentinian businesses to market discipline and allowing international capital to operate freely – this fundamental piece of legislation was the "Reform of the State."[10]

Miguel Roig was Menem's first choice as minister of economy. Roig was the chief executive officer of Bunge y Born. This was a shock to Argentinians, because Menem had the electorate believe that he would pursue a mildly populist policy, having never made himself clear on key issues. The Bunge y Born economist introduced the most radical reform measures that Argentina had known up to that time.[11] The country that pioneered Latin America's populism and statism now would be governed by extremely conservative business leaders.

During the election, Miguel Roig and a prominent Peronist economist, Eduardo Curia, began to draw up an economic recovery and growth plan called "development with justice (*desarrollo con justicia*)," a typical populist-tinted title. The plan was a solid merger between old-line Peronism and Roig's gradualism in reform. The old and new currencies would coexist for the time being, while both being convertible into the dollar. Roig chose Guido Di Tella as his secretary for economic coordination, sending a strong signal to foreign investors that the pro-US Di Tella would be in charge of implementing the new market-friendly economic policies.[12] Not even completing the first week in office, Minister of Economy Miguel Roig died of a heart attack, thus putting Menem's reform policy in jeopardy.

The president quickly named Néstor Rapanelli, a vice-president of Bunge y Born, as the new economy minister. Di Tella was summarily removed, Curia was pushed aside, and Rapanelli's own people were brought into the ministry. Hyperinflation and volatile exchange rates were the two major concerns that Rapanelli and his team confronted. The dollar traded at A\$655 in August and by November the austral depreciated to A\$1000. Since February 1989, inflation had been running at over 110 percent per month and showed no signs of abating. The interest rate was running at 700 percent per month. The Roig-Curia plan, the "Development with Justice," was shelved ingloriously, and Rapanelli announced that the government would increase taxes on bank assets and corporate incomes, would step up vigorous tax collection, and would appropriate assets of state-owned corporations. Such a policy was seen as a thinly disguised attempt to benefit big business. The plan failed miserably. By December, Menem was ready to fire Rapanelli, feeling betrayed by big business.[13]

The initial opposition to Menem's neoliberal economic policies came from all fronts. The traditional Peronists were unhappy with Menem's abandonment of the ideological commitment to the half-a-century-old populist/statist tradition. The bureaucracy and workers of SOEs that constituted 18 percent of all public servants justifiably feared the loss of jobs; the military condemned the privatization policy as a sellout to international capital; and, finally, Argentinian businessmen and contractors deplored the hasty privatization as a recessionary policy and defended the cozy relationships with the state and businesses. At considerable political risk to himself, Menem forged ahead with his neoliberal economic reform.[14]

Menem's early reform

By mid-December 1989, Menem was ready to name his third minister of economy in five months. Antonio Ermán González was one of the president's closest advisers and collaborators. A fellow Riojano, Ermán González was president of the provincial Bank of La Rioja and later provincial minister of economy during Menem's second term as governor in the 1980s. By the time Ermán González took the helm of the Argentinian economy, two key pieces of legislation already in place that aided his policies were: the Economic Emergency Law and State Reform Law. The first law suspended all subsidies for 180 days and then the suspension was extended indefinitely, including industrial promotion projects, export subsidies, subsidies to provinces, and even lawsuits against the federal government. The second piece of legislation guaranteed the transfer of state assets to the private sector, thus defining the process of privatization of SOEs. By then, Menem's economic policy was well in focus: economic stability by controlling inflation, improving national finances, abolishing all price controls, freeing exchange control, and refinancing domestic debts.

In July 1989, inflation hit close to 200 percent and then began to fall rapidly to 6.5 percent by November. Roig's fixed exchange rate could not be sustained and a 50 percent devaluation of the austral shot inflation again to a 40 percent level by the end of the year. The government seized bank term deposits and short-term public sector debts, converting them into ten-year dollar-denominated bonds, known as Bonex 89. The seizure of the deposits and the withdrawal of the austral from the market were intended to lower inflation. The government also suspended all contracts, bids, and payments owed to contractors. Ports, transportation, and petroleum were deregulated and the plans for privatizing the Aerolíneas Argentinas, the national flag carrier, and ENTEL, the telephone monopoly, were moving ahead. The deficits in the provincial finances and national social security system were getting out of hand, however.[15] The situation that Ermán González inherited was anarchic.

The first convertibility-dollarization plan

The floating exchange rate did save the Argentinian economy. All business transactions were conducted in dollars. Stores in the main shopping district of Buenos Aires (Calle Florida) used both the austral and the dollar. Small boutiques had no trouble providing change down to American cents. This de facto dollarization of the economy (*dolarización de hecho*) was spreading to all sectors of business. Five-star hotels routinely calculated bills in dollars, not in australs. Shops would not take Argentinian credit cards that were reimbursed in the austral. Ermán González had little choice but to convert the de facto dollarization of the economy to the *de jure* dollarization.

The plan he proposed was a bimonetization of the economy. The dollar would be used as the currency of transaction until the Argentinian money was stabilized and backed up by a sufficient amount of foreign reserves, gold, and other convertible assets (*respaldo*). But Argentina needed more foreign reserve than its Central Bank had late in December 1989 to launch the convertibility and dollarization plan. The US government was approached for a bridge loan, but the US ambassador told Menem that Washington could not help.[16] This soured the relationship between US Ambassador Terry Todman and Minister of Economy Ermán González, who would hold a grudge against the US envoy until the American's last day in Argentina. By February 1990, the González plan suffered a stillbirth.

By March 1990, the inflation rate hit the record high of 20 000 percent and then began to recede to 1200 percent by the end of the year. Corruption in high places, double-digit unemployment (16 percent), dismantling nonessential state machinery, and even the president's messy marital problems, all threatened to unravel the reforms.

Civilian politicians, especially those of the Peronist party, had been out of power for over 15 years. They were hungry. When Menem came into office, his hangers-on were ready to pounce on the opportunity to use and abuse power. Corruption was by no means invented by the Menem government. Argentina has had a dubious reputation of being a country with corrupt officials, both military and civilian. Susana Angelli, an Italian senator and an heiress of the Fiat fortune, made it clear to Vice-President Eduardo Duhalde that no foreign investor would put money into a corrupt country. Her son, an Argentinian citizen, had been prosecuted for fraud in auto imports and was a prime contractor for the Argentinian-Paraguayan binational hydropower project Yacyretá, which Menem denounced as "the monument of corruption."[17] Menem's men and women simply took advantage of the situation and indulged overtly in excessive personal enrichment. They were endangering the whole reform process. But it was not until the onset of 1992 that Menem was able to rid himself of corrupt in-laws and greedy political cronies. Argentina was losing valuable time in inserting itself into the booming global economy of the early 1990s.

The troika of Menem's advisers

Initially, three factions ingratiated themselves with Menem, each claiming to be the power behind the throne. The first was his in-laws. The Yomas from La Rioja were descendants of Syrians like the president and his family. As the popular story goes, Menem's wife, Zulema Yoma, was not his first love. Zulema also resented the situation and after the birth of their second child, a son named Carlos or Carlitos, the couple began to drift apart. Numerous reconciliations did not work. When Menem became president, Zulema's sister Amira became his appointment secretary, the official gate keeper to the presidency. A brother-in-law, Emir, worked at the president's office and another brother-in-law, Karim, was a high-ranking official in the Ministry of Foreign Affairs. The Yomas and their allies, such as Roberto Vicco, a businessman from Entre Ríos and an official in the president's office, formed a tight clique that sought to take advantage of their access to Menem. Included in this group were one Jorge Antonio, a businessman with not too sterling a reputation, and Ibrahim al Ibrahim, ex-husband of Amira and a former Syrian army colonel. This group cultivated business ties with the Middle East and the Arab business community throughout Europe. It was rumored that they opened up an office, a "parallel private secretariat," downtown to facilitate political appointments and business deals.[18]

The second group of power brokers was made up of Menem's closest political confidants: Eduardo Menem, first brother, federal senate president and his confidant; Eduardo Bauzá, a native of Mendoza but a close ally of Menem's Riojano days, as president's political gate keeper; Raúl Granillo Ocampo, a lawyer and a long-time resident in the US, a key adviser to the president, and Argentinian ambassador to Washington in the mid-1990s; and José Luis Manzano, a Peronist deputy and later an aide to Menem, who would rise to become the minister of the interior and then was disgraced by corruption charges. He would eventually "retire" to the University of California, San Diego, as a fellow at one of its Latin American-related centers, where he would share the residency with another well-known Latino research fellow, Raúl Salinas, the brother of Carlos Salinas de Gortari, president of Mexico, and accused of having conspired to kill his former brother-in-law and partaking in massive corruption.[19]

The third group was made of another coterie of politicians led by Roberto Dromi (minister of public works and services), Ermán González, and Maria Julia Alsogaray (the federal intervenor of ENTEL and its privatizer). They too sought to use access to the president for personal profit. But it was the first two groups that swayed the power of the presidency until 1992.

Menem's troubles with in-laws

Menem has had the reputation as a womanizer (*mujeriego*) which he has never denied. The off-and-on marriage certainly did not help the president's image as a devout husband and family man. Two particular incidents brought the Yomas down from power. A gaggle of Arab businessmen approached the Yomas for favors. One brother-in-law used his contacts with the foreign business community to market milk in Arab countries. Among his contacts were known arms dealers and drug traffickers. A Uruguayan drug dealer arrested in Spain implicated Amira

Yoma, Menem's sister-in-law and her then-husband, Col. Ibrahim, director of customs at the Ezeiza International Airport, among others.[20] The governors of Salta and Catamarca were also named. The US Drug Enforcement Agency confirmed that the provinces of La Rioja, Catamarca, and Salta were known redoubts of drug traffickers. Gaith Pharaon, the Saudi businessman of the Bank for Commerce and Credit International (BCCI) fame, was also named by the Uruguayan drug dealer.[21]

"Yomagate" precipitated accusations, counter-accusations, and scandals of proportions thus far unknown in Argentinian politics. Menem sent in a federal intervenor to relieve his fellow Arab-Argentinian governor of Catamarca, Ramón Saadi, from office. Some said that the move was to please the United States. The United States investigation of the BCCI coincided with the Yomagate, in which Pharaon must have played the role as banker and was accused of laundering drug money. He bitterly complained that all US and European banks did the same. Why pick on an Arab bank? The FBI in New York arrested one Emilio Janjan for laundering drug money. Janjan revealed that his political contacts in Argentina included the highest level up to the office of the president and the ministry of the interior.[22] Also involved in this scandal was a prominent Syrian arms dealer of Franco-era Spain, Munseer al Kassar, whose family was a neighbor of the "Menhems" in Syria. Al Kassar later became a paramour of Amira Yoma. The president was forced to place his sister-in-law on indefinite leave, packing her off to Europe. Also implicated in the drug affair were top aides of the governor of Buenos Aires and former Vice-President Duhalde. A Duhalde supporter and the maker of the Menemobile was fingered by a Madrid daily, *El Sol*, as a drug trafficker.[23] The Yomas were disgraced and the president maintained a discreet distance.

"Swiftgate"

Armour-Swift, the famed meat packer and a subsidiary of the Campbell Soup group, planned to invest $115 million in Rosario to expand and modernize its packing and processing plant. New equipment had to be imported. By the end of Menem's first year in office, the foreign business community was buzzing with the chronic complaints of corruption and even blackmail among Menem's men and women. In December 1990 when George Bush visited Buenos Aires, the US and Argentinian officials discussed ways to clear the roadblocks for US firms willing to do business but unable to do so because of vagaries of corruption, bureaucratic inertia, and outright demands for bribes. Already, the US government heard complaints from many blue chip US firms such as Enron, a Houston energy company, to Firestone, Goodyear, Bell Atlantic, American International Group (an insurance company), and Federal Express. All complained that irregularities in privatization processes or bureaucrats who refused to enforce deregulatory legislation kept them out of the Argentinian market. Then Swift became the symbol of Argentinian corruption, for it involved the president's brother-in-law, Emir Yoma.

Swift officials complained that Emir Yoma would not clear the plant equipment at a customs house until he was paid. No less than Ambassador Todman took the issue to Minister of Economy Ermán González, but heard nothing from the minister.[24] Having waited for a week to confirm a meeting with the minister of economy, the seasoned ambassador decided to write him about the particulars of the complaints of the US firms, including Swift. As it turned out, Menem had called the minister and suggested that Emir himself handle the Swift case of importing equipment.[25] Since González was not going to handle the complaint, Foreign Minister Domingo Cavallo reported Todman's letter to Menem. The president called in his brother-in-law and had Cavallo repeat the story. Emir dismissed the whole accusation as a political attack on the Yomas. In the end he was forced to leave the government. The scandals simmered down as the key players of the Yoma group were removed from the government.[26]

The Argentinian corruption was the appropriation of the state power to maximize personal economic gains by Menem's advisers and followers. Deregulation and privatization created unprecedented opportunities for holders of state power to abuse. There is no evidence that the president himself was implicated in any of the corruption charges. However, when a number of his in-house advisers and key political allies in provinces were charged with corruption, it was inevitable that suspicion of corruption spread and the president could not escape from being tainted. The state power to ensure the economic recovery and growth in Argentina was temporarily sequestered by personal aggrandizement.

The road to divorce

Argentinians suspected that Zulema Yoma de Menem aspired to become another Evita Perón. Her plan to set up a charitable foundation went nowhere. She complained repeatedly to the president, who avoided the whole issue. Soon, arguments degenerated into marital brawls. She accused him being a "son of a bitch (*puto*), drug user (*drogadicto*), and thief (*ladrón*)."[27] She also accused her husband of physical abuse, showing the bruises on her body.[28] Her aides egged her on to fight back by feeding her rumors of the president's extramarital indiscretions. At least two top female aides were named to be among Menem's lovers. Zulema was especially infuriated by the relationship between the federal intervenor of ENTEL, Maria Julia Alsogaray, whom Zulema's aides accused of planning a "political marriage" with Menem by creating a Menemista Party, a party of the "twenty-first century Peronism," bringing together various factions and groups supporting the government. Her father Alvaro Alsogaray was a prominent businessman and politician. Her alleged romance with Menem could reinforce this political tie. First Brother Eduardo, Eduardo Bauzá, José Luis Manzano, Roberto Vicco, and others supported the move to found a new political party.

Zulema's political PR

A threatened Zulema began to surround herself with less than honest politicians. Cultivating the Arabic connections, she adopted as adviser Colonel Mohamed Ali Seindeldín, the leader of the Carapintadas (the group of army rebels in Villa Martelli) who had sought to overthrow the Alfonsín government.[29] Before the election, Seindeldín publicly supported Menem. After the election, he became a frequent visitor to the presidential residence, Olivos, at the invitation of Zulema. The First Lady also collected a variety of political and labor leaders among her supporters such as Saúl Ubaldini (CGT), Rubén Cardozo, former secretary of social action, Guillermo Patricio Kelly, and others.[30] She was making political statements and, when these actions and antics did not go anywhere, resorted to a public relations campaign that finally broke the camel's back.[31]

In a feisty mood, she put up a billboard in Avenida 9 de Julio, the busiest thoroughfare in Buenos Aires, proclaiming: "Loyal to the President but Not to His Delinquents: José Luis *Petroquímica* Manzano; Eduardo *Guardapolvo* Bauzá; Eduardo *Pan de Azúcar* Menem y Roberto *Cometa* Dromi." Manzano was accused of having taken a bribe in a petrochemical plant contract; Bauzá was accused of having received cuts on overbilling government procurement; brother-in-law Eduardo was accused of keeping a secret bank account on his and Carlos's behalf in the Banco de Azúcar in Montevideo, and Dromi was believed to have taken cuts in all privatization projects in his ministry.[32]

This was too much for Menem. During his visit to the World Cup Soccer Game in Italy in 1994 he ordered a military operation to remove Zulema from Olivos, the official residence. One day, the First Lady was out for shopping. The military unit cordoned off the blocks that surround the official residence and kept everyone out. Carlitos called his mother, alerting her to what was happening. When Zulema appeared, the military would not allow the First Lady in. TV camera crews, both national and international, recorded the incident and before the press, the First Lady complained that Menem threw his family out to the street like "dogs."

Menem decided to go for divorce. His principal aide Raúl Granillo Ocampo and brother Eduardo became the champions of keeping the Yomas out of the government and out of the family. The First Lady accused the two of being "the two López Vegas" of the Menem government, the allusion being the courtesan minister of social action of the Isabel de Perón government and the lover of *la presidenta*. The hostility of Zulema to Granillo was more than met the eye. Granillo's younger brother is married to a daughter of Menem's "true love," Ana Maria Lujan. To pacify the warring First Lady and placate her future attacks on him, Menem packed Granillo off to Washington as his ambassador.[33] By the end of 1994, the government was free of the Yomas. And Menem was free of Zulema. Now Menem could devote his energies to state affairs.

The Cordobés from Harvard

A grandson of a socialist and a son of a broom maker in San Francisco, a small town in the province of Córdoba, Domingo Felipe Cavallo was the oldest of three siblings. Precocious and bright as a child, Cavallo was much influenced by Christian socialism in his high school days and was active in school politics. Early on a stickler for details and a superb mobilizer, he would remain as a meticulous organizer of networks throughout his adult life. Cavallo had planned out his whole life well before his twenties: politics and public service were going to be his career. Cavallo was attracted to the discipline of economic sociology. His mentor was Milan Viscovich, a priest and a specialist on Third World development, with whom Cavallo forged a lifelong friendship.[34]

Having distinguished himself as an economics student at the National University of Córdoba, a venerable institution with a distinguished tradition of reform and public service, Cavallo earned his bachelor and doctorate degrees in economics before he turned 25. In 1970, he went to work for the provincial government, which was then in the hands of a military intervenor, as Secretary of Planning and Economic Development, a sub-cabinet post. He adopted a budgeting system ("culture of budget") for the province, identifying clearly the sources of revenues and expenditures, and saw economics as a tool that allowed him to analyze the real problems of society and then find solutions to them. A political change in mid-1970 forced him out of the job, and then he worked briefly at the Bank of the Province of Córdoba. He turned his attention to graduate studies overseas; he was easily admitted to the University of Chicago as a Ford Foundation fellow. But he delayed his departure to the US for a year and then applied to Harvard. In 1974, Cavallo enrolled there in economics and in 1977 he received his Ph.D. in economics from Harvard and returned home.[35]

The making of a technopol

While at Harvard, Cavallo was constantly in touch with Córdoba's leading business leaders and politicians. The province has stood up to the federal government historically and during the military years; provincial leaders were convinced that the military did not care about the economic future of Córdoba. In late May 1969, the provincial capital erupted into the bloodiest revolt against the military junta, known as the *Cordobazo*.[36] It heralded the beginning of political violence and protest of such intensity and to a level so far unknown in Argentinian history. The provincial industrial association (ADIC – Associación de Industriales de Córdoba) and young researchers and professors of the Economics Faculty at the university organized the Fundación Mediterránea and its research arm, the Latin American Economics and Business Research Institute (IEERAL – Instituto de Estudios Económicos sobre la Realidad Argentina y Latinoamericana) in 1977. It is worth mentioning that the doctoral dissertation of Cavallo severely attacked monetarism, an economic policy that many of Latin America's military regimes advocated, including Chile's. Cavallo predicted that monetarism would fail in Latin America.[37]

Months after his return from Harvard, Cavallo was named the director of IEERAL and began to launch a series of research projects on provincial economics and public policy issues, still under the military regime. The funding came from provincial businesses and soon Cavallo established similar research offices in Buenos Aires and Mendoza. At the time of writing the foundation is still supported by corporate membership that includes both Argentinian and foreign corporations. By the mid-1980s it emerged as the country's leading think tank,[38] and Cavallo had forged strong ties with businesses which had supported him financially and politically.

As Minister of Foreign Affairs and the Worship,[39] Cavallo was an important liaison between the Menem government and big business, and more importantly with the United States.[40] In 1981, as the president of the Central Bank, Cavallo "nationalized" all private foreign debt, to the tune of $3.5 billion, thus relieving businesses of the onus of debt burden. The entire debt of the Argentinian industrial sector was estimated at $5.8 billion while the state oil monopoly, YPF, alone owed more than $6 billion. Later, Cavallo's defense was that many Radical economists and politicians had supported the decision.[41] To add more to this formidable store of political clout, Cavallo persuaded Menem to send an Argentinian naval squadron (two ships) to the Gulf War. The president wanted to forge his relationship with President Bush, and both Cavallo and Menem were convinced that their economic revival plan depended on the support of the United States. Argentina became the only Latin American country that participated in the Gulf War of 1990–91. This was symbolic in its embracing globalization, albeit North America-led: Argentina for the first time in decades joined a group of democratic and semi-democratic nations that fought the common cause, thus becoming a full-fledged member of the global community in the eyes of the Western alliance, or, more importantly, to Western and international financial communities.

Menem bets on a new horse

Professionally, Menem respected Cavallo's work and eye for details, but there was never a deep friendship between the two men. Menem thought, like many who knew both men, that Cavallo was temperamental, egocentric, and ambitious. The president was leery of giving the Cordobés a national stage. Menem never disguised his ambition of serving for a second six-year term thus leaving office in 2001.[43] As it turned out, Congress fixed Menem's second term at four years. If Cavallo's economic policy had turned out to be successful, he might have become Menem's most formidable rival within the party. This would have weakened the chances for his own re-election in 1995.

In reality, Menem had little choice. In another round of cabinet-level musical chairs in January 1991, Menem named Cavallo as his Minister of Economy, the fourth in 18 months; his eternal friend Ermán

González was made Defense Minister; and Defense Chief Di Tella was given the foreign affairs portfolio.[43] Cavallo brought to the job another qualification that was important to Menem: his ability to round up support in Washington and Wall Street. The president fretted over the lost prestige and grandeur of Argentina on the international scene. Cavallo demonstrated as foreign minister that he could project Argentina on the world stage as Menem aspired to do.[44]

The economy was in a dire situation. The "bimonetization" policy of the González ministry never took off, since the country had insufficient foreign reserves and the United States refused to grant a bridge loan to launch the plan. By February 1990, the austral was depreciated to 6000 to 1 US dollar. As much as 80 percent of all Argentinian liquid assets were in foreign currencies; at least $45 to $50 billion of Argentinian citizens' money was invested in overseas accounts; and, having been burned from the confiscation of their bank accounts in exchange for Bonex 89, the public's confidence in government policies was almost zero. What Menem asked Cavallo to accomplish was beyond fragile human capabilities. It was not the magic economic and even econometric formulas that Cavallo and his Mediterraneans[45] instituted, but it was the restoration of public confidence and trust in the government that became the bedrock for the successful economic plan. Cavallo better than anyone did not pin all hopes on the economic theories. Winning public confidence and support was his principal strategy.

The Cavallo Plan

Domingo F. Cavallo was sworn in on 31 January 1991 as the fourth minister of economy of the Menem administration. At the end of the first day, the new minister invited a group of leading businessmen to his sumptuous Avenida Libertador apartment for a drink and a chat. Cavallo laid out his plan: abolish the wishy-washy exchange policy; set the same energy price for all consumers; promote the growth of private business; accelerate privatization; revise import and export rules and tariffs; and continue to deregulate the oil and gas sector. His long-standing ties to business during the Mediterranean Foundation days would further assure a good working relationship with the business community and their support.[46] To send an unmistakable message to the business community, he appointed a high executive from a leading conglomerate to be his secretary of planning. Cavallo was determined to have Argentina join the global club of trade and finance.

The 1991 Autumn Plan (popularly known as the Cavallo Plan to the intense disgust of Menem's advisers) launched in April, the autumn of the southern hemisphere, was a stunning success. The architectonics of the Plan were well laid out, yet simply and elegantly. The inflation rate for December 1991 was less than 0.8 percent. By July 1992, the inflation rate rose slightly to 1.7 percent and the annual rate for 1992 hovered a little over 20 percent. The growth of the economy for 1991 was 4 percent, while for 1992 it surpassed 5 percent. Export duties on agricultural products were virtually eliminated. Formerly under the Alfonsín government, the import tariffs ranged from 0 percent to 38 percent, with the exception of electronic goods which were levied between 10 and 90 percent of the value. The exorbitant import taxes were slashed to 22 percent, the highest, and 0 percent for capital goods and raw material inputs that the country did not produce. However, the trade figures for 1989 and 1990 indicated that, in comparison to the 1980 performance, foreign trade during the two years was at 80 percent and 76 percent of the 1980 level, respectively. Furthermore, in March 1991, four Southern Cone countries (Argentina, Brazil, Paraguay, and Uruguay) signed the Treaty of Asunción to forge a common external tariff union, MERCOSUR, effective from 1 January 1995.[47] To improve the country's trade performance, Argentina agreed to eliminate all bilateral barriers with Brazil by the end of 1994.

Peso-dollar parity

Cavallo moored the core of his plan in the currency board on the Convertibility Law, which pegged the Argentinian currency to the US dollar (first A$10 000 and after 1 January 1992 Ps$1.00 to US$1.00) and prohibited the treasury from printing money without its being backed up by gold or fresh foreign reserves, or domestic and foreign public securities redeemable in gold or the US dollar. Hence the austral, and later the peso, were backed up by gold and the US dollar reserves that the treasury had. The law also permitted that contracts could be written in the dollar or the austral (the peso after 1 January 1992). Although the plan was dubbed as the "dollarization" of the economy, the real intent was to make the peso "a unit of account, a store of value, and the common denominator of transactions" that would eventually replace the dollar.[48] The foreign reserves from December 1991 through July 1992 reached the record high of $3.3 billion. By the end of 1994, the Argentinian foreign reserves stood at $18 billion. As of May 1998, the country had $23.4 billion.[49] This currency board became the first building block of Cavallo's macroeconomic reform.

The second pillar of the macroeconomic reform was the fiscal component. Income taxes for individuals and corporations were never faithfully collected in Argentina. To take advantage of the honeymoon with congress, the new economic team produced the draft of a tax law over a weekend and it took congress 12 days to pass it into law. Cavallo's tax measures and better collection system resulted in a 43 percent increase in revenue, compared to a year before, as the hoarding and financial speculation among Argentinian businesses and individual citizens abated, and as the value of the peso had remained strong and on par with the US dollar. Cavallo's political foes were restrained. Former president Alfonsín assured that the Radicals would not oppose the Cavallo plan. Radical deputies and senators remained silent. Eduardo Angeloz, the losing Radical candidate in the 1989 presidential election and then governor of Córdoba, said that he would await the results before he would comment. Incredibly, the Convertibility Law passed in congress in 4 days. The national mood was that Argentina needed to move ahead and there was no time left for political bickering.[50]

On the external debt reduction, Argentina was able to negotiate with international creditors in Santo Domingo in April 1992 and accepted the Brady plan (Table 3.1).[51] It allowed Argentina to write off 35 percent of the current debt at the face value (the total debt being $50 billion plus) and restructure the remainder on a 30-year payment plan with a modest interest rate of 6 percent for the first 7 years and thereafter at 4 percent, backed up by US Treasury zero coupon bonds. Additional reductions of the debt would be coming from the country's unprecedented privatization efforts. Unlike Mexico, all of these changes in Argentina were effected through legislative processes, not by executive fiat. Hence, the stability and longevity of the Argentinian macroeconomic reforms were assured and protected from politically motivated internal disruptions, as in Venezuela. What Argentina could not control were changes in its external economies. It chose to live with and get used to the vagaries of the global economy.

Privatizing inefficient SOEs

The divestment of state-owned enterprises did not exactly begin under Menem. The military began to sell off SOEs on a smaller scale when Alfonsín came into office. The major plan of privatization during the Radical years (1983–89) was to sell the national airline, Aerolíneas Argentinas, and the national telephone monopoly, ENTEL. The entire universe of the SOEs employed 347 000 people in 1989. For the 1970s and 1980s, the SOEs produced around 7 percent of the country's GDP, representing 3 to 4 percent of the total employment. But they consumed a whopping 21 percent of all investment and their expenditure came close to 18 percent of the GDP. Aerolíneas by law had the monopoly share of 60 percent of all domestic routes. On one flight from New York to Buenos Aires, the captain supposedly congratulated one paying customer over the intercom, while the remaining passengers of the 747 flight were on free tickets. The state largesse knew no limits.

During the 1970s and 1980s, like the airline, ENTEL was the epitome of inefficiency. It cost ENTEL $4600 to put in a line, while the international cost was near $1500. The other SOEs were not faring better. The electric utilities SOE spent $6000 to produce one kilowatt of power, while the world's cost was between $1500 and $2700. It was estimated that at least a third of the electricity was stolen due to fraud by users. Between 1965 and 1987, two years before Menem came into office, the government spent $52 billion to prop up its SOEs, or the equivalent of the entire external debt.[52]

The privatization of ENTEL, Aerolíneas Argentinas, and the national highways by the end of 1990 led to the writedown of $7 billion from the country's external debt and an inflow of fresh cash to the tune of $600 million. Some 60 000 jobs were eliminated from the public payroll by privatization. To keep control over the privatization process, the government retained a minority position in the SOEs sold, granting the employees a share of the stocks, normally 10 percent. Menem told visiting US business leaders that workers realized that they would be better off in private-sector companies and now supported the privatization plan. Banks, steel mills, petrochemical plants, ports, and even pension funds were being sold off. In mid-1992, the government passed a law that would finalize the selloff of the country's oldest and most venerable SOE, YPF, by the end of the year.[53] To hasten the process of the privatization of YPF, Cavallo took two bold steps: first, the government corporatized YPF, thus putting a commercial value on the asset, and, second, it hired a US investment bank to prepare for the initial public offering of stocks in New York and Buenos Aires by 1993.[54]

To avoid corruption and to inject some transparency into the privatization process, Cavallo and his team began to weed out the political appointees of Menem, or tolerated their presence if they were unable to fire them but worked to keep them out of the process. The privatization of the telephone company was planned by Maria Julia Alsogaray, the federal intervenor and a Menem hanger on, but Cavallo appointed Wylian Otrera, Secretary of Public Works, to manage it by reporting directly to him. This centralization was necessary, for close supervision over the process was essential for the success of the program. In Mexico, the privatization agency under Carlos Salinas had only seven people who outsourced all other activities to banks and consultancies, while Germany's privatization office had over 3000 people on its staff. According to Mary Shirley of the World Bank, it is essential to have a small but powerful staff for privatization, not a large staff with a cumbersome bureaucracy.[55] Cavallo's team was elitist, trustworthy, and small.

Building a financial market

Realizing that none of Cavallo's Mediterraneans was a specialist on the financial market, Otrera approached Martín Redrado, a Harvard-trained investment banker at the Security Pacific Bank in California, to join the Cavallo economic team. Cavallo knew that unless Argentina's domestic stock market was capitalized enough for the task, privatization would be taken over by foreign investors. Like Brazilians and Mexicans, but unlike Chileans, Argentinians stashed away huge sums (as much as $40 billion) in overseas accounts, and Cavallo needed to convince them to bring the money home. The expansion and modernization of the then small Buenos Aires bourse had to take place first and Redrado was the man to handle the job. Cavallo made him the chairman of the Argentinian securities exchange commission (Comisión Nacional de Valores – CNV).

Redrado immediately informed Cavallo that the entire packaging of the ENTEL privatization was done too hastily. For one, the young chairman of the CNV pointed out that the consortium of five Argentinian banks hired to place ENTEL stocks was taking too much of a commission, 6 percent, or close to $25 million. The globalization of financial markets lowered the cost of money and keen competition kept the commission low. The normal international fee was less than 4 percent. For another, Redrado asked Cavallo to ask for up-front good-faith money from the banks. As it was structured, banks did not take any risk in the privatization of ENTEL; Redrado did not think the banks were sufficiently experienced to handle the placing of stocks throughout the country and around the world; and opportunities for corruption were too tempting. It was proposed that each Argentinian bank should find an international partner, who could advise on the privatization and even send technical specialists to Buenos Aires for the purpose. Otrera and Cavallo blamed all the defects of the plan on Maria Julia Alsogaray. They proceeded to listen to Redrado's recommendations and restructured the privatization process. The final plan was to place 60 percent of the stocks for individual investors, reserving

10 percent for the company employees, with the state holding 30 percent.[56]

To be effective, the monopoly had to be broken up to encourage competition. Alsogaray wanted to split ENTEL into five smaller companies and then changed her mind, deciding on two. In March 1992, three months after the corporatization of Telefónica, one of the two new privatized firms, the value of its stocks soared by 50 percent. It was anticipated that the privatization of the second part, Telecom, would do even better. In August, the Telecom stocks were offered for public sale. By February 1994, the value of the stock soared from $3.99 of the initial offered price to $8.30. The original value of the company as estimated by Maria Julia and her team was $400 million. When the bidding was over, Telecom alone brought in $1.22 billion. To sweeten the pot, foreign investors were allowed to use the debt swap mechanism. The Argentinian debt paper was cheap, 18 cents per dollar. Redrado's complaint was that only foreign investors were permitted to go this route and by allowing it the government was granting a subsidy of 83 cents per debt dollar canceled.[57]

By the end of December 1993, the government sold off 64 SOEs, including YPF, ENTEL, Aerolíneas, the Buenos Aires Electric Power Co. (SEGBA), Gas del Estado, and other nonessential assets. The government also divested 790 real estate holdings and sold concessions on waterworks, railroads, toll roads, the Buenos Aires subway, and television and radio stations. YPF alone attracted $1.3 billion of debt papers. Argentina was able to reduce its external debt by $13.4 billion through privatization until December 1993.[58] The Argentinian privatization is considered one of the most successful and thorough-going in the continent, if not in the world.

Foreign direct investment

A less likely danger was the potential nationalization and statization of private properties that still loomed large in the minds of investors. The government implemented a series of deregulation measures to open the internal market for private investors. Prices, wages, and interest rates were decontrolled. Contracts could be written in either the peso or the dollar. The balance of the current account was restored. Such price distorting regulatory agencies as the national meat and cattle boards, sugar and yerba mate boards, and similar entities were abolished. The insurance sector was deregulated as the state monopoly ended. The government also removed production quotas, price and margin setting, production sharing, and restrictions on the domestic and overseas marketing of oil and natural gas. Finally, small and large companies were given the autonomy of setting up rules for hiring and firing employees, organizing the makeup of crews and work place rules according to business needs. Unnecessary and excessive regulations had all gone.[59] In 1992 and 1993, the high points of the Cavallo plan, Argentina attracted over $10 billion in FDI (Table 5.1).

A deregulated economy

In contrast to earlier times, the structure of foreign investment in Argentina is truly multinational. Between 1990 and 1998, Argentina attracted $45 367 million. For 1999, a staggering amount of $25 153 million entered the country.[60] In addition to US and European investors, Argentina had attracted considerable Asian capital and tech-nologies. In the oil sector alone, there were some 200 international and domestic companies working in the areas of exploration, secondary recovery, refining, and marketing. The country's economic stability plan had been financed by multilateral entities such as the World Bank, the International Monetary Fund, and Inter-American Development Bank. And much of the foreign investment was in joint-venture projects with Argentinian partners, not to speak of compulsory employee shareholding. For instance, almost all privatized former SOEs had Argentinian and international investors. The telephone company (ENTEL) and the airlines (Aerolíneas Argentinas) had even European SOEs as partners. Argentina raised nearly $29 billion in privatization in the 1990s.[61]

The complexity of the globalized economy and the multilaterality of investment strategies actively pursued by the Menem government alone made the old-fashioned nationalization and statization a non-option. At the time of writing, if instability is forthcoming in Argentina, it will be found in the regulatory realm. One regulatory instability is tax rates. Another source of instability is the bankrupt public finances of the provinces. Soon after the Mexican peso melt-down in December 1994 and January 1995, Cavallo fine-tuned the banking laws, tightened the public spending to reduce waste, and increased taxes. Value added taxes went up from 18 percent to 21 percent. However, the national government cannot constitutionally prevent provinces and counties from abusing this fiscal power.

Cavallo and his economic team stoutly resisted all suggestions of devaluing the peso, a deathly signal to the weakening resolve of the

Table 5.1: MERCOSUR Countries: Social Indicators, 1997

	Population (millions)	Life expectancy	Adult literacy (%)	Income distribution (top 20% vs. bottom 20%)	% of people living on less than US$1 a day	UN Human development ranking
Argentina	35.0	72.4	96.0	n.a.	n.a.	36/175
Bolivia*	7.4	60.1	83.0	48.2/5.6	7.6	113/175
Brazil	159.0	66.4	3.0	67.5/2.1	28.7	68/175
Chile*	14.0	75.1	95.0	61/3.5	15	30/175
Paraguay	5.0	68.8	92.0	35.4/9.5	n.a.	94/175
Uruguay	3.0	72.6	97.0	n.a.	n.a.	37/175

Sources: World Bank, *1997 World Development Indicators* (New York: Oxford University Press, 1997); UNDP, *Human Development Report 1997* (New York: Oxford University Press, 1997).
* associate members

Argentinian government to defend the peso. Initially, Argentinian exports suffered. Already, the foreign trade performance during the first three years of Cavallo's reform was below par with the 1980s' figures, with the overhang of the overvalued peso. This was expected, however. Any notion of granting preferential exchange rates to exporters and importers was also dismissed for fear of reinstituting hidden subsidies and rekindling inflation, at the annual rate of around 20 percent in 1994. By 1996, the rate fell to 1 percent, lower than the US inflation rate. The key was to maintain inflationary stability. While these economic and monetary conditions posed potential risks of regulatory and exchange instability, the government stood firm. As long as Cavallo's messianic determination to stay the course remained unaltered, Argentina could count on strong international support and capital.

Menem's new strategy of growth

The global transformation of economic activities preoccupied Argentinian policy-makers in their effort to modernize the current foreign investment laws to attract more capital. Western European companies directed more of their financial resources to Eastern and Central Europe, Russia, and other members of the Commonwealth of Independent States. Geopolitics alone justified this. In view of the economic and financial instabilities that were sweeping Western Europe in the mid-1990s, Argentinians knew that Europe could not provide an enormous amount of necessary capital and technologies that the modernization of the Argentinian economy required. It had to align itself with Washington. To emerge regionally dominant and globally competitive by the end of the twentieth century and the end of Menem's second term in office, Argentina needed a new growth strategy. Developing mining was one. Becoming active in the region-market, MERCOSUR, was another. The friendly relationship that Menem and Cavallo cultivated with the United States could pay off in these turbulent times. The current and future bilateral relations between the United States and Argentina would be reinforced by the expanding trade and investment relationships.[62] Argentina requested to be included in NAFTA along with Chile. Their successful economic recovery first and then future growth would depend on continued deepening ties with the US and Brazil, as well as developing new trade ties with Asia Pacific.

Menem dismisses Cavallo

By fall 1995, a few months into his second term, Menem was confronted with an intractable situation: high unemployment (1 percent higher than when he came into office in 1989) and growing public pressure to relax the austerity program. For the entire year, unemployment remained stubbornly at 16 to 17 percent, while provinces were dragging their feet in economic reform, especially privatizing bankrupt SOE banks, hotels, casinos, and utilities companies. By August 1996, Cavallo was still against any modifications in the economic reform, while Menem was hounded by his supporters to relax the tight money policy. Soon Cavallo was seen as a *political* liability. The relationship between the two men was deteriorating beyond repair. And Menem's hangers-on were eager to see Cavallo go.

In August 1997, Menem and Cavallo had bitter arguments over the course of the country's economic policy. As usual, the minister of economy threatened to resign if he could not have his way. Menem called the bluff. The economic technopol and the political savior of Argentina finally went separate ways. Roque Fernández, president of the Central Bank, replaced Cavallo, and for months international and domestic investors anticipated possible changes in the Convertibility Plan that had been identified so closely with one man for six long years. None came. By the end of 1995, bank deposits recovered to the previous level of 1994, restoring public confidence in the Argentinian financial institutions.[63] Foreign direct investment, especially for long-term projects, had been the lifeblood of Menem's success and began to increase. In 1996, Argentina received $4285 million in direct investment and $4701 million in portfolio investment in 1995.[64] The majority of Argentinians were unwilling to trade slow growth for low inflation. No one wanted back the bad old days of 5000 percent inflation a year. But the Menem government did not succeed in implanting permanent economic stability in the Argentinian psyche, the linchpin of political democracy. Economic stability, so long sought, still remains an elusive dream, beyond the reach of the country's majority. Stability can come only with a change in attitudes, and a change in attitudes will take time.

Argentina at a crossroads

In October 1999, Fernando de la Rúa, mayor of Buenos Aires and a dissident Radical candidate for president of the center-left coalition, the Alliance for Work, Justice and Education, won the election. The losing candidate, Eduardo Duhalde, one-time vice-president for the first Menem administration and governor of Buenos Aires province, was also of the Radical Party (UCR). De la Rúa, known for honesty and integrity, swore that he would wipe out corruption. Once in office and having inherited a budgetary mess, the new president quietly abandoned the campaign rhetoric of a new economic policy of turning away from the IMF and the World Bank handouts. The government signed IMF restructuring terms without fanfare.[65] The 11 years of Menem's rule (1989–99) came to an inglorious end, as the government was tainted by corruption, fiscal profligacy, a popular perception of having abandoned the people, and widespread political abuse by Peronist politicians and Menem's followers. Menem did bring to the country political and economic stability, the longest democratic presidency in history, unprecedented press freedom, and, more importantly, the international respect that Argentina so direly sought. In 1998, one North American political scientist believed that "the prognosis for the survival of Argentinian democracy is extremely positive."[66]

On Thursday, 20 December 2001, Fernando de la Rúa resigned as president, after two days of riots which resulted in the death of 28 people and injured scores of others.[67] This two-year reign of de la Rúa was tumultuous. His cabinet was a composite of former Alfonsín supporters of the Radical Party, center-left politicians of the Front for a Country in Solidarity (Frente País Solidario [Frepaso]), die-hard enemies of Menem, and de la Rúa followers. Unemployment remained stubbornly high at 17 percent at the end of 1999. In 1995, it stood at 18 percent. The lowest rate for the Peronist 11-year rule was in October 1997, when unemployment hit 14 percent. When de la Rúa took office, it was at 18 percent.

To be fair, de la Rúa came into office as the country was already in its second year of recession. To retain the support of Peronist party followers and provincial politicians, Menem freely doled out perks and generous subsidies. The Argentinian federalism, as practiced under Menem, allowed much of the federal revenues to be returned to provinces and municipalities. Many provinces generously increased salaries of public servants, judges, and elected officials, while money lasted.

When the contagion effect of the Asian financial crisis of 1997–98 hit Brazil hard, the government chose to devalue its currency, the *real*. The January 1999 devaluation made Argentinian exports more expensive and the country's exports became stagnant. Cheaper Brazilian goods flooded Argentina, while Brazilians shunned more expensive Argentinian products. In the Southern Cone common market, 97 percent of the trade was conducted by Brazil and

Argentina. The two countries had been the largest trading partners to each other.[68] This aggravated the three-and-a-half-year-old recession of Argentina and indirectly other members of the common market. The currency board which had brought economic stability and wiped out the hyperinflation of the 1980s has been blamed for the overvalued peso. In 2000 alone, the Brazilian government allowed the *real* to slide another 30 percent of its value, making its exports cheaper to Argentinians and to holders of dollars, but making Argentinian imports to Brazil and the world that much more expensive. That did not help the de la Rua government's effort to revive the moribund economy.

The social inequity (half of Argentinians live below the level of 1989) has gotten worse. Argentina spent 18 percent of GDP on social programs during the 1990s, yet pensioners struggled to survive with an average of $500 monthly allowance. Public service employees, especially teachers, went unpaid for months. The World Bank observed that "Argentina is a relatively rich country. Yet despite this wealth, it is also a country with a relatively high level of poverty."[69] In other words, Argentina was suffering from the collapse of sound public policy. The mounting external debt, which in December 2001 stood at $132 billion plus, became unpayable. More than $94 billion of that amount was incurred by the sale of government bonds and commercial papers. The uneven distribution of income, the government's inability to create jobs, and the perception that governmental institutions and officials are corrupt increased popular frustration that came to a head in the months of November and December.

In March 2001, de la Rua appointed Domingo Cavallo to be his third Minister of Economy since taking office. The author of the Convertibility Law and restorer of economic sanity to the country, Cavallo was seen as the bright hope for the country's economic woes. Wall Street welcomed his appointment. By September, the IMF approved $21.57 billion stand-by credit, sending a strong message that the Convertibility Plan and the zero-deficit law "are important pillars of the country's economic strategy and have been vital in helping withstand turbulent financial conditions."[70] In 2001, the IMF rescued Argentina three times, but suspended further aid until the de la Rua government made more progress on its austerity program. Also, in order to avoid being blamed, IMF officials assiduously shunned telling Argentina what to do, a sharp reversal of the past practices, leaving Argentina to stew in its own juice.[71] Frustrated Argentinians invented a board game called "Eternal Debt" (Deuda

Eterna), in which the IMF devastated Mexico, Indonesia, Russia, Turkey and now Argentina with its eternal remedies of fiscal austerity, tax increases, currency devaluation and public spending cuts or freezing. The IMF "help," according to the *Wall Street Journal*, often "left destitute" ordinary citizens of the countries affected. The policies often helped the creditors but not the countries in distress.[72]

Return to populism, again?

But it was not all the fault of the IMF. In Argentina, it was the incessant internal fiscal profligacy and partisan politics to garner more spending resources that bankrupted the government and in the process gave a bad name to globalization, and Menem's neoliberalism. The IMF, globalization and neoliberalism will be blamed in the future. The national congress had been in the hands of Peronist deputies and senators for much of the 1990s. In the October 2001 election, the Peronists won both houses of the congress. They refused to support Cavallo's restructuring package. De la Rúa's last-minute appeal to jointly form a national unity government in late December was flatly rejected. Days before the resignation of the president, the Peronist-dominated chamber of deputies voted to remove the recently imposed bank withdrawal limited to 1000 pesos per month and revoked the March law that gave the executive branch a special power to deal with urgent economic issues without coming to congress for approval.[73] Peronists, eager to return to power, were in no mood to support Cavallo and de la Rúa. Political resistance from provincial governors was equally fierce to the zero-deficit plan, which sought to enforce as much as 13 percent of pay cuts for public employees. Two temporary presidents quit within a week, unable to restore order and sanity without Peronist support in congress. The outcome will be bleak for 2002 and beyond. Duhalde, the third replacement president in two weeks, devalued the peso by 29 percent and publicly acknowledged that default was inevitable. Much of the country's debt is in dollars and devaluation will add more to the debt burden. Tax collection in December 2001 was down by 28 percent. Value-added tax, the chief source of federal rebate to provinces, dropped 47 percent.[74] Back in 1900, Argentina led the continent in fashioning populism and building a dirigiste economic system. The most flamboyantly neoliberal country in Latin America during the 1990s will be the first to turn its back on globalization and its accompanying consequences. In the end,

Argentina needs a fundamental political reform before it can tackle an economy in ruins. A well-known US senator (Everett Dirksen of Illinois) once said that politicians are as good as people who elect them. This time, the democratic liberal Argentinians cannot blame outsiders for the crisis; they have only themselves to blame.

6
"Brazil Is Not a Serious Country"[1]

A new beginning

The pre-Collor Brazil was an exemplar of Third World state capitalism.
To undo the canopy of state interventionism, central planning, and a
jungle of restrictive regulations, Collor's administration had to incul-
cate Brazil with a new culture of antistatist but private market-based
development. The success of his reforms meant a direct confrontation
with the statist tradition which has spawned scores, if not hundreds, of
interest groups, including powerful business enterprises, both public
and private, an ingrained ideology of topdown development, and a
strong dose of national aspirations that Brazil was destined to become
the global player in the South Atlantic. The power of the state steered
the growth of Brazil's economy for decades. As the economy grew, the
state grew. State power led the transition from the agrarian to the
industrial phase in Brazil. The power of the state, as in Pombal's
Portugal and Colbert's France, shortened Brazil's rise from a backward
economy to the world's eighth largest industrial economy within three
decades. The state held the absolute financial lever.[2]

Fernando Collor de Mello, the second civilian president since 1985,
saw his role as one of dismantling the nationalist-populist legacy of six
decades that empowered the country to be sovereign and independent
but in the last decade had become an onerous barrier to the country's
modernization and integration into the global economy. To the baby-
boomer president, the reactivation of Brazil's economy could not occur
until the state was thoroughly restructured. This meant that the public
sector had voluntarily to transfer power and autonomy to the private
sector. Unless the political economy of the state and the market was
reordered, Brazil would not become a winner in the twenty-first century.

Apogee of state capitalism

The economic history of the country, three decades before Collor came to power, tells much about the reform needs of the new government. In 1956, the share of foreign holdings in Brazil represented 34.4 percent of the total equity capital, while by 1979 it shrank to 22.5 percent. In 1982, Brazil's gross domestic product was 55 percent larger than the combined total of the Four Asian Tigers – Korea, Taiwan, Hong Kong, and Singapore. That year, it was equal to 86 percent of Canada's GDP, and, among the developing countries, China's GDP was larger than Brazil's, but only by 5 percent. The manufacturing output of the four Asian Tigers was about 76 percent of Brazil's, although none of the four has natural resources to speak of. It made good sense, given the size of the population and market, for Brazil to opt for import substitutionism, while the four Asian tigers adopted export promotion policies. In 1980, Brazil's exports represented 9.6 percent of the GDP value, which was less than 40 percent of Korea's.

The public sector's control of credit, the financial lever, gave the Brazilian state power and discretion in its industrialization policy. As much as two-thirds of all credit in the 1970s came from SOE banks with the Bank of Brazil controlling as much as 40 percent of all credit. Public sector spending, adding to the credit power, sustained the country's inward-looking economic growth. In 1947, public expenditure equaled 17 percent of the GDP, although by the early 1970s it was nearly 33 percent. The public sector produced as much as 50 percent of the country's output. Of Brazil's 20 largest corporations, 19 were state-owned enterprises.[3] This model was not fitting in the age of globalization, where the engine of growth is private corporations.

Brazil's 'lost decade'

The economic crisis of the 1980s changed all this. For Brazil, it was more than a decade lost. The Four Asian Tigers' combined GDPs came to $450 billion, and Brazil's was $414 billion. If one uses the converter of purchasing power parity in 1995, Brazil's output was $856 billion, while the combined four stood at $880 billion. Brazil lost more than the 55-percent edge in 15 years. In 1980, Brazil's per capita was larger than any of the four Asian Tigers. By 1990, all four Asian countries surpassed Brazil in per capita – Brazil's was $2680 as opposed to Korea's $5400, Taiwan's $6500, Hong Kong's $11 500, and Singapore's $11 600. If compared to the 1995 figures based on purchasing power parity, Brazil's per capita was estimated at $5479, while the four Asian countries were still larger: Korea at $9810, Taiwan at $12 315, Singapore at $20 470, and Hong Kong at $21 670.[4] Furthermore, the Asian countries had more equitable income distribution and higher savings than Brazil (Tables 1.1, 5.1, and 6.1).[5]

'Collor'ed reform

Collor's economic advisers identified the three most excruciating problems of the country: (1) the galloping inflation which reached a monthly rate of 80 percent by January 1990; (2) the federal deficit which was running at an alarming proportion of from 5 to 7 percent of the GDP, or $30 billion per annum; and (3) the combined external and internal debts exceeding over $200 billion.[6] The external debt, when Collor took office, was at US$120 billion and it grew to $122 billion by the end of his first year in office; the payment of interest was suspended in July 1989 under the Sarney government (its second moratorium, and Brazil's fourth since 1982); and the domestic debt hovered at $90 billion, of which $57 billion was owed to the federal government by states. Brazil's managed trade, industrial policy, and cantankerous foreign policy, especially toward the United States since the early 1980s, became a contentious issue of US–Brazilian bilateral relations and has not helped to facilitate the smooth integration of the country into the global economy.[7]

The first priority of the Collor plan, or more precisely the Stabilization Plan, was putting out the fire of the flaming inflation ("liquidating the inflation," as Collor called it) on the one hand, and, on the other, instituting a series of radical administrative reforms to cut state spending. To deal with the first, the government froze all bank accounts, including savings, of people and corporations and foundations, effective from 16 March 1990. Literally, it was like taking drinks away from alcoholics. Collor's economic advisers reasoned that by withdrawing the cruzeiro from the market and by locking all bank deposits up in the vaults of the Central Bank, the spendthrift Brazilians could not spend. The less money in circulation, the less demand for goods and services and therefore less inflation. The government estimated that as much as US$57 billion were taken out of circulation overnight.

The plan was simple and even "elegant" as some Brazilian economists marveled. The plan consisted of (1) freezing all bank deposits above US$1200 (NCz$50 000) for 18 months, after which the citizens could withdraw the sum with 6 percent interest, (2) creating a new currency of the cruzeiro, an equivalent of one old cruzado novo, (3) new taxes and higher taxes on capital gains from all financial operations, (4) rate increases for public utilities, gasoline, and other items – 32 percent for electricity, 32 percent for telephone, 57 percent on gasoline, and 72 percent for postage, (5) a freeze on prices and wages after a one-time salary adjustment of 72.78 percent for March, reflecting the inflation of the month before, and (6) elimination of the subsidies and fiscal incentives, except for those granted to the Free Trade Zone in Manaus.[8]

Also, all foreign exchange control was removed and a mandatory rollback of prices to the level of 12 March 1990 was ordered. Immediately, critics called the policy the "confiscation" of private property and denounced the entire reform package as draconian. The Brazilian government was running a $31 billion deficit for 1990, around 8 percent of its GDP. The specter of the government mismanagement of all this money was pervasive. Within a matter of days, the policy pushed Brazil into a self-inflicted deep recession. Car manufacturers had about 1000 cars on the yard a week before the Collor Plan, but a week later, the average inventory was 12 300 cars per day. The prediction was that the middle class would be the biggest losers.[9] In a show of austerity, Collor proposed to cut many of the perks enjoyed by cabinet members and high-ranking officials of the executive branch and called on congress to do the same.[10]

José Sarney had 27 ministries when he left the office. Collor consolidated them into 12 ministries and 9 secretariats, units reporting either to the president or to a minister. One recent study concludes that the Collor reform radically altered the nature of the entrepreneurial role of the state.[11] He downgraded the ministerial status of the Joint Chiefs of the Armed Forces. And the infamous National Intelligence Service (SNI) was abolished. Two major changes were the creation of the Ministry of Economy, assuming the dual function of finance and planning, and the Ministry of Infrastructure, built on the three old ministries – commerce and industry, communications, and mines and energy. Infrastructure received over 60 percent of all the executive branch's budget. Zélia Cardoso de Mello, Collor's economic adviser during the campaign, was named minister of economy. It was a surprise appointment, for the new minister was only 36 years old, a former member of the Brazilian Communist Party, and a mediocre faculty member of the University of São Paulo. But the rapport between Zélia and Collor was beyond reproach. For Infrastructure, Ozires Silva, the founder and president of Embraer and the chief executive of Petrobrás in the Sarney administration, was appointed. A former colonel of the Brazilian Air Force and a graduate of the California Institute of Technology, Ozires was an ideal choice for the job.[12]

To deal with the second issue of structural reforms of the economy, Collor focused on a three-prong strategy: the privatization of Brazil's some 600 state-owned enterprises – 200 of which were federal corporations; the liberalization of foreign trade; and the deregulation of the marketplace. According to the experience of Latin American and Asian countries, economic reforms must go beyond privatization. Without liberalization and deregulation, privatization had no impact. This chapter will analyze the accomplishments of the three presidents – Collor, Itamar Franco, and Fernando Henrique Cardoso – who have valiantly attempted to carry out democratic state building and economic reform simultaneously.

The legacy of the protected market

Up until 1990, Brazil was a closed market. The Bank of Brazil's foreign trade division (CACEX) maintained a list of tariffs on some 13 500 items, also known as the Annex C. Of the list, close to 3000 items were *forbidden* to enter the country.[13] The Brazilian domestic market protection came in several forms: an outright ban on certain items, such as computers, peripherals, and components; high taxes on automobiles, electronic components, televisions and audio systems, and manufactured wares; and heavily subsidized sectors such as agriculture. One World Bank report estimated that Brazil's tariff rate for industrialized products was three times that of Korea's, a country known for protectionism.[14]

Brazil produced wheat, for instance, but subsidized its producers in order to secure domestic self-sufficiency. Benefitting a small number of wheat farmers of Rio Grande do Sul, this excessive subsidy policy was coupled with restrictive import regulations on cheap wheat, either from Argentina, the United States, or Canada. The whole country was forced to pay dearly for the domestic wheat. By mid-1995, the agricultural subsidies and credit became a political hot potato. The Bank of Brazil held $3.3 billion worth of the unperforming portfolio, an unrecoverable loan to the country's biggest farmers. About 18 000 of 3.5 million farmers used up much of the credit, often diverting the borrowed money to such business ventures as professional football teams, race cars, and speculative ventures in the stock markets. The Cardoso government has clamped down on the abuse. But more precisely, the crackdown began under Collor, who wanted to make Brazilian agriculture more competitive, but could not go far enough because of political pressures.[15]

In addition to legislated trade barriers, Brazil, like other countries, resorted to a series of "non-tariff barriers," or NTBs, that also excluded foreign competition. There were some 40 different types of NTBs practiced in international trade.[16] Examples included the so-called "laws of similars" that tightly regulated packaging and labeling trade marks, often discriminating against imports that had to clear a bureaucratic maze of customs registration and inspections, and refusing to legislate protection and rules for the proper compensation of infringement of international intellectual property rights. To keep foreign competition out, all a Brazilian manufacturer had to do was to register with government authorities, claiming that his product was "similar" to the imported version. The Law of Similars simply placed the suspected item on the Annex C and kept it out of Brazil. Furthermore, the country had a set of "special import regimes," under which the government selectively authorized the import of certain products on a case by case basis.[17]

On the export side, Brazil heavily subsidized certain products. Under the rule of export promotion, or Benefícios Fiscais a Programas Especiais de Exportação (BEFIEX), exporters of industrial products benefitted from an exemption or discount of import duties on capital goods (from 70 to 90 percent) and raw materials (up to 50 percent) for 10 years. Also the federal government actively used the BEFIEX as a key instrument to promote its import-substituting policy. The most favored exporters came from the transportation sector, metals such as iron and steel, chemicals, and heavy machinery. The same World Bank report indicated that more than 80 percent of the BEFIEX benefits went to the sectors: automotive equipment, machinery, and metal products. These sectors produced about 70 percent of Brazil's export earnings. Conversely, 70 percent of the BEFIEX exemptions and reduction of duties during the 1980s favored those Brazilian companies that sold industrialized goods at home, and the remaining 30 percent of exemption was assigned to combat export discrimination against Brazilian products overseas.[18] Exporters of the discriminated products were compensated. In brief, the export promotion law benefitted fewer than 50 companies in a country of 155 million people and an economy of $180 billion in the 1970s and a $414 billion GDP in 1990. By accident the program helped foreign corporations more than domestic firms. In 1978, the government of Brazil approved 30 projects qualifying for BEFIEX benefits. The total value of the exports by the 30 projects was $7.5 billion, of which $5.5 billion or 73 percent represented automobiles, almost all of them manufactured by US and European companies in Brazil. Throughout the 1970s, the export promotion law was responsible for increasing Brazil's exports by 20 percent.[19]

The consequences of such a trade promotion *cum* import substituting policy was both loss of revenue for the state and infusions of heavy subsidies to keep the Brazilian industries afloat. One figure for export subsidies was over $11 billion per year. The real figure should be considerably higher.[20] Brazil's trade fluctuated from $30 billion to $38 billion annually during the first half of the 1990s, and the balance of surplus averaged about $12 and $15 billion. If one deducts the direct subsidies, export bonuses, BEFIEX reductions or exemptions of duties, and special exchange rates that the Central Bank bestowed on premium exporters, Brazil was breaking about even.[21]

Collor dismantles statism

During his first two years in office, Collor brought down trade barriers by removing subsidies and liberalizing trade procedures. Rio Grande wheat farmers fought back bitterly but lost the prized subsidies. Before 1991 the subsidy allowed them to produce a bushel of wheat at $40 above the world price.[22] Abolished was the tight monopoly held by the Banco do Brasil on import–export licensing. Its now defunct foreign trade division, or the CACEX (Carteira de Exportação), was responsible for granting and withdrawing export licenses, as well as arranging short-term credit. This office often made decisions under political influence and pressure, showing favoritism to major corporations and those well connected politically; by the time Collor came to office, it was shot through with corruption. CACEX wielded enormous influence, for the federal government's major portion of foreign currency and revenue came from export activities, especially during the 1980s when foreign direct investment and fresh bank credit began to dry up.

Veja, Brazil's premier weekly and the world's sixth largest news magazine by circulation, observed that during the first two years in office Collor did more to liberalize foreign trade than all his predecessors combined since 1945. Even by Latin American standards, Brazil's tariff structure was antiquated and retained higher rates. In Chile, the state instituted a simple 11 percent import rule on value added products, while maintaining 0 percent for raw materials and capital goods. In

Argentina, it was 0 percent for capital goods and raw materials, while 11 percent for semi-finished items and products that the country does not manufacture and 22 percent for redundant goods. During the first six months, the Collor administration did the impossible by opening up the market: it unveiled the new tariff schedule in January 1991, bringing down the average rate of import taxes to 20 percent; it abolished the list of prohibited goods; it eliminated the bulk of import exemptions and special regimes; it also abolished export incentives; and it did away with BEFIEX, except for those projects under contract. The trade liberalization was more than "sweeping"; rather, it was revolutionary.[23] By the end of 1991, Brazil was importing both capital goods and consumer goods. In 1949, Brazil imported 64.5 percent of its consumer goods and by 1964, thanks to the import substitutionism, the rate steeply declined to 1.6 percent. During the military years, the "nationalization" content rule was pushed up higher, in some cases up to 90 percent, thus making imports unnecessary.

Deregulating the domestic market

Among the myriad regulations that stifled economic activities in Brazil, nothing has aroused more passion at home and abroad than its informatics policy, especially the market reserve for Brazilian-made personal computers. One key dimension of the contentious bilateral relations between the United States and Brazil during the 1980s evolved from the closing of the Brazilian computer market to foreign companies. By the middle of 1991, the Collor government succeeded in convincing the recalcitrant congress to pass a law that would end the market reserve by October 1992, thus allowing the imports of all types of computers, peripherals, and informatics components to Brazil.

Veja observed in a 1986 feature article on the informatics policy that rarely was Brazilian society so engrossed in the polemics of the "market reserve," yet the public knew so little about it.[24] As was discussed in Chapter 3, the intention of the Lei Informática (informatics law) of 1984 was to grant the Special Secretariat of Informatics (SEI) the power to protect only the manufacturers of Brazilian micro- and mini-computers. But the problem was that SEI went beyond its mandate, often branching out into those areas considered matters of "national security." Because SEI worked within the Brazilian intelligence community and reported directly to the National Security Council (from 1985 to 1990, to the Ministry of Science and Technology), its actions were little challenged, were not subject to outside scrutiny, and even had the appearance of being above the law.

In fact, the law was never voted on in a plenary session of the Brazilian congress. Under the gray rules of the authoritarian regime, the Figueiredo government was able to push the informatics bill through the national congress with a "leadership vote." Under this rule, the leader of each party represented the vote of his party in congress. The law so fundamental and so critical to the economic and technological modernization of the country was never read by the congress as a whole. The first civilian president since 1964, and the former federal deputy (later senator) José Sarney, confessed that he could not understand the law's 46 articles and two adjuncts (*anexos*). Two years after its enactment, the law still lacked the enforcement rules (*regulamentos*) that all legislation must have. Yet SEI operated as if there were regulamentos.[25]

In early July 1986, the adherents of the law held a parade in São Paulo's streets. One passer-by asked "what is the informatics?" when he saw the placard saying that "the informatics is ours and so is the talent." Another commented that it meant Brazil was no longer an ally of the United States and this proved that the two countries broke up. It was not just the people who were confused. One federal deputy said that less than 4 percent of his 548 congressional colleagues could explain what the national informatics policy was all about. *Veja* randomly interviewed seven deputies and senators about the law and none was able to explain the content and the purpose. Federal Deputy Jacques D'Ornellas (PDT-RJ) said that, "this is the law with which Senator Roberto Campos was defending the interests of the Americans."[26] The normally erudite Campos did not know when the law would expire. He said 1994. The law granted SEI eight years, or until 1992, to protect the Brazilian computer manufacturing industry. In fact, the senator was one of the most articulate opponents of the law. Why was such a law so powerful and having so many consequences for Brazil never fully debated and voted on in congress?

It came down to a question of economics and populist nationalism. Brazil imported $153 million worth of computers, software, and peripherals in 1983, the year before the law was passed. The US accounted for 50 percent of the imports, or $76 million. In 1984, the imports declined slightly to $149 million, of which the US companies sold 60 percent. And in 1985, the country spent $202 million in imports and the US claimed 50 percent or $112 million. As a whole, the Brazilian computer market was estimated at $2.3 billion, but would grow to be $4 billion within a couple of years, and Brazilians wanted to capture much of it.

The law did allow a foreign computer company to work in the market, if it formed a joint venture partnership and if it held no more than 30 percent of the stocks, paid for the entire cost of the research and development, and agreed to turn over the latest technologies free of charge to the Brazilian partner. It seemed that in the void of the enforcement rules, SEI was taking advantage of the vacuum and interpreting the law according to the bureaucracy's whim, ignoring the spirit of the law.[27] This is what might have been intended by the ultranationalists – the military, the small but growing Brazilian computer industry and its engineers, and university researchers. In fact, the law was written by the National Council of Informatics, the industry group comprised of 23 members, of whom 8 were companies. Brazil was not a military dictatorship; it was a dictatorship of ultranationalistic business men.

Disservice to modernization efforts

By mid-1991, Brazil chose to change the computer policy. After 14 years of a closed computer market, counting from the effective ban in 1977, it was clear that the policy had done more harm to society and the economy than good. The automobile sector, the country's major exporter, had a 4 percent automation rate, while Japan, Germany, and the United States had 38, 30, and 31 percent, respectively. The percentage of the Brazilian small and medium-sized companies using computerized production systems was 10 percent, while those in Japan, Germany, and the United States were 44, 90, and 75 percent each. Hospitals in Brazil that integrated using computers into their operations were less than 4 percent, while the US, Japan, and Germany boasted 98, 100, and 100 percent, respectively. In every other category that *Veja* investigated, Brazil was lagging far behind.[28]

Half of the 800 000 computers that the Brazilians owned in 1991 were obsolete by world standards. The Brazilian computer, it was said, was so out of date that not even African countries would buy it, a supreme insult to the country which had been doing a flourishing business in arms trade in Africa and a country with over 40 percent of its population who can claim African ancestry. The informatics policy was one policy that united the militant Shi'ites of the left, the army of rightwing businessmen, xenophobic military men, and leftist university scientists. But the policy dealt a fatal blow to the Brazilian economy during the "lost decade," the very time when the globalization of the world economy was accelerating and when the country needed fresh foreign capital and technology to pull itself out of the recession. The Informatics Law, unwittingly, did more to contribute to the "lost decade" in the 1980s than its supporters could have imagined. By mid-1995, Brazil had a computerized banking system equal to that of the US. None other than Bill Gates of Microsoft marveled at the tremendous change in the computer market within a few years after the end of the market reserve.[29]

Privatizing state-owned-enterprises (SOEs)

Brazil was not a champion of state enterprises, although it has been Latin America's largest economy. Its nearest rival was Mexico, which matched about half Brazil's gross domestic product in the early 1990s. In the absolute numbers game, Mexico clinched the championship with its 1300 SOEs in the middle of the 1980s. Argentina was in second place with 747. Brazil was third with 687 federal, state, and municipal SOEs. Chile under the Allende government boasted 598, excluding collective farms. And Peru at its peak had 140 state corporations. Together, Argentina, Brazil, Chile, and Mexico at one time created over 3200 SOEs.[30] Between 1980 and 1990, Argentina's share of SOE productively was 2.7 percent of its GDP; Brazil's 7.6 percent; Chile's 14.4 percent, and Mexico's 6.7 percent. For the next five years (1990–95), Argentina's ratio fell to 1.3 percent, while Brazil's *went up* to 8 percent; Chile's declined to 8.1 percent, and Mexico's to 4.9 percent (Table 6.1). In spite of the economic opening and deregulation of the domestic market, Brazil's SOEs accounted for 8.6 percent of the GDP in investment between 1990 and 1995.[31] The state was still a substantial player in the economy. During

Table 6.1: MERCOSUR Countries: Economic Indicators, 1997

	GDP (US$ millions)	Per Capita GNP/PPP	External debt (US$mil)	Exports (US$ millions)	Imports (US$ millions)	Current account as % of GDP
Argentina	281	8,310	89,747	20,969	20,122	–1.4
Bolivia*	6	2,540	5,266	1,101	1,424	–4.0
Brazil	688	5,400	159,130	46,506	53,783	–2.6
Chile*	67	9,520	25,562	16,039	15,914	0.2
Paraguay	7.7	3,650	2,288	817	2,370	–19.0
Uruguay	18	6,630	5,307	2,106	2,867	–2.0

Sources: World Bank, *1997 World Development Indicators* (New York: Oxford University Press, 1997); UNDP, *Human Development Report 1997* (New York: Oxford University Press, 1997).
* associate members

the early 1980s, the peak of Brazil's state-dominated era, the public sector enterprises came to represent somewhere between 60 and 70 percent of the country's production, considerably higher than the 40 percent of Allende's socialist-Marxist Chile.[32]

The core of Collor's privatization plan had to be bold. In Brazil, the law would not allow SOEs to go bankrupt. Import-substituting industrialization required the state to play a bigger role in each decade, as the economy became larger and more complex. By 1990, of the country's 500 largest nonfinancial corporations, SOEs controlled 37.2 percent of the gross revenues, 63.6 percent of the net worth, and 75.5 percent of all fixed assets. In industry, oil and mining, and transportation and telecommunications, the state presence was overwhelming.[33] Collor's privatization strategy was built on the assumption: (1) that the state must reduce its interventionist role in the market place, (2) that private sector ownership and management must be more efficient and productive, and (3) that the federal government must eliminate its $30 billion-plus annual deficit. The legal basis for privatization was built on a combination of two laws (Lei 8031 and Lei 8250), a series of resolutions, circulars, and decisions issued by the Central Bank, the National Monetary Council, and other agencies. By late April 1990, the Collor administration targeted 188 federal SOEs for divestiture.[34] Excluded were approximately 30 SOEs operating in hydrocarbons and electric energy, telecommunications, transportation, and mineral resources. The initial asking price for all the federal SOEs was placed at $14.5 billion.[35]

To oversee the sale of the federal SOEs, the government established the National Commission of Denationalization, chaired by the president of the National Economic and Social Development Bank (BNDES). The commission consisted of from 12 to 15 members from government,[36] business, and the academic world who established the basic rules for privatization by setting the limits on the number of shares individuals and corporations might hold. A foreign investor was limited to 35 percent of the total holding of any SOE if debt for an equity swap was used. The investment had to remain in the country for six years (originally set for 12 years). Another 35 percent of the shares were reserved for Brazilian individual investors; each investor could hold up to 5 percent of the total; and finally, 30 percent of the remaining stocks had to be set aside for employees of the SOE under divestiture. The law still reflected economic nationalism with a strong dose of populist xenophobia.

By the end of 1992, the government intended to sell 92 parastatals, setting the value as high as from $17 to $18 billion. The ambitious plan also included the future sale of ports, roads, and government-held real estate. One government figure placed the value of Portobrás facilities alone at $35 billion. Portobrás is the federal holding company that manages all harbors of Brazil.[37]

Dept swaps, Brazilian style

Although Argentina, Mexico, and Chile used the debt swap mechanism to reduce their *external* debt burden, the Brazilian legislation specifically targeted the reduction of the *internal* debt. Investors could use a whole range of domestic debt papers, many of which had already lost the original value under the assault of inflation. The Collor government required corporations to buy the certificates of privatization as a way of reducing cash in circulation. This in fact was tantamount to deep discounts of SOE assets, when bought with "junk money." Unlike Chile and Mexico, the government did not provide buyers with credit to take SOEs off the state's hands. Unlike Mexico and Argentina, Brazil established stricter regulations on how *foreign* investors could participate. And finally, the xenophobic laws stipulated all Brazilian SOEs could buy up to 15 percent of the total shares of another SOE. Of the 38 SOEs privatized in the 1980s, only 1 had an annual sale of $100 million. Also, philosophically, the privatization of the early 1990s highlighted the government's commitment to the transition from the mixed economy to a free market system.[38]

By the end of 1990, none had sold. For 1991, the federal government was able to privatize 6 companies, all during the last three months of the year, netting $1.7 billion. It was a start. The government also targeted another 18 federal SOEs for sale in 1992.[39] The government was also encouraging private firms to buy the federal infrastructure. To modernize the port systems and federal highways alone would cost Brazil over $10 billion, money that the government did not have. In São Paulo, a group of key industrialists (the Votorantim Group, Camargo Correa, and Itamaraty Group) set up a company (Companhia Paulista de Desenvolvimento) to modernize the Castello Branco Highway (between São Paulo and Mato Grosso) and other state highways. The country's national development bank (BNDES) granted a loan of $150 million and the rest would have to come from private investors.[40]

Opposing camp

To the consternation of Collor, much of the opposition was spearheaded by a band of conservative politicians of Minas Gerais, his own

Vice-President Itamar Franco, and the entire Minas congressional dele-
gation. The only one favoring the privatization was Ronan Tito of
PMDB. Also opposing were leftists such as Federal Deputy Vivaldo
Barbosa of PDT, radical deputies of PT, organized labor like CUT led by
José Meneguelli, and a small segment of the armed forces. Such center-
left politicians as Fernando Henrique Cardoso and José Serra of the
Brazilian Social Democrat Party were not against Collor's privatization.
They in fact favored such an economic reform, although they preferred
Brazil to retain a mixed economy in the style of Italy and Spain.

Late in September 1991, when the country's largest steelworks in
Minas Gerais (USIMINAS) was put up for sale, the opposition from the
ideologically mixed groups sought to stop the process. Earlier several
court injunctions were secured by Minas politicians to stop the sale
and, when this obstructionist tactic failed, the street people (some say
Leonel Brizola, governor of Rio, orchestrated it) blocked the entrance
of the Rio Stock Market building where the auction was held and
several buyers were physically assaulted. The BNDES called off the
auction.[41] A new auction was held a month later without an incident.
Such potential bidders as BRADESCO (Brazil's largest private bank) and
Andrade Gutierrez (a major engineering conglomerate), despite strong
pressure from the government, did not bid. Nor did the foreign holders
of Brazil's debt papers. The final buyers of USIMINAS came from a
group of Brazilian banks (Simonsen Bosano being the consortium
leader), the Companhia Vale do Rio Doce (its Valia pension fund), and
other SOE pension funds. In fact, 42 percent of the stocks of the steelworks was bought up by pension funds of CVRD and other SOEs.[42] As
anticipated, the Brazilian buyers came from the same sectors as SOEs.
The Gerdau Group, Brazil's largest private steel firm, bought several
smaller SOEs which used to be competitors. Chemical companies, met-
allurgical firms, and banks joined in the feast of privatization. The
trend of the divestiture of USIMINAS and subsequently five other
federal SOEs raised more concern among the Brazilian business community than officials of the Collor government. It conjured up an
incestuous relationship of the government using its own funds to buy
its own SOEs. It also conjured up the specter of a socialism through
pension funds, most widely used in Austria and Sweden.

Sex, corruption, and globalization

Within six months of gaining office, the Collor government was rocked
by a sex scandal. Justice Minister Bernardo Cabral, a married man and a

federal deputy from Amazônia, and Minister of Economy Zélia Cardoso de Mello, Collor's chief economic architect, were having an affair. She wanted to get married, he did not want to leave his wife, and things got rather messy. Zélia gave Bernardo an ultimatum and the man failed to meet it. She was not going to be a mistress, she said. That was against her middle-class values. The president was in a bind. The justice minister was a political coordinator of the government who handled the relations between congress and the executive branch. Zélia was the economic linchpin of Collor's reform. In the end, the agonizing president let both go. By May 1991, Brazil was deep in recession but with single-digit inflation. Business and the media argued that Zélia "liquidated the inflation" but in the process killed the economic goose.

This was as it turned out the first of the soap-opera scandals that would eventually bring down the Collor government. The First Lady, by custom, served as the head of the Brazilian Assistance Legion, a government-funded social services agency. It distributes foods, clothes, medicine, and other necessities to the needy. It had a budget of about $1 billion a year and employed 9400 people. The allegation was that the First Lady (Rosane de Malta) was diverting some of the money (around $11 million) to her relatives in the home state of Alagoas.[43] Only 26 years old, the First Lady was inexperienced in politics. Along the way, Rosane accumulated enemies in and out of the family circle. A month before the formal investigation of her mismanagement of the fund was launched, the books of the social services agency were audited and irregularities were found.[44] She proclaimed her innocence but under pressure resigned.

Collor and the man named PC

The clean-cut image of Fernando Collor was his asset and liability at once when he became president. The accomplishment of the first 100 days in office was impressive. Inflation was down from 85 percent in March to 10 percent by May. He held down wage rises, yet granted workers and management the freedom to negotiate. The minimum wage actually went down from $95 to $69 a month. The federal government also announced plans to retire 68 000 functionaries. In São Paulo, industries laid off 50 000 workers because of the recession. There was a de facto moratorium of interest payments to the holders of government bonds and external creditors.[45] Collor's initial austerity measures such as proposals to sell the official mansions of ministers, reduce the fleet of official limousines, and eliminate other perks convinced the public that he would continue to push for drastic reforms. But the crescendo of scandals and corruption charges against relatives of the president and his political cronies was sapping much of his energy. No one doubted that the crowd from Alagoas was usurping the presidential power and gaining access to the federal coffers to enrich themselves. The trouble was that "the Republic of Alagoas" was not sharing the spoils with other power elites.[46]

Paulo César Farias, or PC, was already a successful businessman when he came aboard the Collor campaign as treasurer. It is not clear how he financed the campaign, but there are plenty of speculations, one of which was that he promised access to the federal government for contributors. It was the best-financed campaign in history. There were several million dollars left in the campaign chest that PC controlled when the election was over. After the election, he put three of his brothers in strategic places for money making. One brother was secretary of public sanitary work for Alagoas. The incumbent governor owed his election to PC's financial prowess. Another brother held the number two position in the federal ministry of health. And the third brother was a federal deputy.

The name of the game was to garner federal funds for public works projects and economic development projects for specific individuals and companies. PC needed supporters at three levels: the state, the federal executive branch, and the federal congress. To start a project and to implement the project, state and local governments must request it and lobby the appropriate ministries and congress. To approve it and fund it, the executive branch and congress must go along. And PC chose contractors.

The money-collecting scheme that PC set up was a company in São Paulo, called EPC, presumably Empresa Paulo César. The EPC was a facilitator, greaser, and influence-peddling company. From here, PC and staff worked the country's major banks, industrial firms, construction companies, agricultural producers, and anyone who needed the Brazilian federal government to make money. Among them were Brazil's top 20 corporations, such as Norberto Odebrecht, Andrade Gutierrez, and Votorantim.[47]

Justice on the Lam

As soon as the government issued an arrest warrant in late June 1992, PC fled to Buenos Aires. From there, he traveled to London. While in London, PC's lawyers sought to work out a deal with the Brazilian judiciary. Unable to secure it, the fugitive left England for Thailand. In

Bangkok, PC planned to meet with his family for Christmas of 1992. By chance, he spotted a Brazilian businessman in a hotel restaurant and, homesick, he wanted some company for dinner. The businessman learned the real identity of PC and immediately called the Brazilian ambassador, who in turn requested the Thai police to arrest PC. Within days, PC was on his way back home under Brazilian police escort.

Tried and found guilty, PC was sentenced to seven years in prison. His wife died of heart failure while PC was imprisoned in Brasília. Their children returned home from their Swiss boarding school. Under the circumstances, PC's lawyers secured a writ that allowed PC to serve out the rest of the sentence in an "open regime" in Maceió, his home town. The court defined the open regime: Pedro César Farias had the right to serve the prison term in the Alagoas State Fire Brigade head-quarters, permitting him to leave the prison during the day and return at night to his cell.[48]

In April 1996, Paulo César Farias was murdered by his jealous lover at his beach house in Maceió, the capital of Alagoas. The death of Collor's treasurer was a national shock. PC never fully revealed how the shake-down scheme worked and who was involved in it, to his last day. The official story was that when PC was planning to marry another woman, the jilted lover who had regularly visited him in his cell for the past two years killed him. There was a palpable sigh of relief from many politicians, businessmen, and even his relatives who preferred the dead PC to a talkative PC.[49] A year after his death, the Italian police accused PC of importing cocaine into the country and laundering drug money.[50]

Resigned and impeached

By October 1992 the congressional impeachment proceedings were going in full swing. As Collor planned to foil the impeachment vote, pious politicians condemned him even before evidence was in. Ambitious and less scrupulous ones traded their votes of support for public projects or jobs for friends and relatives. Collor was confident that having bought and co-opted bushels of deputies, the chamber would not vote for impeachment. The government party held the majority. Collor was equally confident that he could not lose.

But things began to sour. When the chamber decided to cast the vote during a live television broadcast, many deputies suddenly found morality and anticorruption a useful plank to stand on rather than their sworn loyalty to and friendship with the beleaguered president. His political creatures such as Federal Deputy Cleto Falcão of Alagoas turned against him. Collor had been a *padrinho* at the wedding of the deputy and his wife and again served as godfather to their daughter. Federal Deputy Raquel Cândido of Roraima traded her vote for 10 000 sq. meters of choice federal land, but then the former taxi-driver-turned-deputy voted against Collor at the last minute, proclaiming the victory of "morality." She kept the land. Another deputy, failing to get his nominee a job at Light of Rio, a utilities SOE, voted against Collor, shouting he was "against corruption, against corruption." In late September, the chamber voted to ask the senate to impeach Collor.[51] When the senate voted for impeachment, his older brother Leopoldo was in Miami; his other family supporters vanished; his die-hard political hangers-on of 1989 were out of town; and Fernando Affonso Collor de Mello was all alone at the end.[52]

Itamar the *President Pífio*

The changes Vice-President Itamar Augusto Cauteiro Franco brought to the government were both substantial and cosmetic. He wanted only honest but "crudely common" (*pífio*) men in his cabinet, as he called them "ministros pífios." No more Hermes ties, Rolex watches, imported cigars, and Logan whisky. Many men and women who served in the Itamar government conformed to this image. He wanted people to see where he worked by ordering the removal of shades that blocked the view to the third-floor office of the president at Planalto from the street. Also banished was the "intimate room" where Collor used to keep a bed. Itamar wanted to restore dignity to the office and succeeded. In his inaugural speech, he promised that "the country can be sure that there won't be corruption in this government."[53] He nearly kept that promise.

Detractors said that the only contribution of Itamar, an uncommon man, was to reintroduce the Volkswagen beetle. For years it had been discontinued in favor of more expensive and flashy models. The president deplored the loss of the common man's car and persuaded Volkswagen to resume production. The company obliged. Naturally, the Brazilians called the beetle "itamar." Divorced with two grown-up daughters, he was extremely thin-skinned. He was easily upset by cartoons that made fun of his wig or his dress manners. Everything the press criticized about his government was taken as a personal affront.

Itamar and Cardoso, an odd couple

Initially, Itamar appointed friends from Minas Gerais to key economic posts and soon learned that they had neither talent nor political clout to pull off daring economic reform. Like Menem before him, Itamar was forced to turn to more prominent outsiders. He chose the then-foreign minister, Fernando Henrique Cardoso and a founder of the Brazilian Social Democrat Party (PSDB), as his chief economic mandarin.

Cardoso was his third finance minister, an internationally known political sociologist and a social democratic gadfly during the military years. Like Itamar, Cardoso was a federal senator, but it was said that they were only acquaintances, not friends. Cardoso brought with him solid academics such as Edmar Bacha, Pedro Malan, Pérsio Arida, and other economists who had been architects of the Cruzado Plan of the Sarney government. Together, they crafted the *Real* plan to stabilize the economy by July 1994. Unlike others before him, Cardoso had expert knowledge of Latin American economic reform and was thoroughly familiar with the intricate workings of the globalized economy. In fact, Cardoso has been one of the strong advocates of global integration.

Brazil was a late comer in this game of economic stabilization and reform. Chile, Argentina, and Mexico among the big economies of Latin America had done it. Argentina, the perennial butt of jokes to Brazilians as a colossal economic failure, was booming; everyone was attracting foreign direct investment and portfolio money to emerging markets from Mexico City to Buenos Aires, except Brazil. The Brazilian inflation in April and May 1994 was running close to 50 percent a month and short-term interest rates reached an unfathomable 11 900 percent. Bank certificates of deposit paid 5600 percent in interest.[54] Brazil was sinking rapidly into hyperinflation. Much touted reforms were not implemented and were even unimplementable under the circumstances.

The Real *Plan*

Cardoso's economists came up with an ingenious plan. Months before the *Real* Plan was introduced on 1 July, Brazil was living with a "real unit of value (URV)" which was equal to one US dollar. Unlike the Cavallo plan in Argentina, the Brazilian plan offered a two-step stabilization plan. First, the URV's value to the cruzeiro was changed each day; as of the first week of May 1994, one URV was worth Cr$1302.65 and one US dollar Cr$1302.40.[55] All contracts were written in the URV. Salaries were pegged to the URV. By June 1994, prices in stores were marked in the URV. When paid, the units were simply converted into the current daily exchange rate of the cruzeiro. Since the URV was tied to the dollar, the economy functioned for months as if it were dollarized. The inflation rate began to stabilize, although it was still high. By the third week of June, one URV was worth Cr$2547.09, while one US dollar was traded at Cr$2546.70. The Cardoso team planned to with-draw the URV and to replace it with the new currency, the *real*. On the day the new money was introduced, one URV was valued at Cr$2750, the official exchange or conversion value set by the Central Bank for all transactions. One URV was replaced by one *real*.

Cardoso, the Savior of Brazil

Three months before the new money was introduced, Cardoso had left his cabinet post to run for president. While the government would not allow the *real* to be exchanged for the dollar on demand as in Argentina, it did allow the value of the *real* to remain within a small band, close to a one-to-one rate. Initially like the peso, the *real* was more valuable than the dollar by a few cents. Prices were decontrolled; indexation was removed; negotiations for salaries were left to workers and management. The government reduced first and then eliminated much of the subsidies to agriculture, industry, and export sectors. The government undertook further liberalization of foreign trade to expose Brazilian products to stiff competition. Until 15 July 1994, the old and new currencies circulated side by side; and on 16 July the *real* would be the only currency of transaction.[56]

By early October, inflation was down to less than 2 percent per month (50 percent in May) and the grateful Brazilians elected Cardoso as their president. The plan worked, not because of the elixir of the *real*, but because the Brazilians wanted it to work, as with the Argentinians of 1991. In fact, the people who planned the policy were the same technocrats who had worked for the Cruzado Plan in 1986. Remarkably, one of the economists published an article in 1985, proposing a monetary reform similar to the *Real* Plan.[57] Brazil had hit bottom. No more lofty promises, no more politics as usual. The Brazilians, like their southern neighbors, wanted a new beginning and Cardoso was the man to give it to them. As the *Economist* pointed out, the country's return to "economic sanity" would be good for its neighbors as well.

A die-hard political culture

The main task of the Cardoso administration was to consolidate the gains made by the *real* and to advance on the substantive reforms so that the economic growth plan could become a reality. Months into office, Cardoso was unable to push his reform through congress.

Politics since Sarney had degenerated into "what's in it for me" and unless the president reciprocated pork for vote it became impossible to get a bill approved in congress. Ministries were distributed to key parties, whose votes Cardoso needed. Masterfully, he manipulated political loyalty as well as regional rivalry to forge and reforge his congressional power base.[58]

In order to manage this Herculean task, Cardoso pushed several broad reform measures: forging a broad society-wide consensus to accept bitter medicines such as paying taxes, trimming fiscal fat, restraining excessive wage demands by powerful unions, and convincing congress to think boldly. Congress in May 1995 passed a law that would break up the telecom monopoly, and a groundswell was seen for the privatization of the oil monopoly, Petrobrás, as the month-long strike by the workers of the petroleum and natural gas sector perilously threatened to shut down the national economy. To avoid messy political meddling by powerful senators and deputies, let alone businessmen with money, in stopping privatization, Cardoso established a US-styled independent commission or agency. By 1998, the Agência Nacional de Petróleo (ANP-National Petroleum Agency) was managing all contracts for exploration, production, and marketing of petroleum and hydrocarbon products. By taking the power away from Petrobrás, Cardoso was able to inject a measure of transparency. Other state-dominated activities such as mining, utilities, and telecommunications soon came under the control of similar federal agencies, which reported directly to the president.

The two terms of Cardoso between 1995 and 2002 should be remembered as an era of unprecedented transformation for Brazil in history. Not only was he the first Brazilian president elected to two consecutive terms but also was instrumental in inserting Brazil into the global economy. A month after his re-election in November 1998, the full impact of the Asian financial crisis was felt. Brazil sealed an agreement with the IMF to reform its fiscal system radically, reduce bourgeoning public spending, and accelerate state administrative reforms. The IMF agreed to contribute $41.5 billion to Brazil's effort. Nonetheless, by mid-January 1999, Cardoso was forced to devalue the *real* by 40 percent. The initial impact was devastating. The fear of inflation flaring up again was foremost among Brazilians. Against bitter criticism, Cardoso forged ahead with tough measures of increasing interest rates, tightening credit, and resisting all temptations to bring back protectionism and close the economy. In the end, his policies prevailed. The exchange rate settled down by mid-1999, the interest rate was declining, and Brazil's exports were once again bouncing up. In 1999, a record high of $30 billion entered Brazil as foreign direct investment. But the addiction to state handouts and easy foreign money dependency was hard to break. Without reining in the runaway spending of states (the 1988 Constitution requires sharing revenues among the federation, states, and municipalities), Cardoso knew that the Brazilian economy could not be stabilized. To break such an old habit would take indeed all the political skills that Cardoso could muster. If anyone could do it, it would be Fernando Henrique Cardoso.[59]

Cardoso leaves an intractable Brazil

Historians will remember Fernando Henrique Cardoso as one of the greatest presidents in history. His economic stabilization policy had worked well during his two terms in office. The limited engagement in neoliberalism allowed the positive impact of globalization to seep into the country, while Cardoso consolidated political democracy, endorsed press freedom, and improved on human rights. Where Brazil did not score well was in the area of political modernization, eradication of corruption in high places, and inability to forge a national political party system.[60] With multiple regional parties with strong personalities in charge (there are 18 political parties present in congress at the time of writing), the collaboration between the executive and legislative branches degenerated into bartering favors. Powerful senators and deputies often traded with the president their votes for public works projects and extra funds for their states and districts. In 2000 and 2001, several key deputies and senators, many of whom were supporters of Cardoso, were driven out of office under the allegations and charges of corruption and abuse of public power. The energy crisis, including the shortage of electricity, in early 2001 tarnished the image of Cardoso as an efficient manager. The Constitution Committee of the Senate introduced a bill to prohibit all future privatization of state-owned power facilities, as the government announced the construction of 21 new hydropower and 26 gas-driven thermal plants.[61]

Although Cardoso had done much to alleviate mass poverty in the country, one recent government study showed that income inequality had become worse. In fact, Brazil's inequity was worse than any African country's. The top 10 percent of Brazilians garnered 50 percent of all national income, while the poorest 50 percent took home 10 percent of the income.[62] On average Brazilians receive 6.3 years of schooling. Social instability, lack of civil liberty among the poor, police brutality, unequal income distribution, and the inability of the congress and presidency to effectively solve the problems will remain intractable beyond Cardoso's term in office. In fact, Freedom House in New York classified Brazil as "partially free" since 1993, while civil liberty in Brazil received 4 out of 7 (7 being "not free" and 1 being "most free").[63] The October 2002 election will likely be a boring contest among such political perennials as José Serra and Tasso Jereissati of Cardoso's party (PSDB) of the center-left persuasion, Luís Inácio Lula da Silva (PT) of the workers, and Itamar Franco, governor of Minas Gerais and an eternal thorn in the side of Cardoso from the populist wing of the PMDB party.[64] Or, there will be a surprise candidate, as in 1989 when an obscure former governor of a northeastern state captured the presidency. That candidate may be Roseana Sarney, governor of Maranhão, a northeastern state, and daughter of former president and senator José Sarney.[65] Brazilians see women politicians as less corrupt than men. Whatever the outcome, one thing is sure: Cardoso will turn over a country in better shape than when he received it in 1994.

7
Chile: Pinochet's Not Too Silent Revolution

Consolidating market authoritarianism

Henry Kissinger, the consummate geopolitician and the secretary of state for the Nixon and Ford administrations, considered the Soviet Union a problem, Chile a nuisance, and Cuba something in between. To Pinochet, Chile was a problem, Cuba a nuisance, and the Soviet Union the problem of the United States. These two divergent perspectives would place the United States and Chile on a collision course. Those working in Chile on behalf of and in behalf of Cuba and the Soviet Union were Pinochet's enemies. Years later, many in the know would recall that Pinochet was not one of the original and inner plotters to overthrow the Allende regime. In fact, as Allende's last army chief of staff, Pinochet was vacillating until the chief of the navy gave him the ultimatum either to join or to get off.[1] The armed forces were stricken with the fear of the immediate Marxist takeover of the country, especially by followers of the Movimiento Izquierda Revolucionario (MIR), and were prepared to oppose the Allende government and the extreme leftist supporters at all cost. One of the founders of the MIR was Allende's nephew, for whom the president had respect and admiration, but whom he was unable to control. It was suspected that the Marxists and other leftists were receiving a small amount of financial and material aid from Cuba and Eastern bloc countries including the Soviet Union. This connection was sufficient for the armed forces.

When the armed forces overthrew the constitutional government and took power from it, four men controlled the ruling junta: the army chief Augusto Pinochet Ugarte, the air force chief Gustavo Leigh, the navy chief José Toribio Merino, and the national police

146

chief (carabineros) César Mendoza. Their stated objective for the coup was to defend the Constitution of 1925, the document that General Carlos Ibáñez and the army wrote, but Juan Gabriel Valdés observed that the junta was a group of "authoritarians without a project."[2] The group's initial agreement was to rotate the presidency of the junta amongst the four, but soon the wily Pinochet outmaneuvered his rivals by seizing the title of the "Supreme Chief of the Nation." The irate Leigh shouted back: "You think you're God!"[3] Pinochet was extremely insecure about his power and did not hesitate to retire those posing threats to himself. At one time a close aide spoke out against the junta's human rights violations and the general fired him on the spot. By June 1974, he granted himself the supreme power to rule the country by issuing Decree No. 527. Pinochet placed spies throughout the government, thus keeping tabs on his opponents.[4] Soon after that, no one dared to challenge Pinochet for his authority and his power within the armed forces.

Pinochet's suppression of the critics of the junta did not stop in Chile. In Argentina and the United States, the regime's critics and opponents were silenced and even assassinated. In broad daylight in Washington, DC, Allende's foreign minister Orlando Letelier was murdered. The first accusing finger was directed at MIR members, whom the US authorities suspected of having exiled themselves in America soon after September 1973. Many sought asylum in the US, and Washington had to dispatch a group of Immigration and Naturalization Service officials to Chile so that radical MIR members whom the US government considered "terrorists" could be excluded. Soon after the involvement of the FBI and other investigative agencies in the murder case, it was learned that the Chilean military intelligence, working closely with anti-Castro organizations in Miami, sent two killers to Washington. The Chilean intelligence officers first secured US visas with Paraguayan passports. When the US consulate in Santiago discovered the fraud, the visas were speedily revoked. It was 9 August 1976. Incredibly, the same officers reapplied for visas, this time with Chilean official passports. The US consulate issued them multiple entry official visas on 16 August, a week after the original visas were revoked. It was suspected that the Chilean security agents could not have gotten visas without knowledge of the US Government. American law is strict about one thing: anyone using a fraudulent passport to receive a visa is automatically excluded from the United States when caught. But in this case, someone made an exception.[5]

"The brick layers"

The "silent revolution," or, more precisely, the great economic transformation of this century that the junta fathered, was not originally
intended by the coup makers. Roberto Kelly was a retired naval officer
with solid connections with Chile's business community, including
El Mercurio, the country's largest newspaper, and its owner, the
Edwards clan. A year before the fall of the Allende regime, conservative
business groups with the support of the CIA and foreign business
began to mobilize neoliberal economists and businessmen to draw up a
"battle plan" to counter the Marxist command economy. The chief
architect of the massive 500-page document, affectionately known as
"The Brick" (*el ladrillo*) was Sergio de Castro, a Chicago Ph.D. Navy
cronies of Kelly and the chief coup maker, Admiral José Toribio
Merino, were convinced that the market economy was the only way to
move Chile from underdevelopment to development. When the report
was completed, it received scant attention outside the small group. But
Chile now had an alternative to the socialism-Marxism of Allende. It
was doubtful if many in the navy, not to speak of the army, the air
force, and the national police, ever heard of "The Brick."

When the junta put Merino in charge of the economy, the admiral
brought in Kelly to lead the economic planning ministry, ODEPLAN.
Kelly in turn tapped a German-born naturalized Chilean, Miguel Kast
Rist, to be his top aide. A graduate of Chicago, Kast was a fanatic about
market economies, exuding Teutonic enthusiasm for public service,
and persuaded his students and colleagues to accept self-sacrifice for
the good of the country. He was a committed free marketer. At one
time, Kast told his friends that if Chile had 100 economists trained in
Chicago and they all came back to work for the country's private and
public sectors, Chile would not have to worry about Marxism and
socialism.[6]

Together Kelly and Kast brought in Chicago Boys as second-echelon
officials during the first two years of the junta's rule. They laid foundations for the reform and shaped development policies of the Chilean
junta between 1975 and 1985. The peak of the power and fame of the
Chicago Boys was in 1979 and by 1982 their luster was beginning to
fade, as Chile plunged into a deep economic crisis. By 1985, the military banished them from government agencies. Historians seldom
commented on the role Miguel Kast played in the early years of the
junta's economic policy formulation, but there was no doubt that he
was among the most articulate proselytizers of neoliberal economics.
Kast would serve as president of the Central Bank and minister of labor

and social welfare, and in these posts he left an indelible mark on the future of Chile.

The Chilean military dictatorship was different from the Asian variety in that Pinochet and the junta were extremely confident about their power and were not "suspicious of people trained abroad."[7] Unlike Myanmar's junta and the early years of the Korean junta under Park Chung Hee, the Pinochet regime never feared ideas from outsiders. In fact, there is evidence that the junta interviewed several civilian groups in search of a right formula for the country's economic recovery and growth. The Chicago Boys and the junta created market authoritarianism.

Group of 26

José Piñera recalled that what unified the Pinochet economists was what they believed in: a swift abandonment of the statist policies, implanting sound macroeconomic fundamentals, and undying patriotism for the country. The foundation for the on-coming revolution of the Western Hemisphere's most daring open-market economy was laid by a group of technocrats and technopols, most of whom were trained at the Catholic University of Chile and the University of Chicago. Collectively, this elite group was made up of 26 people, whose most senior member was Sergio de Castro, the chief Brick Layer and the regime's first architect of the economic transformation. Together the group had an enduring impact of Chile and Latin America. For the next 16 years, the regime's economic policies were guided by the trio of Sergio de Castro, Jorge Cauás, and Hernán Büchi. The first two men held economics graduate degrees. The third held an MBA.

Contrary to popular belief, not everyone in the inner group of 26 was Chilean and not all members of the group studied in Chicago.[8] Hernán Büchi (minister of finance and planning minister), José Piñera E. (minister of mining and minister of labor), Felipe Lamarca (director of Chile's Internal Revenue Service), Jorge Cauás (minister of finance), and Carlos Cáceres (minister of finance, minister of the interior, and president of the central bank) did not go to Chicago. Cauás, who was the key economic point man in 1975, studied at Columbia. Büchi, who was instrumental in reviving the recessed economy in the mid-1980s, was a Columbia MBA. José Piñera was a Harvard Ph.D. in economics. All held secondary posts in the economy, finance, planning, and banking sectors of the national government at the outset of the junta rule.[9] All of them shared common neoliberal,[10] economic perspectives and were determined to salvage the country from the ruinous legacy of the Allende regime by applying what was then known as the world's most revolutionary economic policy to a fragile Chile.

Only 2 of the technocrats, Büchi and Piñera, became prominent politicians or technopols, and were unsuccessful presidential candidates in 1989. Only 1 of them, Rolf Lüders, held the accumulated post of "biminister" of finance and economy concurrently. Thirteen of the group of 26 held teaching posts at the Catholic University and 5 at the University of Chile. The rest had no teaching experience. Some of the most revolutionary policies, such as public housing, privatized pension funds, labor reforms, educational reforms, banking reforms, and debt swaps were introduced by those technocrats who did not study in Chicago, but at Harvard (Piñera), or Columbia (Cauás and Büchi). Yet all shared a visceral fear of socialism, disdain toward partisan democracy, and the abhorrence of populism.

It was their common rejection of Chile's past and their consensus on the pathway to an economic revolution that brought them together to establish the condominium of the 16-year dictatorial rule.

Roots of Chile's malaise

The Brick's neoliberal analysis of Chile's economic crisis by late 1973 read like a textbook case study. According to Sergio de Castro, the regime's durable economist (minister of economy of 1974–76 and minister of finance of 1976–82), Chile had suffered from chronically anemic and erratic low growth rates since 1940 and the unfortunate consequences were the dismal performance of the key economic sectors, exaggerated statist interventionism, a shortage of productive employment, persistent inflation, an underdeveloped agricultural sector, and extreme mass poverty.[11] These problems were not the creation of the three short years under the Marxist-socialist regime, but of over four decades of Chilean democracy going back to the late 1930s and the 1940s. Often the economic woes and low growth were blamed on the prevailing industrial monopolies and unproductive agricultural estates. The concentration of economic wealth in the hands of the country's oligarchy was accentuated, and by unraveling it many politicians and academics thought Chile could solve the problem. High taxes during the 1960s and the redistribution policy in the early 1970s proved to be a failure.

Also, de Castro and his fellow Brick Layers pointed out that the growing state interventionism was rooted in the Keynesian thinking that the low-growth problem could be solved by expanding public spending. Interest rates were set and regulated by the state; so were the exchange rates, prices and wages, food costs, and public services. And powerful pressure and interest groups garnered public resources for their own benefits. The Chilean state also invested heavily in those areas of low or scarce productivity, thus reducing further national savings, especially in the private sector that paid heavy taxes to support these programs. In 1970, the national savings represented 17 percent of Chile's GDP, while in 1972, the penultimate year of Allende's rule, it declined to 12 percent.[12]

If one were to take de Castro's analysis at its face value, Chile in 1973 was at the historical peak of the statist expansionism with all of its inherent negative trimmings. The role of the state in itself, as shown in Asia Pacific and other Latin American countries, is not bad and cannot be condemned. The problem is the way the state expanded itself in the marketplace and the way its bureaucracy abused power going beyond the basic needs of correction, regulation, and supervision. De Castro like other neoliberals of his generation lamented the atrophying private sector and the hypertrophying state as unwelcome symptoms, which by the early 1970s proved to be deadly. Dirigistes, including the followers of Salvador Allende, turned Chile into an autocratic polity and an inefficient economy in the vortex of the globalizing world economy. Chile, in brief, was uncompetitive, decoupled from the global systems, and autarkic to the extreme. As high as 85 percent of all incoming capital was channeled through the country's official banks like CORFO and the Central Bank.[13] As in Brazil and Argentina, the borrowed credit was rationed according to political exigencies, and the beneficiaries of such external credit were SOEs. Also like other countries with similar economic and political growth policies, Chile needed to be "reinserted" into the global economy so that it could grow with the rest of the world.

The state commits hara-kiri

To accomplish these objectives, the Chicago Boys had to launch a revolution by wiping out the onerous legacy of half a century. They established three broad policy goals: *deregulating* the domestic economy (the market), *liberalizing* international trade, and finally *privatizing* some 600 state-owned enterprises. The timing and Chile's conditions were perfect. The globalization of the world economy was like a train, slowly pulling out of the Latin American station, and Chile had to get on it by double trekking. The economic policies that Frei and Allende pursued created a new fertile ground and mechanisms for the Chicago

Boys to tap and use. The centralized command structure of implementing reforms was in place to be exploited. Frei's massive tree-planting campaign would result in the lumber export boom and Allende's nationalization and statization of industry, agriculture, mining, and forestry centralized the country's economic structure in the hands of the state bureaucracy. No longer did the industrial and agricultural elites pose a threat to a new economic transformation. Copper mining, firmly in the hands of the state, produced revenues that the military could use to fund its own modernization and much needed Chilean development programs.[14] It should be pointed out that for all the zeal of implanting a market economy, the Chicago Boys were unable to privatize the national copper monopoly, CODELCO.

Pinochet protected the copper monopoly from his zealous privatizers. The copper price was up and the military continued to derive a hefty amount of revenues annually from it. Pinochet, when asked why he did not authorize the privatization of CODELCO, said that he liked a business that made money! Furthermore, the armed forces receive 10 percent of the total sale of copper by CODELCO.[15] In vain, many Chicago Boys argued that unless Chile changed its economic structure completely there was no point getting on the global train.

Much of the success of the economic reform introduced and implemented by the regime's economists was owed to the authoritarianism that required no popular consultation and public accounting. The dictatorship created a political space for the Chicago Boys and their successors to work in. It also created the right psychological environment for the neoliberal economic program to thrive. Chileans had nowhere to go when Allende was overthrown. Socialism-Marxism failed them miserably. The gung-ho zeal for change, the high-level contempt for partisan politics, and the strong conviction among the Chicago Boys to subordinate personal interests to the good of the country washed well with the military. In some ways, such an attitude insulated the economic technocrats and technopols from outside criticism. How the Chicago Boys developed their working relationship with the junta was a critical avenue for Chile's economic transformation in the 1970s and 1980s. Chile succeeded because there were the right kinds of internal and external conditions that permitted such a chemistry of a bureaucratic-authoritarian regime to work. More importantly, like Argentinians, the Chileans wanted a change after years of stagnation and the three years of socialist-Marxist chaos.

Perhaps Celso Furtado was correct in observing that Allende's men only cared about Chile as the bearer of Latin America's first elected socialist-Marxist government. And Kissinger was right: Allende's men had no sense of history. Ideologically miles apart, Furtado and Kissinger were saying the same thing: a revolution could be won only by a people with a sense of history.

In search of the right fundamentals

At the outset, the military did not have a plan for saving the economy. Inflation in September 1973 was running at 900 percent, growth was almost nil, the economy's productivity was declining, and the world was just entering the first leg of the global business recession provoked by the price hike of OPEC's oil.

The junta invited several political and business groups for ideas and policy recommendations. Initially, key junta economic advisers came from the ranks of the private sector with strong Christian Democratic ties, such as Raúl Sáez, Fernando Léniz, Alvaro Bardón, and Jorge Cauás. Raúl Sáez, a Frei minister, was a founder of CORFO, father of all SOEs, a strong advocate of state-sponsored industrialization, and one of "seven wise men" of the Alliance for Progress of the Kennedy administration in the early 1960s. Léniz came from *El Mercurio* where he served as executive director. Bardón had a close relationship with the banking sector. Cauás worked for the World Bank in Washington. Many career technocrats, hold-overs from the previous Marxist government, continued to work for the junta, however. Christian Democratic economists like Cauás and Bardón were given key posts. Merino, one of the four top junta leaders, appointed a navy man to be a finance minister, who in turn relied on Christian Democratic advisers. Léniz served as economy minister, while Sáez held the portfolio of economic coordination. Cauás's goal was to restore "a modern, mixed economy," true to the tradition of the Christian Democrats.[16]

Business leaders turned out be disappointing advisers. While welcoming the return to a market economy, they strongly lobbied for state support for their own companies, especially subsidies and other forms of favoritism as a quick fix for economic recovery. And daily, military leaders were being lectured by Christian Democrat politicians on the merit of an open-market economy while at the same time calling for a strong guiding hand of the state. The military found the PDC advice both anachronistic and a wishful return to a Frei era of mixed economy. Gradually, Christian Democrat leadership began to lose influence in the policy-making arena, and by mid-1974 the party and the junta became estranged. The party fathers ordered its economists in the junta to leave. All but Cauás and Bardón quit.[17]

Empowering the Chicago Boys

The result of the first year's attempt to reform under Léniz and Sáez and working with Christian Democrats was precariously meager: inflation ran at 375.9 percent per year, unemployment rose, and real wages stagnated. Furthermore, state revenue fell by a third. Chile, a net importer of oil, was reeling from high oil prices, while the income from copper plummeted. Kelly went to Pinochet and told him that more drastic measures were needed and persuaded the general to empower the Chicago Boys to reorganize the economy. At the same time, Kelly, Kast, and other Chicago Boys were leading a sordid power struggle against the entrenched career bureaucrats and centrists like Léniz and Sáez, the minister of economy and the minister for economic coordination, respectively.

By April 1975, the Chicago Boys won. The junta gave them the power to design a plan of "shock treatment" for the country, and Cauás was installed as the new finance minister receiving broad authority over the country's economy. A somber Cauás announced the first shock plan, and with it the consolidation of the Chicago Boys' power was complete. Sáez resigned quickly.[18]

The military was preparing for wars against Argentina and Peru over territorial disputes and was convinced that the country must have economic growth and stability to confront the two historical foes. The military knew that it did not have economic specialists within its own ranks, that partisan economists would hamper the reform, and that the fanaticism of the Chicago Boys was viewed as unyielding patriotism with which the junta leaders and the rank-and-file of the armed forces could easily identify. The Boys and the armed forces were made for each other and Chile needed them in 1974, as the global economy plunged into recession. Years later, Kast would write to Pinochet, shortly before he (Kast) died of cancer, that the general was the savior of Chile and the free world; and another Chicago Boy who was running for political office in 1989, the last year Pinochet was in office, acclaimed the general as "the true author of the silent revolution and rising society."[19]

Draconian measures

Cauás's team produced one of the most draconian stabilization plans ever adopted by a Latin American country.[20] Known as the Economic Recuperation Program, it had a deficit-cutting budget that drastically reduced inflation, lowered import tariffs, dismissed tens of thousands of public functionaries, and restored a fiscal balance and stability. The SOE deficit decreased by 27 percent in 1975, public investment was cut by half, and by 1978 one out of four officials was sent home for good.

Inflation in 1976 and in 1977 was cut by half. Public investment was down to the level of the 1960s. Unemployment shot up, tripling to 16.3 percent in 1976 and 14 percent by 1977.[21] The Boys did not stop there. Rates for public utilities and other services were increased, income tax was increased by 10 percent, a heavy consumption tax was levied on imported luxury goods, and all exemptions to VAT were eliminated. A plan to privatize SOEs – CORFO alone held 507 companies – and to deregulate the domestic banking sector was laid. The Cauás plan was a *government-induced* recession.

The results were both swift and stunning. Unemployment climbed to 19 percent, as if there was no limit; imports flooded the country – the import tax was down to 44 percent from the historic high of 200 percent – forcing inefficient domestic manufacturers out of business; deregulated banks were competing for deposits by paying higher interest rates; the deficit declined from 27.7 percent of GDP in 1973 to 2.9 percent in 1975; and weakened labor unions and political parties failed to challenge the junta's policies. The GDP declined by 12.9 percent and per capita by 14.4 percent. The industrial sector and civil construction suffered the worse decline: 25.5 percent and 26 percent respectively. And the stubborn inflation remained at the annual rate of 340.7 percent, according to the junta's own figures.[22]

This first phase of the junta policy worked but with considerable negative impact on the economy and society. Chile now needed a policy of economic recovery first and then growth, requiring a more detailed plan of converting the statist economy into a market-oriented one. But the recession was too profound and painful. The junta replaced Cauás with de Castro. A new group of Boys was brought in. Sergio de Castro, the former dean of the Faculty of Economics at the Catholic University, became the undisputed doyen of the Chicago Boys. It was a full three years after the junta took power that the Boys consolidated their position. A thoughtful technocrat like Kast was concerned about the ascending power and arrogance of some of the Boys and urged them to "humanize" their behavior.[23] The military's trust in them was total. De Castro was among a handful of officials who could argue with Pinochet. The crisis both at home and abroad called for a radical departure from the previous policy.

The junta's long-term development policy

There were four distinct phases of the economic policy that the junta adopted between 1973 and 1990. The first phase (1973–78) implanted a stringent stabilization plan to reverse the economic malaise and to reignite economic growth; the second phase (1979–80) introduced a series of structural changes, known as "Seven Modernizations," by which the junta sought to institutionalize the changes wrought up to that time; the third period dealt with the financial crisis of 1981–83 and briefly reverted to state intervention in the economy; and finally, the fourth period (1984–90) deepened the reforms by re-privatizing those SOEs that the state took back in 1982 and 1983 and initiating a second round of privatization of those SOEs not affected before then, which attracted foreign direct investment and promoted exports.[24]

The Seven Modernizations focused on the areas of labor, social security, education, health, decentralization of regional administration, agriculture, and justice. Without modernization in these seven areas, no gains from both the economic and social changes could be sustained and be permanent, and, more importantly, growth *with development* could not be had. By any measure, the Pinochet regime succeeded in implementing its modernization policies in all seven fields with equal impact and consequences. This chapter will focus on four of the seven areas that have fundamentally altered Chile during the 16 years of the bureaucratic-authoritarian rule: privatization, pension reform, labor reform, and foreign direct investment, especially in mining.

Two privatizations

The proliferation of SOEs or parastatals in Chile can be traced to two historical developments. First, the role of the interventionist state in economic development and growth was well defined in the mid-1930s, as CORFO began to establish production companies in steel, energy, beet sugar, and public utilities. These were the sectors where foreign and domestic capital had been most active but became depressed in the 1930s. The logic of the public sector's entry into the formerly private sectors of the economy was to revive the faltering economy and produce goods and services for all classes. And create employment. The universal accessibility to credit, goods, and services by Chileans was the rationale for CORFO's establishment.

The second wave of proliferating parastatals in Chile came from a series of business failures. As private companies in debt to state banks and governmental agencies were unable to liquidate (pay off) their debt, CORFO took them over. Instead of closing the failed businesses, the government turned them into public companies to maintain the stability of employment and to keep business going. Chile's pattern of creating SOEs was not that different from Argentina's and Brazil's:

import-substituting industrialization necessitated the involvement of the state in the market and private investors were not always eager to invest in all sectors of the economy. As Mário Henrique Simonsen would say, the state filled the vacuum.

By 1965, the country had 68 SOEs, which were controlled by 16 giant holding companies, also parastatals. At the end of the Allende rule in 1973, the tally soared to 596. Of these, 325 were industrial SOEs and 18 banks. In that year, the combined output of all parastatals reached about 40 percent of Chile's GDP, but they accounted for 100 percent in utilities, 85 percent in mining, 70 percent in transportation, and 85 percent in banking.[25] The first round of privatization between 1974 and 1979 either returned 492 SOEs to the original owners or resulted in their sale. During the business recession of 1982–83, as many as 50 privatized companies were returned to the state custody, for the new owners were unable to run the businesses profitably.[26]

The 1981–82 business recession, or more precisely bank failure, in fact lasted until the spring of 1984 and had several causes: one was a global business recession in the wake of the second oil price hike imposed by OPEC in 1979–80, when the price of oil per barrel reached the historic high of $40. The second reason was the break-down of the Chicago Boys' "monetarism" which pegged the peso "forever" at 39 to 1 dollar. The rationale was that once the public sector deficit in the fiscal account was eliminated, as it had been by 1978, and deregulated trade and investment began to work, inflation would fall.[27] Throughout the 1970s, this policy worked wonders, as long as international capital flocked to Chile, the only Latin country with investment barriers down and liberalized foreign trade. Third, by the early 1980s, interest rates were going up, money became scarce, and oil at $40 a barrel began to pinch the global economy, forcing recently privatized but heavily leveraged Chilean banks to cut back. The interest rate for business borrowing stood at 40 percent[28] in 1981, as all the projections of 7 to 8 percent growth of the economy trumpeted by the junta became an elusive dream. Fourth, between 1977 and 1981, the bankruptcies of private firms increased by four-fold. In 1981, the current account deficit of Chile went over $4.8 billion.[29] During the same period, employment in Latin America increased by 3 percent, while Chile's shrank by 6 percent. A think tank closely tied to the Christian Democrat Party, CIEPLAN, pro-duced an alternate plan of development and growth to the policy implemented by the Chicago Boys. CIEPLAN economists complained that Chile opened its market too much and too fast to foreign competition; that Chile had too much foreign debt and had no coherent development strategy; that the regime was abandoning the dirigiste role of the state too hastily; and, finally, that the government failed to create jobs.[30] To make matters worse, the price of copper plummeted from 99 cents a pound in 1980 to 67 cents by 1982. And the country's foreign reserve shrank by 45 percent.[31]

The opposition economists proposed that the government invest in productive sectors to create jobs and ease macroeconomic adjustment policies. By labeling the regime's technocrats "monetarists" CIEPLAN economists launched an international campaign of discrediting junta economists by drawing foreign criticism. Ricardo Ffrench-Davis, a Chicago Ph.D. and an articulate critic of the Chicago Boys, argued that Chile was going contrary to world trends. Monetarism never gained popularity in developed and developing countries, and all it did in Chile was to set off the new alarming trend of the concentration of wealth in the hands of a few conglomerates. Of the 177 largest companies in the country, 10 percent of the shareholders held 72 percent of the capital of each company.[32] It was akin to the Japanese government's public relations strategy of calling all US critics of its trade policy "Japan bashers." In fact, José Piñera commented with hindsight that none of the Chicago Boys was a "sophisticated monetarist" or knew much about Milton Friedman's brand of neoliberal monetarism. What the regime's economists knew well was the basic tenets of supply and demand in an open economy and the fundamentals of efficiency of competition in a free enterprise system. The "detoxification of a state-hobbled economy" was the goal; this had to be carried out with an element of surprise. Towards this goal, there was a unity among the regime's economists trained at Chicago, Harvard, and Columbia and the generals, both groups of whom sought to end the role of the activist state in the economy once and for all.[33]

Months before Black September in Mexico, which defaulted on its payment to international banks in 1982, the Chilean economy was slowly sinking. The government chose to devalue the peso by 18 percent, but the market sent the peso down further. The normally muzzled labor and press joined the business community to block in vain the Chicago Boys' policy. Chile was in its worst economic crisis ever: the unemployment rate was at 32 percent and its GDP fell by 14.1 percent. Unrest was spreading throughout 1983 and 1984, forcing Pinochet to declare a state of siege. The "political crime" rate went up: over 40 000 opponents of the regime landed in jail in 1984, compared to 1000 in 1981, the last year of the boom of the 1970s and the marvel of the Chicago Boys.[34]

A comparison with the earlier crisis is in order. Between 1974 and 1977, 2.5 percent of the national workforce was laid off because of Pinochet's retrenching and dismantling policies. In 1973, the parastatals' combined deficit equaled 33 percent of the national current account deficit, but by 1976 Chile succeeded in eliminating all public sector deficits. The central bank was forbidden from lending money to SOEs, a policy subsequently written into the Constitution of 1980. Also between 1974 and 1979, the first privatization period, Chile's tariff rates tumbled down from 750 percent at the highest to an average of 10 percent. Foreign direct investment flowed in massively in 1979 as the exchange rate was set permanently. So much money came into the country that Chilean banks were tripping over each other to lend money to customers, worthy and unworthy. The credit volume grew between 1978 and 1981 by 100 percent. Soon after that, Chilean banks were unable to borrow money from overseas sources. Many buyers of SOE banks had not used their own money but leveraged the purchase with overseas money, or the state-lent credit. In 1981, 16 new banks were opened to join the existing 27 privately owned banks. The privatization led to a borrowing binge and between 1979 and 1981 the country's external debt tripled, all by private banks and firms. The problem was still with the country's depressed productive capacity. Chile was importing more than producing at home, and, borrowing heavily from the credit glut, consumers spent as if there was no tomorrow. The Chicago Boys' policy of privatization, liberalization, and deregulation reversed the macroeconomic disequilibria, but their economic policy created an artificial boom. By the end of 1982, 16 banks went belly up, including the two largest, Banco de Chile and Banco de Santiago. The economy's output fell by 14.1 percent; unemployment soared; and the country entered into the worst depression in history.[35]

Büchi-instilled stability

Brutal and inhumane as it was, Chile's privatization accomplished what the Pinochet regime set out to achieve: to stabilize the economy and set it in motion for growth by production.[36] And also, it was the time for Pinochet to fine-tune and calibrate the economic policy. The basic premises of privatization, liberalization, and deregulation were sound and remained as the regime's policy cornerstones. The regime needed to focus on how to reignite economic growth to make itself politically popular to Chileans, and time was running out. To attract more foreign direct investment to all sectors by fully implementing the 1974 Foreign Investment Code (Decree-Law No. 600), the government needed a new strategy going beyond stabilization and adjustment. The current policy was seen as inflationary. Between 1982 and 1985, the junta began to lose faith in the Chicago Boys and changed finance ministers five times. In 1985, a Columbia University graduate, Hernán Büchi, was chosen to lead the country to prosperity.[37] The era of the Chicago Boys came to a close.

Büchi was one of the earliest collaborators of the Chicago Boys in the 1970s. Like Cavallo of Argentina, Büchi was almost messianic in his commitment to Chile's well-being and his vision of how to accomplish it. In 1973, he worked in the planning secretariat as a second-echelon official and emerged as one of the key players in the government. In 1985, Büchi wanted to push the structural and policy reform beyond the point at which Chile could not turn back to the "bad old days" in the event of another economic crisis.[38] Like all good reformers, Büchi knew that the fracasomania, the culture of dependency, and living off the state subsidies and largesse were a political culture hard to break.

Büchi went after reforms with a vengeance. Firmly believing in the passion for the possible, he balanced the budget by cutting spending, including payments to retirees, the military, and civilians. Companies that reinvested profits rather than disbursing them to stockholders were given tax incentives. He abandoned the earlier policy of using a strong peso (by tying it permanently to the dollar) to fight inflation; rather, by maintaining the peso at an internationally competitive level, he was able to reignite growth and especially increase exports. The economy was growing at 5 percent per year and inflation was down to 20 percent by 1988. In 1986, foreign direct investment equaled 6 percent of the GDP, but by 1988 it rose to 17 percent. And domestic savings reached 22 percent of the country's output, nearly the level of the Asian Tigers.

Debt-for-equity swaps

Büchi launched a program that the Chicago Boys didn't or couldn't contemplate in the 1970s: debt swaps. To attract international capital, Büchi combined the Central Bank's rules (Chapter 19 of the Foreign Exchange Regulations) and the 1974 Foreign Investment Law. The government of Chile allowed anyone to buy Chilean debt papers at the current market price. In 1984, one Chilean debt dollar was traded below 59 cents.

Once an investor declared his intention of buying the promissory notes (debt papers) from a commercial lender, whether a Chilean, United States, Japanese, or European bank, he was committed to exchanging them for the peso. The peso could be used to buy assets and invest in projects such as privatization. The Central Bank offered to buy back the dollar-denominated debt papers at face value, less a service charge of about 13 cents per dollar. Chapter 19 allowed the conversion of a dollar bought at 59 cents into 87 cents but in pesos. This meant that a mining company could buy a mining property from the government at a steep discount price.

The government imposed fair but anti-speculative conditions for all capital coming to Chile under Chapter 19: capital must remain in the country for ten years; profits could be expatriated beginning in the fifth year; in the event that the original capital was expatriated, the investor had to sell all or parts of the Chilean property acquired under Chapter 19. This was a boon for investors who wanted to acquire SOE properties. Both Chile and the investors were winning: Chile was able to reduce its foreign debts, while investors bought assets at a discount. Under this scheme, Chile converted $3.6 billion of debt, about a quarter of the country's total, into equity, now in the hands of private investors. Foreign investors were particularly active. US investors were not the only ones being bullish about Chile. Alan Bond of Australia, for instance, acquired the Santiago Power Company, the country's largest, from the government through debt swaps.[39]

This debt-for-equity swap policy was further buttressed by eliminating public sector deficits, a reasonable monetary policy, competitive exchange rates, opening the long cocooned economy through tariff reduction and adopting a unitary rate for all imports, ending subsidies, and an all-out privatization of SOE properties as well as the social security and pension systems. Under Büchi, Chile consolidated its place as a country with a rule of law, property rights firmly spelled out, and regulatory regimes being developed and written clearly for all players in the economy.

The second privatization

The second privatization after 1985 was often criticized as a giveaway. One study shows that the Pinochet government granted an average of 25 percent of the subsidies to buyers of privatized parastatals and, in the case of reprivatized banks, a hefty 52 percent in subsidies. Non-financial parastatals which had been weaned from generous state handouts required only 12 percent in subsidies to go private. The financial reform of 1974–82 eliminated the public sector deficits including those of SOEs, and some critics of the regime wondered if there was any need to privatize state companies at all. Chile had to continue to deepen its structural reform. It was now or never. Büchi and his supporters were convinced that in 1985 Chile was still in danger of reverting back to populist macroeconomics. It had not crossed the point of no return. Chile was an attractive investment alternative to international capital in the maelstrom of the global depression, but the economic team wanted to consolidate that position and reputation. For four years (1985–89), the government auctioned off an additional 28 SOEs, whose book value was estimated at $2.8 billion but which netted half, or $1.4 billion.[40]

What made Chile a good risk was its sound macroeconomic policy foundations, the "fire sale" of SOEs and private assets under Chapter 19 of debt-for-equity swaps, and the Pinochet regime's fervor to expand the ownership of private properties. Lüders, who was the finance minister in 1982, later realized that, had it not been for the dictatorship, the country could not have come out of the crisis. He was not alone on this. Unlike Mexico in 1995, the Chile of 1982 had one strong advantage: dissent could be easily controlled and even silenced; and the junta imposed reform policies at will and without society-wide consultation.[41]

Pension fund reform

The junta unveiled its retirement or pension fund reforms in November 1980 by Decree Laws Nos. 3.500 and 3.501, soon to be modified by two additional decrees the following year. The business slowdown and escalating company bankruptcies in the early 1980s followed by the banking crisis of 1982 delayed the full implementation of the decrees. Against the backdrop of the economic downturns and the subsequent business recession of 1982, an earlier analysis of the pension reform was gloomy and was given little chance to succeed. In fact, one study attempted to show that, under the new plan, the total amount of return or remuneration stood to be less than half the rate under Allende's rule.[42] This projection turned out to be unfulfilled and untrue. Another study by CIEPLAN ten years later still warned that the pension funds could go broke and even lead to public indebtedness.[43]

In 1985, the government allowed SOE employees the right to buy stocks in their own companies, as they were being privatized. The law further permitted employees to use their own pension funds to acquire individual stocks, thus opening up the possibility of investing pension funds in publicly held corporations. This idea of privatizing pension funds has been often associated with José Piñera who, like

Büchi, believed that to be successful the Chilean reforms had to be pushed to boundaries thus far unknown to history. Appearing in weekly television interviews on economic and social policies, Piñera convinced the country that pension funds must be part of the market economy.

Under the plan, all workers of the public and private sectors, including the self-employed if willing, but excluding all members of the armed forces and the police, contributed 10 percent of their monthly wages, plus an additional 3.44 percent for unemployment, disability compensation, and survivor's benefits to a private fund. These percentages applied to the first $22 000 of yearly income. Each contributor had an "investment account" with a brokerage, chosen by the contributor. The fund manager invested money in stocks, bonds, and financial market instruments, but by practice much of the funds was invested in government-controlled and –approved stocks and funds.[44] The pension fund management companies, known as AFPs (administradoras de fondos de pensiones) invested in stocks, bonds, mutual funds, and overseas accounts, as they saw fit. There were some 15 AFPs, many of whom were associated with banks, insurance companies, trade unions, and even workers' co-ops. Such international investors as AIG, Aetna, and Banco de Santander of Spain were full participants. The average cost of maintaining the account was around 2.9 percent of the worker's salary.

The superintendency of AFPs watched over how the funds were invested and managed and checked potential abuses. The length of time for contributions (the retirement age being 65 years for men and 60 years for women),[45] the monthly amount of contributions, and the manner of withdrawal, after retirement, would determine the type of portfolios that the contributor could choose: an insurance policy, annuity, or a mutual fund. Each person was required to make a minimum payment of US$1000 per year and to choose one of the three methods of benefit withdrawals, when retired: withdrawing one lump sum; establishing monthly payments over a fixed period of time; or withdrawing the money in five, ten or fifteen installments. The contributor, not the fund manger or the state, was to choose one of the three options.[46] One study of the pension funds showed that in 1995 an average of 78 percent of the mean annual salary of the last ten years was paid out. When the system was open, the workers had a choice of converting to the private fund or remaining with the old, pay-as-you go system. A fourth of the eligible workers, or 500 000, chose the new system immediately. Over 90 percent of the workers who belonged to the old system eventually switched to the private system and by 1995 five million Chileans owned private pension accounts.[47]

The past performance and future prospects for the AFP portfolios were good. Between 1981 and 1990, the lowest return on investment was 5.41 percent (1998) and the highest was 21.36 percent (in 1981, a year before the bank collapse). In 1991, an impressive 15.64 percent was turned in. Chile was one of the hottest "emerging markets" in the world and the AFP funds benefited from the boom. The state guaranteed a minimum retirement benefit as a social safety net. In 1990, the AFP funds amounted to 15 percent of Chile's GDP; in 1994, 40 percent; and by 2030, the retirement fund should be equal to the country's GDP. The AFPs in 1995 exceeded all portfolios held by non-banking institutions with $15 billion in assets.[48] In order to protect the investment, Chilean law required that all AFPs and investment accounts such as mutual funds should be two separate legal entities. If an AFP should become bankrupt, the investment account should remain intact and untouched.[49]

Since the inception of the private pension system in 1981, the total value of such units of the system in 1995 as old age, disability, and survivor's benefits was higher by 50 to 100 percent than the old pay-as-you-go system. Between 1985 and 1988, the AFP funds held 18 percent of all stocks and bonds in the Chilean financial market. In 1994, the fastest growing sector in the Chilean economy was financial (4.3 percent), followed by personal services (3.4 percent), construction (2.7 percent), and commerce (2.3 percent).[50] As of 1995, the pension funds were valued at $25 billion, or equivalent to 40 percent of the GNP.[51] Chile might be the only country where cab drivers and janitors read the daily stock market performance in the newspapers!

Labor reform

Through the years since the Second World War, Chilean organized labor remained fragmented. Communist influence spread slowly in the Central Única de Trabajadores (CUT), which became an adjunct of the Chilean Communist Party (PCC). Christian Democrats and Socialists had labor unions and worker followers of their own.[52] The Frei years were devoted to the control of labor, often pitting Christian Democrat unions against Communist-dominated CUT. But it was during the Allende years that labor transformed itself. Once having tasted power as one of the supporters of the Allende coalition – two of CUT's leaders became cabinet members – the country's labor was afflicted with internal ideological and power struggles, thus never succeeding in consolidating its power base, as in Argentina under Perón. Socialists and the MIR set up *cordones industriales*, or unions organized along geographic lines, which bitterly opposed CUT rallies and demonstrations. CUT members in turn opposed cordones' tactics of the direct takeover of factories and plants in response to Allende's call for workers' defense of his government.[53] To the end of Allende's rule, Chilean workers never united but remained militant.

The regime implemented the reform in several steps: wage suppression, outright disbanding of the leftist unions, intimidation by dispatching tanks to the Christian Democrat Party union headquarters, and hauling off to jail some of the vocal and militant leaders. After 1973, unionism as known before that period ceased to exist. Decree Law No. 203 of 1973 excluded anyone involved in prior land seizure from family land grants. The worker with a record was excluded from the benefit of the reform. The junta also repealed several labor laws that the Christian Democratic government introduced, such as the rural workers union act.[54] As a result, the real wage of Chilean workers and the poor in general eroded considerably under the military rule. Wage increases were shunned, lest they could spark inflation and hamper growth.

Resurgent democracy

In 1990, the victorious Center-Left coalition of 17 political parties, knows as the *Concertación*, brought Patricio Aylwin to power. The very economists of CIEPLAN who had bitterly criticized in 1983 the regime's reforms and adjustment came to occupy first- and second-level posts in the new democratic government. Curiously, this group was not eager to reinstate the old statist and populist economic policies, thus becoming silent partners to the military's economic transformation. Instead, they were willing to continue with Pinochet's policies with a series of minor modifications. Alejandro Foxley Rioseco, a Wisconsin, Madison-trained economist, the president of CIEPLAN, and the architect of the 1983 alternative policy, became the minister of finance. Foxley had strong ties with Christian Democrats, once working for the Frei government (ODEPLAN) as a young economist.[55] René Cortázar, an MIT Ph.D. and also a sharp critic of the regime's social welfare policy, became the minister of labor and social welfare, choosing not to reverse the labor reform. And Ricardo Ffrench-Davis, a close collaborator of Foxley, went to the Central Bank. All these former critics of the regime's "monetarist" policies acquiesced to the success of the Büchi-built economic foundations: money supply must be reduced to dampen inflation; a fixed exchange rate system was harmful to export sectors; the strong labor unionism and the hypertrophied state were inimical to the growth of the economy. The Aylwin government focused on how to embrace the convergence of the left, the center, and the right, while maintaining the economic course set by the Pinochet government. Foxley graciously admitted that his criticism in 1983 was too harsh and even too premature.[56]

Aylwin embraces Pinochet's policies

Some alleged that Aylwin and his economic advisers were not free marketers. To them, the market represented "the paradigm of cruelty,"[57] CIEPLAN economists included a diverse group or philosophical *dirigistes* and even socialists. Their writings in the 1970s and 1980s showed a strong proclivity toward state regulation and state domination of the market. But, as Alejandro Foxley admitted, they might have gone too far. More specifically, the economic architects of the Aylwin government defined greater needs as: (1) to increase investment so that the economy could grow at least 5 percent per annum; (2) to establish a mechanism to restore social equity so that all Chileans could benefit from the economic growth, past, present, and future; (3) to balance the past growth objectives with the current limited financial resources at home and abroad; and, finally, (4) to be prepared to face the consequences of the excessive macroeconomic expansion in 1988–89, thanks to higher copper prices.[58] As will be seen, the Aylwin–Foxley objective was to diversify the economy, thus moving away from the monocultural dependency on copper, while continuing to attract investment to the mining sector.

The transformation was both political and economic. The new civilian government inherited an expansive economy that was growing at 6.2 percent for each of the previous five years, yet the benefits were not evenly shared. There was no social equity. Hence, it was growth without development. Also, a new democratic Chile had to face the situation of how to adjust minimum wages for the working class.[59] The economic planners were palpably caught between their old habits of resorting to the rhetoric of developmentalism and populist social policies, but at the same time the new world economy and its realities forced them to moderate their raw impulses. In the end, the Aylwin government and its economists reined in all temptations to undo the economic accomplishments of the dictatorial regime and chose to continue the same policy with cosmetic modifications.

Copper is still king

Well before the Aylwin government came into office in March 1990, Chile began to deregulate and liberalize its mining sector. The mining policy that the new civilian government pursued was one and the same that the Pinochet regime put on course. Foreign investors increased their confidence level in Chile, as little or no fundamental economic policy change was instituted by the Aylwin government. The fundamentals of sound macroeconomic policy, sensible foreign investment policies, and the equal treatment of foreign and national capital continued. Alejandro Hales, twice minister of mines (once under the Ibañez government and then again under the Eduardo Frei M. – the father – administration), was selected to lead the mining sector for the third time. A gentlemen lawyer of considerable prestige and business reputation among the international mining community, Hales was a perfect choice to send a message to current and prospective investors that Chile would not change its mining policy radically and would do business as usual. The boom continued.

The mining boom was made possible by a variety of policy foundations, such as short-term incentives and long-term changes mentioned earlier. The fiscal deficit was gone; the economy was free from the distortions caused by parastatals, all of which were privatized by 1990, except for a dozen or so (CODELCO and the unsellables); and the Foreign Investment Law of 1974 allowed investors to keep overseas bank accounts for corporate profits, setting the maximum tax rate which could be renegotiated after the first ten years and guaranteeing the expatriation of capital and profit after a minimum of three years of residency. The last requirement was eased in 1994.

Other fine tuning of social and economic regulations also spurred mining investment. The Labor Code of 1980 and its amendments in 1987 curbed labor militancy and made it easier to hire and lay off workers. The devaluation of the peso in 1982 and the elimination of the fixed exchange system made the Chilean currency more competitive and less expensive for investors to do business in the country. The new Mining Code of 1984 and its implementation regulations treated both foreign and domestic investors equally, shortened the length of time to secure exploration permits, and assured the right of the exploration company to continue to exploit minerals that it discovered. The Tax Code of 1984 and its amendments in 1988 brought the Chilean tax rates to the world level in the range of the mid-thirties in percentage. By allowing a generous deduction of direct business expenses, the effective rate came down still more to 15 percent or less. The privatization opened up untapped reserves that were in public lands for private exploration and exploitation. By using the debt-for-equity swaps, undercapitalized small and medium-sized firms launched projects that were normally beyond their financial means.

When the Aylwin government came into office in March 1990, the mining projects were valued at $3 billion. During the next four years, the total mining investment from the private sources alone soared to $16 billion. Some 500 US firms invested $3.3 billion in Chile between 1974 and 1993, of which about 70 percent was in mining. The US firms received authorization for an additional $9.6 billion to be invested. Roughly 42 percent of all foreign investment came from the US. In mining the US remained the largest investor (48 percent of the total), closely followed by Canada with 44 percent. The stampede for mining investment was on and was still strong in March 1994, when Aylwin turned over the reins of government to his successor Eduardo Frei, son of the founder of the Christian Democratic Party and former president.[60]

New twists in Chilean economic policy

The Aylwin government added minor modifications to the earlier investment policies set on course by the Pinochet regime. Debt-for-equity swaps were continued, but no longer could the investor use debt papers to buy SOEs. Swaps could be used for new projects such as the modernization of infrastructure and productive activities that created jobs. The government stopped all plans to privatize CODELCO, ENAMI, and ENCAR – the three major mining parastatals – to allay all fears about the foreign takeover of mining. Instead, the government encouraged joint ventures. As government social spending rose, the SOEs received less funding. Chile's copper parastatal, CODELCO, successfully put together a joint venture with foreign companies. The list of its partners reads like who's who in the world mining industry. Most recently, Cyprus-Amax, a Colorado mining company (now Asarco-Cyprus), LAC Minerals of Canada, and CODELCO agreed to develop the E1 Abra copper property. After initial difficulties, the project finally took off.[61]

Diversifying the economy

Although Chile has 24 percent of the world's confirmed copper reserves, it aggressively began to diversify its economy. In the 1960s, minerals represented 85.6 percent of Chile's exports. In the 1970s, the proportion declined to 70.6 percent, then to 57.2 percent between 1981 and 1984, and 53.1 percent for 1985–89, a year before Aylwin was elected. By the mid-1990s, between 40 and 45 percent of the exports were copper. Manufactured and industrial products expanded steadily from 10.5 percent in the 1960s to 24.3 percent in the 1970s and to 32.8 percent for 1985–89.[62] Economic diversification was on the way. Government promotion of fruit growing, fisheries, wine, and forestry products paid off. Winter fruits were marketed in the US, Europe, and Asia. Chile invested for nine years in developing high-quality salmon farming to meet the Japanese standards. The country was the world's second largest salmon grower (but the third largest producer from both salmon farming and from catches), exporting to Japan and the United States. Chile ranked only after Norway and Britain with an annual production of 45 000 tons recorded in 1995. Chilean vintners, once export adverse, are now most aggressive in tapping the world market. Finally, the tree planting campaign that the government promoted in the late 1960s had been paying off handsomely. The Compañía Acera Pacífica, formerly a steel SOE, was the country's largest lumber exporter, in addition to being the largest iron ore mining company and steel maker. The privatized conglomerate exported in 1994 more than 1500 containers of wood moldings per month and other construction-grade materials to the United State alone.[63]

Chile goes global

Chile was also becoming a global important investor in Argentina, Peru, and Mexico. Between 1990 and 1994, Chilean companies and individuals invested $1.8 billion in Argentina, or 62 percent of all foreign direct investment in that country. Cavallo's stabilization policy and improved bilateral relations between the two countries helped. In fact, Chile was more than Argentina's investor. It offered access to Asia Pacific for Argentinian products. With higher per capita income and three times the Chilean population, Argentina offered an attractive market for Chile. Former SOEs of Argentina received Chilean capital, from Buenos Aires utilities to food processors. According to the Argentinian government, Chile invested $691.5 million in the Argentinian privatization. Peru received $441 million of Chilean money and one of Lima's largest super-market chains was Chilean owned. Chile was also a key player in Peru's privatization of state-owned mining companies.[64]

Mexico was Chile's third favored place of investment. About 20 percent of Chile's annual exports went to Latin America, and Argentina, Brazil, and Mexico collectively accounted for 12 percent of all Chile's exports.[65] In 1994, Japan emerged as Chile's most important trading partner in imports, and a full third of the country's exports went to Asian countries in 1996. Chile's crossborder investment and trade are expected to grow and expand, now that it has become an associate member of the Southern Cone Common Market (MERCOSUR) and is an active member of the 19-country Asia Pacific Economic Cooperation (APEC).[66] But the Asian financial crisis of 1997–98 dampened Chile's prospects for expanding exports to the Pacific Basin and, by mid-1999, its economy lurched into a deep recession.

The second civilian government since 1990

The whole issue of Chile's growth under the military has been reviewed critically both at home and abroad. Eduardo Frei Ruíz-Tagle, a week after he took office, admitted that the priority of his government was to end poverty. When Aylwin became the president, 40 percent of Chileans lived in poverty. When he left in March 1994, the misery index was reduced to 27 percent. Frei was determined to wipe out poverty when he left the office at the dawn of the twenty-first century. Chile could very well be the first Latin American country that would have eliminated poverty.[67] In a way, Chile's political stability was based on the Concertación's continuity. Frei pointed out that the armed forces understood this, when the Christian Democrat-led Concertación was able to pass on the reins of the government to one of its younger leaders. It was the first time since 1915 that the Chileans elected a government that pledged the continuity of the former government's policies. Frei emphasized that the people should make decisions, while the state should only create opportunities and make them available to the people. Although Chile did not suffer from the problem of corruption, Frei wanted his administration to be an honest one. Also he reinforced and defended the sense of public service and national identity. Chile should not become a society of consumerism, one of the tenets of globalization.

On the political front, Frei assigned top priority to recovering the power to appoint service chiefs by 1997, until which time the armed forces would function as a self-administered corporation. In contrast to Argentina and Brazil, the Chilean armed forces could not be pushed to the back seat of national politics, at least not for the immediate future. He also saw a strong need to reform the national supreme court which, as a creature of the junta, was not a partisan to democratic institutions and practices. Another institution from the military days was the National Security Council: the upper chamber had a portion of senators appointed by the junta, whose mandate expired in 1997. The government negotiated with the opposition on the new agenda for stability and harmony after 1997 as the largest institutional vestige of the military rule disappeared. While Frei did not consider himself an heir to the Christian Democratic movement that his father founded and nurtured, his government marked an important generational transition.[68]

Income inequality?

A 1995 book by Joseph Collins and John Lear made a compelling point that Chile had experienced growth without development. Compared to the 1970 poverty index, Chile doubled the number of its poor from 20 percent in 1970 to 41 percent in 1990. The authors mention that the poverty index declined to 27 percent by 1994. Like the United States and Brazil, the rich in Chile increased their share of national income from 37 percent in 1978 to 47 percent in 1988; and the percentage of citizens without decent housing went up from 27 in 1972 to 40 in 1988.[69] Although the book did not dwell on the improvements made after 1988, it was nevertheless a cogent view that the military years saw material growth at the expense of the poor (Table 7.1). Both the Aylwin and Frei governments were determined to correct these policy mistakes and the figures in 1990 in housing, education, health, and poverty have improved considerably and show every sign of continuing to ameliorate. The Lagos government in 2001 is equally determined to improve the efficiency of the economy that is just recovering from the aftermath of the Asian financial crisis.

It is a mistake to think that Chile was a thorough-going laissez-faire market economy. On the contrary, the state exerted enormous regulatory power in many areas of the economy. In this sense, Chile's political economy was different from that of Argentina but similar to that of Brazil. For instance, rules governing the entry and exit of foreign capital –

Table 7.1: State-Owned Enterprises: Their Shares in GDP and Investment as Percentage of GDP, 1985–95

	Shares in GDP: 1985–90 (%)	Shares in GDP: 1990–95 (%)	Investment as % of GDP: 1985–90	Investment as % of GDP: 1990–95
Argentina	2.7	1.3	9.4	3.0
Brazil	7.6	8.0	13.0	8.6
Chile	14.4	8.1	15.3	6.1
Mexico	6.7	4.9	10.5	6.5
Indonesia	14.5	n.a.	8.9	15.7
Korea	10.3	n.a.	14.3	n.a.
Malaysia	n.a.	n.a.	n.a.	25.9
Thailand	n.a.	n.a.	11.5	10.4

Sources: World Bank, *1998 World Development Indicators* (Washington, DC: World Bank, 1998), pp. 182–4.

debt-swap investment had to remain in the country for ten years and all other capital investment for three years – were more stringent than those of other countries in Latin America. The case was similar with administrative centralization, although both the Aylwin and Frei administrations emphasized decentralization and still deposited power in Santiago, whose bureaucrats were no administrative eunuchs. Mining represented less than 45 percent of the exports in 1995 and less than half the production came from the state-owned enterprises, yet the state had not taken a bold step in privatizing CODELCO and ENAMI. Workers and employees, unions were still a political force to contend with, in spite of the labor reform. Statism was a political chameleon. With one of the first privatization projects, the merchant marine company (EMPREMAR – Empresa Marítima S.A.), the Frei government assigned 32.33 percent to the employees, 67 percent to investors, and 0.68 percent to the government.[70] As Frei stated in his interview with *Veja*, his administration's priority was *the people* and their welfare, rather than institutions or growth theories. If the trend seen in the EMPREMAR divestment continued, Chile would restore equity by wiping out the "social debt" the military regime incurred during its 16-year rule.

The years 1997 and 1998 were crucial for the future consolidation of Chile's democracy and market economy. Four years before the civilian government was restored, Edgardo Boeninger, then a senator, foresaw that the military-appointed supreme court, the independent central bank, the armed forces, appointed governors and mayors, and similar institutions preempted the power of future civilian presidents, and, more importantly, the ability of Christian Democrats to introduce "a modern, mixed economy" and "a social market economy" would be hampered.[71] To die-hard CD followers, social democracy was still an unfulfilled dream.

The senate was packed with rightwing legislators, while the commanders of the armed forces and national police by the Constitution of 1980 could not be removed by the president. In October 1997, President Frei appointed General Ricardo Izurieta to replace Pinochet in early January 1998. Pinochet changed his mind and remained as the supreme commander of the armed forces until the spring of 1998. This threw a damper on Frei's state reform. All former presidents who had served for a six-year term were given a choice of becoming senators for life, after leaving office. Patrico Aylwin served for four years, and was thus unqualified for the senate. But Pinochet was and made it clear that he intended to serve in the upper chamber of the Chilean congress.[72] The Chilean Communist Party sought to keep the general from taking up his senatorial seat by charging him with genocide. The husband of the party's secretary general disappeared (presumed to be murdered) during Pinochet's watch. The Santiago court agreed to hear the case.[73] By April 1998, Pinochet was sworn in as senator for life.

The 1998 economic woes

The economic stability of Chile was not unshakable. In June 1998, the Asian financial turmoil and the low copper price (around 80 cents a pound) dealt Chile a severe blow. About 30 percent of the country's exports (salmon, fishmeal, copper, and winter fruits) went to Asia, and the recession in Japan, particularly, hurt Chile's external account badly. The Central Bank of Chile introduced a series of reforms, including lowering the level of required reserves for foreign companies down from 30 percent to 10 percent, narrowing the foreign exchange band (down from 25 percent to 5 percent), and letting the interest rate rise.[74] Chile used to turn away speculative capital, but in 1998 welcomed it (Table 7.2). Unemployment in the mining sector rose steadily for the year, as the copper price fell and a record number of small mining companies declared bankruptcy.

The beginning of the end?

In October 1998, General Pinochet, then a senator for life, visited Europe on a "diplomatic mission." While in London, the British

Table 7.2: Foreign Portfolio Investment: Argentina, Brazil, Chile, and
Mexico, 1990 and 1999

	1990 Bonds (US$million)	1999 Bonds (US$million)	1990 Equity (US$million)	1999 Equity (US$million)
Argentina	–857	8000	13	404
Brazil	129	2683	0	1961
Chile	–7	862	320	1192
Mexico	661	5621	562	1129

Source: World Bank, *2001 World Development Indicators* (Washington, DC: World Bank,
2001), pp. 340–1.

authorities placed him under house arrest, pending the final decision
on Spain's request for the general's extradition. Instigated by a Spanish
lawyer activist and a former aide to Allende, the Spanish court claimed
the right to try Pinochet for "the crimes of terrorism and genocide."[75]
Whether Spain or any other country in Europe which lost its citizens
to the military terrors of Chile during the 1970s and 1980s had the
jurisdiction over Pinochet was not disputed, at least not in Europe. The
Spanish judge relied on historical materials, including those from the
Rettig commission (Chile's truth and reconciliation group made up of
the country's most eminent citizens and jurists) as well as documents
gathered by the archbishopric of Santiago.[76] What emerged from this
episode was a severe test for Chile's democracy in transition. In 1992,
many leaders of the Concertación asserted that the transition was completed.[77] But the arrest of Pinochet reopened the old political wound,
which lacerated the country once more: Pinochet's conservative supporters and those on the center-left sought to end the saddest chapter
in history and move on. It was clear that the deeds of the 17-year military dictatorship could not be cleansed by a decade of democracy and
economic progress alone. More was needed, but no one could say for
sure what that was.

A long good-bye to authoritarianism

The campaign for the presidential election in 1999 began badly. The
leftwing partners in the Concertación alliance were pushing hard the
candidacy of Ricardo Lagos, a cabinet minister in the Allende government and a die-hard socialist. The December 1997 congressional election went badly for the Christian Democrat Party wing of the alliance.
The PDC share in the national congress reduced to 23 percent, down
from 27 percent in 1993. Its other partners (the Party for Democracy –

PPD [Partido por la Democracia], the Socialist Party – PS [Partido Socialista], and the Social Democratic Radical Party – PRSD [Partido Radical Social Demócrata]) were able to hold on or increased their shares. This did not bode well for the Christian Democrats' chances for nomination and presidency. Once Lagos won the nomination, his candidacy was opposed by Joaquín Lavín, a popular mayor of Los Condes, a suburb of greater Santiago and a former economist for the Pinochet government. The election was fair but harsh, bringing back the memories of the Pinochet era and the threat of dividing the country. Lagos, to win the election and to continue the conciliation begun by the Concertación, distanced himself from his own followers and joined the Frei government in demanding the return of Pinochet. Lavín worked hard to convince the voters that he was no Pinochet in mufti, while Lagos painted himself as a European-style "Third Way" socialist who would bury the violent past and move forward to a bright future. The first round of the election was so close that the result was indecisive. The second round of the election was held and Lagos won narrowly. The politics of accommodation with the military and the right worked well in the two presidencies following the end of Pinochet's rule.[78] Lagos was no less willing to change the policy that worked than Lavín.

History has it that in 1970 it was Eduardo Frei M. who passed the presidential sash to a socialist–Marxist and in 2000 it was his son, Eduardo Frei R. T. who turned over the government to another socialist.[79] All indications were that Lagos was no Allende. He toned down the leftist rhetoric, extended the olive branch to the business community, the traditional supporter of Pinochet, and actively pursued trade and investment ties with MERCOSUR, APEC, and the EU. The government was unwilling to join the Southern Cone Common Market as a full member. Lagos insisted on the right to pursue separate bilateral trade and investment relationships with non-MERCOSUR members, as if the common market was an open regionalism. This position has been stoutly rejected by Brazil.[80]

In the legislative elections in December 2001, the Alliance for Chile made up of Pinochet's followers gained 44 percent of the seats in the chamber of deputies, up from the 30 percent it held in the 1997 election. The government's edge of the 70-50 majority shrank to 64–56. The Concertación of Lagos slid from 50 percent to 47.9 percent in the lower house. In the senate race, the government lost one seat, thus creating a 24 to 24 tie.[81] The Lagos government was likely to experience difficulty in pushing its reform agenda through congress. In fact, the Pinochet party had emerged as Chile's largest political party. The transition to democracy and a society of open liberal values had still a way to go. Chile in 2000 managed to grow, but the effects of the economic recession, caused by the Asian financial crisis, still lingered in 2001. The country had a 9.7 percent rate of unemployment, half that of Argentina. At the time of writing, for the remaining two years of the government, the space for Lagos to manoeuver is limited, unless he is willing to work with the Pinochet followers. This is not an unthinkable political reality for a socialist-turned Third Way president. This in fact can consolidate the transition to democracy.

Conclusion: Will the Past Overtake the Future in Latin America?

Globalization versus sovereignty

In the globalization debate, there is a school of thought that the unchecked expansion of crossborder finances, investment, trade, manufacturing, and consumerism has destroyed sovereignty as well as weakened the social safety net, seriously threatening the economic stability of nations.[1] Whether globalization will dismantle the current system of nation states and replace them with something different is not just a possibility, but a reality. Nation-states are forming region-markets and region-states. The oldest and the first entity to emerge from the supranational movement of the 1990s, the European Union, began to form soon after the end of the Second World War.[2] In the Western Hemisphere, the Rio Pact of the American nations, a military and security alliance, dates back to 1948. Its moral and economic successor was the first Summit of the Americas meeting in Miami of December 1995 when 34 of the 35 countries of the Americas agreed to negotiate a free-market agreement by 2005. Non-democratic Cuba was excluded. In 1992, Canada, the United States, and Mexico agreed to establish the North American Free Trade Agreement (NAFTA). In 1994, it became a reality. Further south, Argentina, Brazil, Paraguay and Uruguay signed the Asunción Treaty in 1991, by which the four nations established a common external tariff agreement in 1995, MERCOSUR/MERCOSUL.[3]

Asia Pacific, Southeast Asia, South Asia, the Middle East and North Africa, and Sub-Saharan Africa have moved forward with establishing regional trade blocs or common external tariff agreements.[4] The current mood (in 2001) in Latin America is that globalization offers new opportunities for the continent to redesign its economy and in the process to prosper by taking advantage of global financial and trade integration. The fact that not all Latin countries are prepared to take full advantage of the globalization now in fulmination concerns policymakers of the hemisphere. Argentina, Brazil, Chile, and Mexico are relatively better positioned to do so than others. But the collapse of Argentina's neoliberalism does not augur well for others.

Before the age of globalization, a country was assumed to be sovereign, if it could do three things: (1) defend its territorial integrity by effectively enforcing its laws and militarily fending off invaders; (2) influence its neighbors' foreign trade and defense policies to advance its own national interests; and (3) regionally and globally advance its territorial claims and politico-economic interests against those of other states.[5] In the age of globalization, when money can be transferred by a few computer key strokes, multinational and global corporations are constantly in search of cheaper and more efficient factors of production across borders and when money, services, and goods are traded with less and less restrictions from nation states, the historical notion of sovereignty is no longer valid. The ultimate test of whether a country has retained or lost its sovereign power and autonomy to make key decisions is how well it has met the challenges of globalization since the 1980s. New challenges will require improving its share of the global economy by heavily investing in education, health, infrastructure, and modern processing technologies. To realists and neomercantilists, wealth grants the power to be sovereign and even to become a great power.[6] But this is outmoded thinking. Whether Latin America – and more precisely Argentina, Brazil, and Chile – can meet these new challenges of globalization remains to be seen.

Democracy or market, but not both

One sure way to judge how well Latin America has confronted the globalization challenge for the past three decades is to compare it to East Asia. The fundamental differences between Latin America (which, initially, followed Adam Smith's notion of development) and East Asia (which embraced Friedrich List's model) go beyond the obvious realms of political and economic cultures. In 1960, the per capita GNP of Korea was $500, while Brazil's was $1400. Some three and a half decades later in 1998, Korea boasted a per capita/ppp of $13 990, while Brazil's was only $5710.[7] Yet all four countries (Argentina, Brazil, Chile, and Korea) went through similar phases of statist planning, military-dominated governance, the proliferation of state-owned enterprises, except in Korea, and resorting to export-promotion policies as in Korea and Brazil. Between the mid-1980s and early 1990s, all four countries launched the transition process to democracy. According to United Nations and World Bank studies, the Asian countries as a whole invested more per capita in education, health, and infrastructure than Latin American countries.[8] Also, Asians saved more than Latin Americans.[9]

Latin America thrived in xenophobic statist populism until the late 1970s and then began to contract economically. East Asia did not show anti-imperialist attitudes toward foreign capital, although all except for Japan and Thailand were recent colonies of Europe, Japan, or the United States. Both Latin America and East Asia have also experimented with Marxism and communism. Communist China and Vietnam have sought to integrate their economies with the global systems, while Sandinista Nicaragua and Castro's Cuba have regarded such attempts as the recolonization of their economies. Asia grew in spite of history, while history has held back Latin America.

Before the Asian financial crisis of 1997–98, the World Bank considered Latin America and Asia Pacific the two growth poles of the world economy.[10] In Asia and Latin America, the state dwarfed the market historically by begetting "state capitalism." However, the historical similarity ends here. In Asia, there have been two prevalent trends: (1) either the state has prudently stayed out of the market, as long as market failures could be corrected with minimal intervention as in Japan, Hong Kong, Korea, and Taiwan; and (2) in such multiethnic societies like Malaysia, Singapore, and Indonesia, the state directly participated in the market as equity holders and managers to assure social stability.

The supremacy of the state

In Latin America, the state relished taking up economic space, thus competing against the private sector in the market, while Asia considered less drastic and less statist alternatives. The degree of foreign domination of the market both in Asia Pacific and Latin America mattered. In Asia, the colonial retreat and independence in the late 1940s and 1950s palpably reduced the presence of foreign overlords. In Latin America, the United States continued to exercise its economic hegemony and was soon joined by European and Japanese multinationals by the 1960s. On both continents, economic crises inevitably provoked state interventions, but the style differed. Asia begat a state-*led* or *managed* capitalism, while Latin America embraced state-owned capitalism. The international political economies of Latin America and Asia Pacific have been affected by similar forces of the globalization of the economy since the 1970s, and yet the latter has continued to expand during the 1980s while the former experienced the "lost decade" causing the continent's economy to contract and in some countries to dissipate the gains of the past three decades under statist-populist policies.[11] Latin America lost sovereign power and autonomy over its life, while Asia did not.

SOE: an engine of growth or a breeder of corruption?

There is no doubt that Latin America before the mid-1980s was benefitting from a multitude of state-owned enterprises, the principal vehicle of economic growth. The fundamental difference between the Asian and Latin America SOEs was found in their respective management principles and practices. In Asia Pacific, state capitalism has been essentially market-driven. Even when the state predominated in credit, for instance, pricing always reflected the realities of the market. This was not the case in Latin America, however. Hence, the financing of SOEs in Asia and Latin America differed. The rationale for building SOEs in Asian countries was more sociopolitical and even ethnicity-driven, while that in Latin America, where the leftist and nationalist-populist ideologies often served as the guiding principles, was to keep foreign competition out. The market has determined the viability of the SOEs in Asia, but seldom was this the case in Latin America.

In Asia, top executives who lead SOEs and GLCs (government-linked companies of Singapore) are often technocrats and civil servants, while in Latin America the top managers have come from the ranks of political appointees and retired or active military officers. Hence, overstaffing, inefficient resource allocation, corruption, factor pricing rigidity, low quality management, and less than average performance have been the hallmark of Latin America's SOEs. In Singapore, the best civil servants working in GLCs are rewarded or punished according to the performance of the companies they direct. Their salaries are often equivalent to those of private-sector executives. The management principle for Asian SOEs was (and still is) competitive pricing, while Latin America's has been to provide underpriced and subsidized goods and services to the public. Except for the Suharto era of Indonesia, both retired and active military officers running SOEs in Asia are rare. In Latin America, retired officers were often rewarded with second-career jobs in SOEs, or are silent partners with civilians in "strategic" enterprises such as airport duty free shops, gas and oil distributorships, petrochemicals, and even the computer industry.[12] Today, they continue to work in the interstices of power.

Organized labor has also benefited from association with SOEs in Latin America. Militant labor movements required a stronger state presence in the market, often pitting the state against multinationals and domestic conglomerates, than in Asia where organized labor belongs to the companies they work for and are easily manipulated by the government. Hence, the socialist tinge has always been present in Latin America's state capitalism while in Asia it has been less apparent and less real. When Latin America was going through privatization in the 1980s and 1990s, opposition from organized labor was strongest in Brazil, Venezuela, and Mexico. Ideological and power struggles and purges of communist-Marxist leadership crippled the unions in the Southern Cone countries. The labor unions of Argentina and Chile suffered considerable setbacks during the military years and hence were in no position to oppose the privatization processes.

ISI: a double-edged sword?

Import-substituting industrialization also reshaped Latin America politically and socially by bringing populist and military regimes to power throughout the continent. The regimes' central purpose was to nationalize and statize the economy without going through overt Marxist revolutionary processes. In the end, a good populist government could do more for the masses than a socialist or a Marxist regime in the backyard of the United States, which has consistently shown historical hostility to such regimes and has often overthrown them. Populism gave a semblance of electoral democracy, often manipulated, but, once in power, the elected could implement programs and policies that for all intents and purposes even socialist and Marxist governments could not have adopted.[13] Nationalist populism provided a good cover to hide Marxist-socialist intent. This was especially important for Argentina, Brazil, and Chile, which firmly endorsed the anti-communist pact of the Cold War, the inter-American defense alliance of Rio in 1948.

In Argentina, Brazil, and Chile, a new alliance of ISI was forged. Nationalist but undercapitalized industrialists and managers of SOEs considered such a policy a boon: it kept foreign competition out and monopolized the closed market. The populist and leftist organized labor supported such a policy, for the state often set and regulated wages and provided generous social benefits. The middle class accepted the policy, for the national pride of being self-sufficient in industrial goods and offering free social services to all was important. Intellectuals of the left and the right endorsed the policy, because ISI gave them the satisfaction of having the sense of autonomous development and, more importantly, of seeing the decline of European and American economic hegemony. Notably, the military in Latin America called for and supported a nationalist policy of economic sovereignty. For decades, ISI was Latin America's rallying cry and a political, social, and economic canopy that accommodated everyone.

Is democracy compatible with market?

Economists for a long time have believed that faster economic growth is achieved under authoritarian rule than under liberal democracy. Robert Barro has argued that countries under "autocracy" grow faster than those under democracy.[14] Barro also found that once "autocratic" countries attain democracy they tend to spend more on social programs than invest in infrastructure and similar productive projects; hence the economy grows more slowly. Furthermore, countries with a low level of economic development do not retain democracy.[15] This coincides well with Sebastian Edwards's analysis of the historically low savings rates in Latin America, resulting in lower growth rates than Asia's.

A group of Swiss researchers has found that the relationship between democracy and market (or more precisely, economic growth) is "inconclusive."[16] Earlier thinking in economic development was that democracy and market are incompatible, but the most recent theoretical trend has been that they are compatible. The failure of socialist economies in the 1980s and early 1990s further reinforces the thinking that autocracy and economic growth are mutually incompatible. What is clear is that weak democratic government can wreak havoc as well as strong interventionist governments in the marketplace. Economic and financial globalization has enhanced the opportunities to engender political democracies in those countries in the vortex of the world economy. Over time, however, democracy can be an obstacle to economic growth, the life blood of market capitalism.[17]

Economic fundamentals are one key to all countries' success: these include sound macroeconomic policies, low inflation and interest

rates, stable exchange rates tied to market forces, high private investment and savings, long-term investment in human capital formation,
low or no deficit in current accounts, and so forth. Asia's early abandonment of ISI and closed markets, the indulgence in using SOEs as
the principal tool for development and growth, excessive politicization
of populist groups, and ideologically divisive xenophobia helped pave
the way for greater and longer prosperity. Culturally, Asians were (and
still are) more willing to accept authoritarian or peculiarly Asian styles
of paternalistic governance than Latin Americans, so long as their rice
bowls were filled.[18] Economic and social security came before political
democracy. The events of the past few years in Korea, Taiwan, and
even Singapore support this hypothesis: having built a prosperous
economy, the people now demand more political openness and secure
their rights to participate in government. Democratic regimes will
increasingly come under pressure to adopt and expand social safety net
measures and invest less. In turn, this may adversely affect the economic growth rate. It is worth remembering that the current democratic regimes in Latin America and Asia emerged from the collapse of the
military bureaucratic-authoritarian governments of the 1960s and
1980s. The transition to democracy was provoked by a series of external economic crises (Argentina and Brazil) as well as civic movements
to restore an open liberal society (Chile).[19]

   In Latin America, the political pressure from the left to build democracy often occurred during the times of economic crises, thus contributing to civil disorder and inviting stiff resistance from the right.
Often, such confrontations led to the advent of rightwing regimes,
which further suppressed democratic processes.[20] Although Asia and
Latin America grew fastest under authoritarian rule, the Asian governments distributed wealth more equitably than the Latin American
regimes, but Latin America has offered the needy greater benefits from
social programs than Asia.

Globalization: an elixir or a nadir?

Two other significant differences, aside from economic policies and
authoritarian tendencies, are worth mentioning. Korea, Taiwan, and
Singapore did not liberalize trade and investment regimes before the
early 1980s. Unlike Latin America, Asian intra-regional trade and
investment (from Japan and overseas Chinese scattered throughout
Southeast Asia) were far more intense, thus forcing Asian states to be
more competitive regionally and globally.[21] Hence, in dealing with

international banks, for instance, Asian countries acted individually. Latin America often used collective bargaining power such as the Andean Pact to protect its ISI policies and to restrict foreign direct investment flows. In the mid-1980s, Argentina and Brazil consorted briefly to declare a joint moratorium, or to form a debtors' cartel, until the Sarney government decided not to challenge the global banking system at the last minute. Asia lacked a coordinated regional policy of sustaining ISI or common statist development strategies, while Central America, the Andean countries, and the Caribbean sought to forge such collective platforms. The pack instinct of the Latin America of similar cultures and heritage has hurt its interest over time, while the individual case-by-case approach taken by the Asian countries of diverse and even conflicting cultures and history has helped the continent partake of the benefits of globalization, as seen in the recovery from the financial crisis throughout Asia in 1998 and 1999.

Backlash to globalization

Nancy Birdsall has raised a fascinating concern about the potentially negative impact of globalization on Latin America and by extension on all developing countries. Globalization through the spread of consumer values, mass customization, unrestricted access to factors of production in manufacturing, democratic institutions, and capitalist enterprises has often been blamed for a host of ills for developed and developing countries.[22] Crossborder trade, investment, and manufacturing can benefit, not all, but those most prepared to take advantage of such innovation. Within developed countries, low-skilled workers suffer most, as in Western Europe, the United States, and Japan.[23] Similarly, less competitive countries will gain less or even lose more in the global marketplace.[24] Birdsall's concern is that prosperity begat by Latin America's participation in globalization can result in inequality, or, more precisely, can worsen the current inequity. Latin America has a bad history of social inequality. In 1950, Birdsall reports, 65 percent of all land in Latin America was owned by 1.5 percent of farmers. Since then, the situation has become worse.[25] In Argentina, Brazil, and Chile, the upper class succeeded in garnering a greater share of national income and consumption power during the last three decades of the twentieth century than previously.[26] The richest 20 percent of the urban population in Argentina expanded its consumption power from 45.3 percent in 1980 to 51.1 percent in 1994. In Brazil, the contrasting numbers were: 56 percent in 1979 and 58.7 percent in 1993. In Chile, the rich lost a bit: 56 percent in 1980 and 55.6 percent in 1994. The poorest 40 percent fared less well: 17.4 percent of the national income in 1980 and 13.8 percent in 1990 (Argentina); 11.8 percent in 1979 and the same in 1993 (Brazil); and 12 percent in 1987 and l3.4 percent in 1994.[27] If the social and economic equity issues continue to be ignored, Latin America will not be able to maintain democracy and hence will sunder its market economy. Bad policies will be adopted and the threat to democratic regimes will ensue. Globalization will do the rest of the damage.

Contested globalization: state over market?

How to balance the power of the state and the wealth potential of the market in a democratic way is a coming challenge for Latin America and Asia in the twenty-first century. Scholarly review and scrutiny of globalization and its positive and negative impacts on nation states has been on the rise. Between 1980 and 1984, there were 13 monographs that analyzed the phenomena of globalization. Between 1992 and 1996, there were over 580 works. In the single year of 1996, the *Social Science Citation Index* listed more than 200 treatises.[28] During the last five years of the twentieth century, more books, articles, and scientific papers raised countless questions about globalization, whose one-time proponents are just about outnumbered by today's critics.[29] The emerging criticism of globalization has drawn both scholarly and media attention, as the public outcry against integrated world trade and finance in the period 1998–2001 has so convincingly demonstrated during such events as the WTO meeting in Seattle, the IMF-World Bank annual meetings in Washington and Prague, the World Economic Forum in Davos, and the Third Summit of the Americas in Quebec. Globalization is increasingly seen as a demon, not a panacea, for human development. Public policy makers in Latin America and Asia have increasingly spoken out against unfettered globalization, particularly in Venezuela and Malaysia.[30] Calls for regulating global financial markets, free trade, foreign direct investment, and foreign portfolio investment have been on the rise.[31] Opponents of global financial reform argue that countries should adopt sound public policies that can take advantage of globalization, rather than shout at the rain. More reforms, they assert, inevitably mean more regulation.[32]

The contrast of the international political economies of globalization in Latin America and Asia has been stark. In both regions, the state has expanded, but for different reasons. In both regions, the state has been contracting, also, for different reasons but abetted by similar external forces of globalization. The Asian state has promoted private corporations to be regionally and globally competitive; the Latin American state replaced the private sectors and seized the market with its proliferating SOEs. The Asian state has not competed against the private sector at home or abroad. The Latin American state often became a vital source of contracts, an overbearing partner, and a milk cow that the private entrepreneurs learned to use and abuse. In the process, it has bred corruption. The Latin American state was predatory and parasitic, going beyond the economic, political, and social logic of intervention and appropriation. The Asian state has calibrated its need to intervene and to reinforce its economic instruments to expand the competitiveness of its multinationals, government-linked companies, and state-owned enterprises in the global economy. In both cases, history has proven that state intervention is a useful mechanism and even a necessary one for economic development and growth. But intervention is like drink: society must learn how to drink responsibly and know when to stop. If unchecked, the excess can destroy society and economy. Asia in 1998 was paying the price of such moral hazards as crony capitalism, sloppy banking practices, state patronage to relatives of governing elites and their friends, and too much speculation on real estate projects, in spite of the sound macroeconomic policy foundations.[33] In a peculiar way, prosperity in Asia was the root cause of the 1997–98 turmoil: the elites became too greedy and came to abuse public power. Arrogance and avarice backfired on them. The consequences of this mistake will take years, if not decades, to overcome. In Latin America, based on the lessons learned from Mexico's peso meltdown in 1994–95, Brazil's *real* devaluation in early 1999, deep business recessions in Argentina and Chile in 1999–2001, and the collapse of Argentina in January 2002, it can be argued that the elites also abused prosperity, but, unlike Asia, the state failed to distribute prosperity and misery more equitably. Castañeda, now Mexico's foreign minister, warns that obsessive popular demand for redistribution, social justice, and rectification of the past sins can undo the current democratic consolidation and market achievements.[34] Birdsall's preoccupation is also eminently justified. Unless the current leaders of Latin America do their job right – balancing the nurturing of democracy and the growth of the market – the past will overtake the future.

Notes

Introduction

1. Ruth Capriles and Marisol Rodríguez de Gonzalo, "Economic and Business History in Venezuela," in *Business History in Latin America: the Experience of Seven Countries*, eds. Carlos Dávila and Rory Miller (Liverpool, UK: Liverpool University Press, 1999), pp. 158–75; the quote is from p. 160. Octávio Rodriguez, *Teoria do subdesenvolvimento da Cepal* (Rio: Forense-Universitário, 1981).
2. World Bank, *World Development Report 1999/2000* (New York: Oxford University Press, 1999), pp. 258–59; World Bank, *1999 World Development Indicators* (Washington, DC: World Bank, 1999), pp. 204–10 for the merchandise trade and pp. 212–18 for the service trade.
3. Thomas L. Friedman, *The Lexus and the Olive Tree* (New York: Farr, Straus and Giroux, 1999), p. 52.
4. "World Stocks," *Asia Week* (9 April 1999), p. 67.
5. United Nations Conference on Trade and Development (UNCTAD), *World Investment Report 1997: Transnational Corporations, Market Structure and Competition Policy* (New York: United Nations, 1997), pp. 72, 303.
6. *World Development Report 1999/2000*, p. 15.
7. Horacio Verbitsky, *El vuelo* (Buenos Aires: Planeta-Espejo de la Argentina, 1995). This is a remarkable *mea culpa* story by a naval officer who was involved in the operation that routinely eliminated opponents of the regime and subversives by drugging them first, then flying them out to the ocean, and finally dumping them into the ocean.
8. Maria Celina D'Araújo and Celso Castro, org., *Ernesto Geisel*, 2nd ed. (Rio: Fundação Getúlio Vargas, 1997), p. 230.
9. Angelo Codevilla, "Is Pinochet the Model?" *Foreign Affairs* (November–December 1993), pp. 127–41. James F. Hoge, Jr., "A Conversation with President Cardoso," *Foreign Affairs* (July–August 1995), pp. 62–75.
10. Emma Rothschild, "Globalization and the Return of History," *Foreign Policy* (Summer 1999), pp. 106–17, esp. , 107.
11. David Held, Anthony McGrew, David Goldblatt and Jonathan Perraton, *Global Transformation: Politics, Economics and Culture* (Stanford: Stanford University Press, 1999), pp. 1–10.
12. Daniel Cohen, *The Wealth of the World and the Poverty of Nations* (Cambridge, MA: MIT Press, 1998); Andre Gunder Frank, *Re-Orient: Global Economy in the Asian Age* (Berkeley: University of California Press, 1998); Jean-Marie Guéhenno, *The End of the Nation State* (Minneapolis: University of Minnesota Press, 1995); David Held, *Democracy and the Global Order: From the Modern State to Cosmopolitan Governance* (Stanford: Stanford University Press, 1996); James Rosenau and Ernst-Otto Czempiel, eds., *Governance without Government: Order and Change in the World Politics* (New York: Cambridge University Press, 1992); and Susan Strange, *The Retreat of the*

State: the Diffusion of Power in the World Economy (New York: Cambridge University Press, 1996).

13. Paul Hirst and Graeham Thompson, *The Globalization in Question: the International Economy of the Possibilities of Governance* (Cambridge, UK: Polity Press, 1996).

14. Dani Rodrik, *Has Globalization Gone Too Far?* (Washington, DC: Institute for International Economics, 1997).

15. Linda Weiss, "Globalization and the Myth of the Powerless State," *New Left Review* (September–October 1997), pp. 2–27, and her book, *The Myth of the Powerless State* (Ithaca, NY: Cornell University Press, 1998).

16. David Price, *Before the Bulldozer: the Namiquara Indians and the World Bank* (New York: Seven Locks Press, 1989).

17. Manuel Castells, *The Rise of the Network Society*, Vol. 1: *The Information Age: Economy, Society and Culture* (Malden, MA: Blackwell Publishers, 1996), pp. 92–6.

18. "New Ideas for the Old Left," *The Economist* (17 January 1998), pp. 29–30. The word "rightwing" is mine.

19. Edgardo Boeninger, "The Chilean Political Transition to Democracy," in *From Dictatorship to Democracy: Rebuilding Political Consensus in Chile*, eds. Joseph S. Tulchin and Augusto Varas (Boulder, CO: Lynne Rienner Publishers, 1991), pp. 50–61, esp. , 58.

20. The quote is coming from: Antônio Carlos Pojo do Rêgo and João Paulo M. Peixoto, *A política econômica das reformas administrativas no Brasil* (Rio: Expressão e Cultura, 1998), p. 111.

21. Jorge Dominguez, "Latin American's Crisis of Representation," *Foreign Affairs* (January–February 1997), pp. 100–13.

22. Abraham Lowenthal, "Latin America: Ready for Partnership?" *Foreign Affairs. America & the World 1993* (1993), pp. 74–92.

23. Jorge G. Castañeda, *The Mexican Shock: Its Meaning for the U.S.*, trans. Maria Castañeda (New York: New Press, 1995), pp. 211–13.

24. George Soros, *The Crisis of Global Capitalism (Open Society Endangered)* (New York: Public Affairs, 1999), pp. 109–12.

25. Paul Krugman, "Dutch Tulips and Emerging Markets," *Foreign Affairs* (July–August 1995), pp. 28–40, esp. , 29–30, and *The Return of Depression Economics* (New York: W.W. Norton, 1999).

1   Latin America in the Age of Globalization

1. Martin Carnoy, Manuel Castells, Stephen S. Cohen and Fernando Henrique Cardoso, *The New Global Economy in the Information Age: Reflections on Our Changing World* (University Park, PA: The Pennsylvania State University Press, 1993).

2. Fernando Henrique Cardoso, "North–South Relations in the Present Context: a New Dependency?" in Carnoy et al., *The New Global Economy.*, pp. 149–59 (154–5).

3. Ibid., p. 156.

4. World Bank, *1999 World Development Indicators*, p. 14, *World Development Report 1997: the State in a Changing World* (New York: Oxford University Press, 1997), p. 237.

5. "World Stocks."
6. William Greider, *One World, Ready or Not: the Manic Logic of Global Capitalism* (New York: Simon & Schuster, 1997), pp. 23–4.
7. Lowell Bryan and Diana Farrell, *Market Unbound: Unleashing Global Capitalism* (New York: John Wiley & Sons, 1996), p. 4.
8. Kenichi Ohmae, *The End of the Nation State: How New Engines of Prosperity Are Reshaping Global Markets* (New York: The Free Press, 1995), p. 5.
9. Kenichi Ohmae, "Putting Global Logic First," in *The Evolving Global Economy: Making Sense of the New World Order*, ed. Kenichi Ohmae (Cambridge, MA: Harvard Business School Press, 1995), pp. 129–37 (130). Bryan and Farrell, *Market Unbound*, pp. 2–3.
10. Jeffrey Sachs, "International Economics: Unlocking the Mysteries of Globalization," *Foreign Policy* (Spring 1998), pp. 97–111 (107).
11. John Stopford and Susan Strange, with John S. Henley, *Rival States, Rival Firms: Competition for World Market Shares* (New York: Cambridge University Press, 1992), pp. 35–6.
12. Hirst and Thompson, *Globalization in Question*. Rothschild, "Globalization and the Return of History."
13. Robert B. Reich, *The Works of Nations: Preparing Ourselves for 21st-Century Capitalism* (New York: Vintage Books, 1991), pp. 13–15.
14. Paul Kennedy, *The Rise and Fall of the Great Powers: Economic Change and Military Conflicts from 1500 to 2000* (New York: Random House, 1987).
15. This is the title of Dicken's chapter 3. *Global Shift: Transforming the World Economy*, 3rd ed. (New York: The Guilford Press, 1998), p. 79.
16. Strange, *The Retreat of the State*, pp. 3–15.
17. Jeremy Brecher and Tim Costello, *Global Village or Global Pillage: Economic Reconstruction from the Bottom Up* (Boston: South End Press, 1994), p. 4.
18. In Indonesia, peasants who lost land to the modernization and development projects during the Suharto years are wanting their lands back: Margot Cohen, "Tackling a Bitter Legacy," *Asia Week* (2 July 1998), pp. 22–7. Price, *Before the Bulldozer*. A highway construction project in Western Brazil destroyed vast tracts of indigenous land, and had been financed by the World Bank.
19. Ralph Nader and Lori Wallach, "GATT, NAFTA, and the Subversion of the Democratic Process," in *The Case against the Global Economy and for a Turn toward the Local*, eds. Jerry Mander and Edward Goldsmith (San Francisco: Sierra Club, 1996), pp. 92–107. Reinaldo Gonçalves, *Globalização e desnacionalização* (São Paulo: Paz e Terra, 1999), pp. 11–18.
20. The editors of the *New Political Economy* devoted a whole issue to this issue of the negative impact of globalization on how to prevent the erosion of the past gains by liberal and socialist states. See John Kenneth Galbraith, "Preface," *New Political Economy* (March 1997), pp. 5–9.
21. *The Case against the Global Economy*, p. 12.
22. United Nations Conference on Trade and Development, *World Investment Report 1997*, pp. 5, 303, 304.
23. "Front Notes" and Scott Weeks, "Debt Research on the Rise," *Latin Finance* (July/August 1997), p. 9 and pp. 21–2, respectively.
24. World Bank, *1999 World Development Indicators*, pp. 298–300.
25. International Monetary Fund, *World Economic Outlook May 1998* (Washington, DC: IMF, 1998), pp. 3–5. Sachs. "International Economics," p. 108.

26. World Bank, *The East Asian Miracle: Economic Growth and Public Policy* (New York: Oxford University Press, 1993).
27. "Introduction," in *States against Markets: the Limits of Globalization*, eds. Robert Droyer and Daniel Drache (London and New York: Routledge, 1996), p. 1.
28. A. Kim Clark, *The Redemptive Work: Railway and Nation in Ecuador, 1895–1930* (Wilmington, DE: Scholarly Research Books, 1998).
29. ISI is generally known as import substitution industrialization.
30. Alain Roquié, *The Military and the State in Latin America*, trans. Paul E. Sigmund (Berkeley: University of California Press, 1987).
31. Manuel Antonio Garretón, "Political Processes in an Authoritarian Regime: the Dynamics of Institutionalization and Opposition in Chile, 1973–1980," in *Military Rule in Chile: Dictatorship and Oppositions*, eds. J. Samuel Valenzuela and Arturo Valenzuela (Baltimore: The Johns Hopkins University Press, 1986), pp. 144–83, esp. 145–6.
32. Nigel Grimwade, *International Trade: New Patterns of Trade, Production and Investment* (New York: Routledge, 1989), Chapters 3 and 4 on the growth of world trade. John H. Jackson, "Managing the Trading System: the World Trade Organization and the Post-Uruguay Round GATT Agenda," in *Managing the World Economy: Fifty Years after Bretton Woods*, ed. Peter B. Kenen (Washington, DC: Institute for International Economics, 1994), pp. 131–51. DeAnne Julius, *Global Companies & Public Policy: the Growing Challenge of Foreign Direct Investment* (New York: Council on Foreign Relations, 1990), pp. 14, 41–7, 67–70.
33. Alfred Stepan, *The State and Society: Peru in Comparative Perspective* (Princeton: Princeton University Press, 1978) and *The Military in Politics: Changing Patterns in Brazil* (Princeton: Princeton University Press, 1971).
34. David Collier, "Overview of the Bureaucratic-Authoritarian Model," in *The New Authoritarianism in Latin America*, ed. David Collier (Princeton: Princeton University Press, 1979), pp. 20–32, esp., 23–5. For the tripartite alliance of the B–A regime in Brazil, consult: Peter Evans, *Dependent Development: the Alliance of Multinational, State, and Local Capital in Brazil* (Princeton: Princeton University Press, 1979).
35. Paul W. Drake, *Labor Movements and Dictatorship: the Southern Cone in Comparative Perspective* (Baltimore and London: The Johns Hopkins University Press, 1996), p. 79.
36. Fernando Henrique Cardoso, *O model político brasileiro e outros ensaios*, 2nd ed. (São Paulo: DIFEL, 1973), pp. 50–103.
37. Guillermo A. O'Donnell, *Modernization and Bureaucratic–Authoritarianism: Studies in South American Politics* (Berkeley: University of California Institute of International Studies, 1973), pp. 53–7, 94–6. Fernando Henrique Cardoso, *Autoritarismo e democratização* (Rio: Paz e Terra, 1978), pp. 25–43.
38. Sebastian Edwards, "Why Are Latin America's Saving Rates So Low?" in *Pathways to Growth: Comparing East Asia and Latin America*, eds. Nancy Birdsall and Frederick Jaspersen (Washington, DC: Inter-American Development Bank, 1997), pp. 131–60, esp. 132–7.
39. For Argentina, consult Norberto Galasso, *Gatos y sardinas en la economía argentina: de Martínez de Hoz a Cavallo* (Buenos Aires: Editorial Fraterna, 1992). For a more rigorous economic study of the collapse of the Argentine public sector, consult: Osvaldo H. Schenone, "El comportamiento del sector público

en la Argentina," in *El sector público y la crisis de la América Latina*, eds. Felipe Larrain and Marcelo Selowsky (Mexico City: El Trimestre Económico, 1990), pp. 16–66. For Chile, consult: Centro de Estudios Públicos, *"El Ladrillo": Bases de la política económica del gobierno militar chileno* (Santiago: CEP, 1992), which is an economic document prepared during the last years of the Allende government by opposition economists and businessmen as an alternate policy proposal. It became the basic economic doctrine of the military regime and its successors with little modification.

40. Karl Polanyi was the first to raise doubts about the self-regulating laissez-faire system. More recently, Robert Kuttner cogently argued that there is no market economy: Polanyi, *The Great Transformation: the Political and Economic Origins of Our Time* (Boston: Beacon Press, 1957 [1944]). The success depends on how well the state crafts its interventionist or regulatory policies. Kuttner, *The End of Laissez-Faire: National Purpose and the Global Economy after the Cold War* (Philadelphia, PA: University of Pennsylvania Press, 1991).

41. Martin Carnoy, *The State & Political Theory* (Princeton: Princeton University Press, 1984), pp. 32–3. Polanyi, *The Great Transformation*, pp. 130–50, esp., 139–42.

42. For Argentina, consult: CEPAL/CET, *Las empresas transnacionales en la Argentina*, Estudios e Informes de la CEPAL, No. 56 (Santiago: CEPAL, 1986). For Brazil, consult: Marcos Arruda, Herbet de Souza, and Carlos Afonso, *Multinationals and Brazil: the Impact of Multinational Corporations in Contemporary Brazil* (Kitcher, Ont., Canada: Moir Press, 1975), and David Teixeira Vieira and Lenita Correa Camargo, *Multinacionais no Brasil: Diagnóstico e prognóstico* (Rio: Saraiva, 1976). For Chile, consult: Patricio Rozas, *Inversión estranjera y empresas transnacionales en la economia de Chile (1974–1989): Prática de inversión y estrategia de las empresas transnacionales* (Santiago: CEPAL, 1992).

43. Jorge I. Dominguez, ed., *Technopols: Freeing Politics and Markets in Latin America in the 1990s* (University Park, PA: Pennsylvania State University Press, 1996); "The Technopols," *Latin Trade* (April 1997), p. 10.

44. Luis Varela and Jorge Zicolillo, *Un Domingo en el purgatorio* (Buenos Aires: Ediciones Beas, 1992), pp. 57–84.

45. For the Chicago Boys, consult: Manuel Delano and Hugo Translaviña, *La herencia de los Chicago Boys* (Santiago: Ornitorrinco, 1989), and Juan Gabriel Valdés, *Pinochet's Economists: the Chicago School in Chile* (New York: Cambridge University Press, 1995).

46. Jorge G. Castañeda, *Utopia Unarmed: the Latin American Left after the Cold War* (New York: Alfred A. Knopf, 1993), pp. 164–9, 245–6. "Introduction: the Right and Latin American Democracies," in *The Right and Democracy in Latin America*, eds. Douglas A. Chalmers, Maria do Carmo Campello, and Atilio A. Boron (New York: Praeger, 1992), pp. 1–9, esp. 4–5. For Franco's legacy, consult: Roberto Pompeu de Toledo, "Enfim, um presidente que deu certo," *Veja* (16 November 1994), pp. 34–45.

47. Alfredo Leuco and José Díaz, *El herdero de Perón, entre dios e el diablo* (Buenos Aires: Planeta, 1989).

48. Gustavo Cuevas Farren, *Renovación ideológica en Chile: los partidos y su nueva visión estratégica* (Santiago: Universidad de Chile, 1993).

49. Ezequiel Gallo and Estabán F. Thomsen, "Electoral Evolution of the Political Parties of the Right: Argentina, 1983–1989," pp. 142–60; for Peru, consult Francisco Durand, "The New Right and Political Change in Peru," pp. 239–58; and for Brazil, consult Ben Ross Schneider, "Privatization in the Collor Government: Triumph of Liberalism or the Collapse of the Developmental State?," pp. 225–38, all in *The Right and Democracy,* eds. Chalmers, Campello, and Boron.

50. The term "cosmopolitical" comes from Friedrich List, a nineteenth-century political economist. *The National System of Political Economy,* trans. Sampson S. Lloyd (Fairfield, NJ: August M. Kelley Publishers, 1991), pp. 121–2.

51. Andres Wyatt-Walter, "Regionalism, Globalization, and World Economic Order," in *Regionalism in World Politics: Regional Organizations and International Order,* eds. Louise Fawcett and Andrew Hurell (New York: Oxford University Press, 1995), pp. 74–121, esp. 115.

52. Marjorie Deane and Robert Pringle, *The Central Banks* (New York: Viking, 1995).

53. Steve Solomon, *The Confidence Game: How Unelected Central Bankers Are Governing the Changed World Economy* (New York: Simon & Schuster,1995), is a study on how democratic governments lost the power to regulate their economies to central bankers.

54. The concept of sovereignty emerged in the Late Middle Ages, as the then feudal system began to collapse. Hendrik Spruyt, *The Sovereign State and Its Competitors* (Princeton: Princeton University Press, 1994), p. 3. Gene M. Lyons and Michael Mastanduno, eds., *Beyond Westphalia? State Sovereignty and International Intervention* (Baltimore, MD, and London: The Johns Hopkins University Press, 1995), p. 5.

55. "Global Banks," *Business Week* (International edition) (24 May 1994), p. 42.

56. Clyde V. Prestowvitz, Jr., *Trading Places: How We Are Giving Our Future to Japan and How to Reclaim It* (New York: Basic Books, 1988).

57. Paul Volcker and Toyoo Gyohten, *Changing Fortunes: The World's Money and the Threat to American Leadership* (New York: Times Books, 1992), pp. 228–30, 241–6. Prestowitz, *Trading Places,* pp. 65–6, 106–10.

58. Kenneth P. Jameson, "Dollar Bloc Dependency in Latin America: Beyond Bretton Woods," *International Studies Quarterly* (1990), pp. 519–41.

59. Lester C. Thurow, *The Future of Capitalism: How Today's Economic Forces Shape Tomorrow's World* (New York: William Morrow and Company, 1996), p. 17.

2   Argentina: the Birth of Latin American Populism

1. Alexander Gerschenkron, *Economic Backwardness in Historical Perspective* (New York: Frederick A. Praeger, 1962), pp. 19–20, 362.

2. Good general histories of Argentina in English are hard to find: David Rock, *Argentina 1516–1987: From Spanish Colonization to Alfonsin* (Berkeley and Los Angeles: University of California Press, 1987). Rock's more recent book picks up where he left off: *Authoritarian Argentina: the Nationalist Movement, Its History and Its Impact* (Berkeley and Los Angeles: University of California Press, 1995). Guido Di Tella and Carlos Rodriguez Braun, *Argentina, 1946–83: the Economic Ministers Speak* (New York: St. Martins Press, 1990).

3. Michael L. Conniff, "Introduction: Toward a Comparative Definition of Populism," in *Latin American Populism in Comparative Perspective*, ed. Michael L. Conniff (Albuquerque, NM: University of New Mexico Press, 1982), pp. 5–13, esp., 5–7, 13. Conniff places the populist era of Latin America between 1920 and 1965. The clientelistic aspect of populism is discussed by: Claudio Véliz, *The Centralist Tradition of Latin America* (Princeton: Princeton University Press, 1980), p. 287. The World Bank introduced a confusing but politically correct typology of lumping together the Perón regime of Argentina, the Allende government of Chile, and the García administration of Peru in a single category of populist. See World Bank, *World Development Report 1991: the Challenge of Development* (New York: Oxford University Press, 1991), Box 7.2, p. 133.

4. Castañeda, *Utopia Unarmed*, pp. 40–4, 45–6. On García, Mario Vargas Llosa, *A Fish in the Water*, trans. Helen Lane (London: Faber & Faber, 1993), pp. 85–96, 152–79.

5. Stepan, *The State and Society*, pp. 117–27, 144–51. Stepan offers two types of military regimes: "inclusionary" such as Peru's and "exclusionary" such as Argentina's, Brazil's, and Chile's. However, Stepan does not address one critical issue that the inclusionary and exclusionary regimes all shared: non-market and statist economic policies and the retention of populist redistributive systems that their civilian adversaries had built, but both continued to a varying degree.

6. Castañeda, *Utopia Unarmed*, pp. 24, 34–5.

7. Ruth Berins Collier and David Collier, *Shaping the Political Arena: Critical Junctures, the Labor Movement, and Regime Dynamics in Latin America* (Princeton: Princeton University Press, 1991), Chapter 5, esp., pp. 162–8.

8. Rudiger Dornbusch and Sebastian Edwards, "The Macroeconomics of Populism," in *The Macroeconomics of Populism in Latin America*, eds. Rudiger Dornbusch and Sebastian Edwards (Chicago: University of Chicago Press, 1991), pp. 7–13, esp., 8–10.

9. For Menem's comments, see United States Department of Commerce, International Trade Administration, "Argentina: Menem on Privatization," IM1910426, 2 October 1992, *National Trade Data Bank*, CD-ROM (November 1992), hereinafter cited as USDOC, *NTDB*, CD-ROM with date. For the historical ranking of Argentina's economy, consult Carlos H. Waisman, *Reversal of Development in Argentina: Postwar Counterrevolutionary Policies and Their Structural Consequences* (Princeton: Princeton University Press, 1987), pp. 4–6.

10. World Bank, *World Development Report 1992: Development and the Environment* (New York: Oxford University Press, 1992), pp. 218–19, 222–3, Tables 1 and 3. Inter-American Development Bank, *Economic and Social Progress in Latin America: 1991 Report: Special Edition – Social Security* (Washington, DC: IDB, 1991), pp. 23–7, 273, Tables B-1 and B-2.

11. Inter-American Development Bank, *Economic and Social Progress in Latin America: 1994 Report: Special Report: Fiscal Decentralization* (Washington, DC: IDB, 1994), p. 21.

12. Domingo F. Cavallo, "Argentina," in *The Open Economy: Tools for Policymakers in Developing Countries*, eds. Rudiger Dornbusch and Leslie C. H. Helmers (New York: Oxford University Press, 1988), pp. 267–8 and Table 12–1.

13. Rock, *Argentina 1516–1987*, pp. 162–9, 196–9. Charles Jones, "Commercial Banks and Mortgage Companies," in *Business Imperialism 1840–1930*, ed. D. C. M. Platt (Oxford, Eng.: Oxford University Press, 1977), pp. 17–52.

14. Paul H. Lewis, *The Crisis of Argentine Capitalism* (Chapel Hill, NC: University of North Carolina Press, 1992 [paper]), pp. 34–5.

15. Herman M. Schwartz, *States versus Markets: History, Geography, and the Development of the International Political Economy* (New York: St. Martin's Press, 1994), p. 263.

16. Raul Prebisch, "Five Stages in My Thinking on Development," in *Pioneers in Development*, eds. Gerald M. Meier and Dudley Sears (New York: Oxford University Press, 1984), pp. 175–91, esp., 184.

17. Lewis, *Crisis*, pp. 36–7.

18. Ibid., p. 38.

19. United Nations Economic Commission for Latin America, *El desarrollo económico de la Argentina* (Santiago: CEPAL, 1958), pp. 135–6.

20. Waisman, *Reversal*, pp. 46–53.

21. Ibid.

22. Rock, *Argentina 1516–1987*, pp. 263–4.

23. Sylvia Maxfield and James H. Nolt, "Protectionism and the Internationalization of Capital: U.S. Sponsorship of Import Substitution Industrialization in the Philippines, Turkey, and Argentina," *International Studies Quarterly* (March 1990), pp. 49–81, esp., 73–8.

24. Donald C. Hodges, *Argentina, 1943–1987: the National Revolution and Resistance*, rev. ed. (Albuquerque, NM: University of New Mexico Press, 1988), pp. 34–5.

25. Rock, *Argentina 1516–1987*, p. 328. C. Fred Bergsten, Thomas Horst, and Theodore H. Moran, *American Multinationals and American Interests* (Washington, DC: Brookings Institution, 1978), pp. 354, 370, Footnote 1.

26. Ibid., pp. 355–8, 375–6.

27. Bergsten, Horst, and Moran, *American Multinationals*, pp. 355–6 (on taxes) and p. 355, Footnote 3.

28. Ibid., p. 389. For the details of this conflict, see Gertrude G. Edwards, "The Frondizi Contracts and Petroleum Self-Sufficiency in Argentina," in *Foreign Investment in the Petroleum and Mineral Industries: Case Studies of Investor-Host Country Relations*, eds. Raymond F. Mikesell and William Bartsch (Baltimore, MD: The Johns Hopkins University Press, 1971), pp. 157–215.

29. Castañeda, *Utopia Unarmed*, p. 45.

30. Celso Furtado, *Os ares do mundo* (Rio: Paz e Terra, 1991), pp. 195–9.

31. Ronaldo Munck, *Argentina: From Anarchism to Peronism* (London: Zed Press, 1987), pp. 195–203.

32. Davide G. Erro, *Resolving the Argentine Paradox: Politics and Development, 1966–1992* (Boulder, CO: Lynne Rienner Publishers, 1993), pp. 99–101.

33. Hodges, *Argentina, 1943–1987*, p. 197.

34. Albert O. Hirschman, "The Case against 'One Thing at a Time,'" *World Development* (August 1990), pp. 1119–22. Onganía's deputy told Hirschman that the government had the following priorities: to solve the economic problems, then to address social equity, and finally to attempt the cosmetic restoration of civil liberties and political democracy. On the reflection of his government, Onganía broke silence: Hector D'Amico, Silvia Fesquet,

Gustavo González, and Maria Grinstein, "Onganía: 30 años no es nada," *Noticias* (19 February 1995), pp. 50–6.

35. Some argue that the US economy was also built on the premise that the mobilization of war resources can prolong its growth. Seymour Melman, *The Permanent War Economy: American Capitalism in Decline* (New York: A Touchstone Book, 1985).

36. Donald C. Hodges, *Argentina's "Dirty War": an Intellectual Biography* (Austin, TX: University of Texas Press, 1991). A mind-bending chronicle of the era was written by a well-known journalist: Jacobo Timerman, *A Prisoner without a Name, Cell without a Number*, trans. Toby Talbot (New York: Vintage Books, 1981). According to the official commission that investigated human rights abuses, little under 10 000 Argentines of all ages were jailed, killed, and/or missing ("disappeared"): The Sábato Commission, *Nunca Más: Informe da Comissão Nacional sobre o desaparacimento de pessoas na Argentina, presidida por Ernesto Sábato* (Porto Alegre: L&PM Editores, 1984).

37. David Pion-Berlin, *Through Corridors of Power: Institutions and Civil-Military Relations in Argentina* (University Park, PA: Pennsylvania State University Press, 1997), p. 45.

38. Bergsten, Horst, and Moran, *American Multinationals*, p. 384.

39. For this period, the following three works are worth consulting: Guillermo A. Calvo, "Fractured Liberalism: Argentina under Martínez de Hoz," *Economic Development and Culture Change* (April 1986), pp. 511–33; William C. Smith, *Authoritarianism and the Crisis of the Argentine Political Economy* (Stanford: Stanford University Press, 1991), pp. 231–66; and José María Dagnino Pastore, *Crónicas económicas: Argentina, 1969–1988* (Buenos Aires: Editorial Crespillo, 1989).

40. Erro, *Resolving the Argentine Paradox*, pp. 103–4. Domingo F. Cavallo, "Argentina: Trade Reform, 1976–1982," in *Trade Reform Lessons from Eight Countries*, eds. Geoffrey Shepherd and Carlos Geraldo Langoni (San Francisco: ICS Press, 1991), pp. 27–39, esp., 31.

41. Roberto Cirilo Perdia and Fernando Vaca Narvaja, *Plano Austral: Nova estratégia do FMI*, trans. Maria Isabel Ekhvanossafa (Porto Alegre: Editora Tschê, 1986), p. 75.

42. Erro, *Resolving the Argentine Paradox*, pp. 108–9.

43. Ibid., pp. 102–3.

44. Ibid., pp. 18–21. Cavallo, "Argentina: Trade Reform," p. 30.

45. Erro, *Resolving the Argentine Paradox*, pp. 124–6.

46. Pion-Berlin, *Through Corridors*, p. 58.

47. On the Falkland war, several items are worth looking at: Alejandro Davata and Luis Lorenzano, *Argentina: the Malvinas and the End of the Military Rule*, trans. Ralph Johnston (London: Verso, 1983); Max Hastings and Simon Jenkins, *The Battle for the Falklands* (London: Michael Joseph Publishers, 1983); Christopher Dobson, John Miller, and Ronald Payne, *The Falklands Conflict* (London: Coronet Books, 1982); The Sunday Times Insight Team, *The Falklands War: the True Story* (London: Sphere Books, 1982); Robert Fox, *Eyewitness Falklands: a Personal Account of the Falklands Campaign* (London: Methuen, 1982).

48. Pion-Berlin, *Through Corridors*, pp. 111–12, 141–51.

49. Deborah L. Norden, *Military Rebellion in Argentina: Between Coups and Consolidation* (Lincoln, NE, and London: University of Nebraska Press, 1996), pp. 183–6.
50. Erro, *Resolving the Argentine Paradox*, p. 127.
51. Ibid., pp. 132–4. Pablo Giussani, *¿Por qué, doctor Alfonsín?* (Buenos Aires: Sudamericana-Planeta, 1987), pp. 195–6.
52. Luigi Manzetti, *The International Monetary Fund and Economic Stabilization: the Argentine Case* (New York: Praeger, 1991), pp. 141–2).
53. Ibid., pp. 142–3.
54. Giussani, *¿Por qué, doctor Alfonsin?*, p. 134. Perdia and Narvaja, *Plano Austral*, pp. 120–1. For an excellent study of how the conglomerates behaved in the 1980s, consult Pierre Ostiguy, *Los capitanes de la industria: Grandes empresarios, política y economía en la Argentina de los años 80* (Buenos Aires: Editorial Legasa, 1990). The book identified 23 such holding companies, whose names appear in Cuadro 2.
55. Luis Majul, *Por qué cayó Alfonsín: el nuevo terrorismo económico* (Buenos Aires: Sudamérica, 1990), p. 19. The financial speculation raged because of the high interest rates: for every six months, the Argentinian banks paid 50 percent in interest, or one million dollars deposited netted $500 000 every 180 days.
56. Manzetti, *The International Monetary Fund*, p. 145.
57. Perdia and Narvaja, *Plano Austral*, pp. 101–6, 119–20.
58. Monica Peralta-Ramos, "Economic Policy and Distributional Conflict among Business Groups in Argentina: From Alfonsin to Menem (1989–1990)," in *The New Argentine Democracy: the Search for a Successful Formula*, ed. Edward C. Epstein (Westport, CT: Praeger, 1992), pp. 97–123, esp., 103.
59. FIEL (Fundación de Investigaciones Económicas Latino-Americanas), "El regimen de compre nacional: una aplicación a la industria petrolera" (ms), Buenos Aires, October 1988, FIEL Library.
60. "Argentina's Economic Chief Replaced in Bid to Boost Radical's Election Chances," *Latin American Regional Reports: Southern Cone Report* (20 April 1989), p. 1.

3   Brazil: Building a Capitalism without Risk

1. The two books by Skidmore are now classics: *Politics in Brazil, 1930–1964: an Experiment in Democracy* (New York: Oxford University Press, 1967) and *The Politics of Military Rule in Brazil, 1964–85* (New York: Oxford University Press, 1988).
2. D'Araújo and Castro, orgs., *Ernesto Geisel*; Jarbas Passarinho, *Um híbrido fértil*, 3rd ed. (Rio: Expressão e Cultura, 1996); Armando Falcão, *Tudo a declarar* (Rio: Editora Nova Fronteira, 1989); Robert Campos, *Reflexões do crepúsculo* (Rio: Topbooks Editora, 1991), and *Além do cotidiano*, 2nd ed. (Rio: Record, 1985); João Paulo dos Reis Velloso, *O último trem para Paris: De Getúlio a Sarney: "Milagres," choques e crises do Brasil moderno* (Rio: Editora Nova Fronteira, 1986); and Alexandre Garcia, *Nos bastidores da notícia*, 5th ed. (Rio: Editora Globo, 1990).

3. Maria Helena Moreira Alves, *State and Opposition in Military Brazil* (Austin, TX: University of Texas Press, 1985).
4. Peter B. Evans and Paulo Bastos Tigre, "Going beyond Clones in Brazil and Korea: a Comparative Analysis of NIC Strategies in the Computer Industry," *World Development* (November 1989), pp. 1751–68.
5. SEST/SEPLAN [Brasil], *Cadastro das empresas estatais 1984* (Brasília: SEST, 1984), pp. vii–xi. An excellent analysis of the Brazilian SOE trajectory through the 1950s to 1980s is found in: Fernando Rezende, "O crescimento (descontrolado) da intervenção governmental na economia brasileira," in *Seminário sobre planejamento e controle do setor de empresas estatais: Casos nacionais*, eds. IPEA and CEPAL (Brasília: IPEA, 1983), pp. 151–91. Rezende gives the four categories defined by Decree-Law No. 200 of 25 February 1967.
6. Thomas J. Trebat, *Brazil's State-Owned Enterprises: a Case Study of the State as Entrepreneur* (New York: Cambridge University Press, 1983), argues that not all SOEs were money losers; in fact, he praises the performance of some SOEs.
7. Jeffry A. Frieden, *Debt, Development, & Democracy: Modern Political Economy and Latin America, 1965–1985* (Princeton: Princeton University Press, 1991), p. 123.
8. Antônio Delfim Netto, *Delfim: "Não olhe só a dívida: Veja o que ela represe-senta: Itaipu, Tucuruí, o programa siderúrgico, os metrôs, Caraíba, a petro-química, Tubarão … "* (Brasília: Secretaria de Planejamento, 1983). Nelson Mortada, *Estatais: Menores gastos, maior produtividade* (Brasília: Secretaria de Planejamento, 1984). Presidência da República [Brasil], Secretaria de Planejamento, *Razões para acreditar em 1984 apesar dos dez anos de crise mundial* (Brasília: SEPLAN 1984). SEPLAN [Brasil]/CNPq, *Setor produtivo estatal: Dispêndio em ciências e tecnologia 1978/82* (Brasília: SEPLAN, 1982), p. 61. On Brazil's external borrowing, consult: Frieden, *Debt, Development, & Democracy*, pp. 95–142, 122–31.
9. Petrobrás [Brazil], *Relatório Annual* and *Relatório Annual Consolidado*, various years.
10. SEST/SEPLAN [Brasil], *Sinopse da atuação da Sest no período 1980/84* (Brasília: SEST, 1984), pp. 51, 90–1.
11. SEST/SEPLAN, *Legislação básica* (Brasília: SEST, 1984), p. 521.
12. João Paulo dos Reis Velloso, *O estado e a economia* (Brasília: SEPLAN, 1975). The left also agreed with Velloso. Roberto Saturno Braga, *Política, economia e estatização (debates parlamentares)* (Rio: Civilização Brasileira, 1976).
13. Ibid. João Paulo dos Reis Velloso, *Os 20 anos do BNDE* (Brasília: SEPLAN, 1972).
14. João Paulo dos Reis Velloso, et al., *O real e o futuro da economia* (Rio: José Olympio, 1995), is a superb analysis of the national economy.
15. BNDE System, *Annual Report: 1980* (Rio: BNDE, 1981), pp. 11–12.
16. *Visão* (29 March 1982) and *Gazeta Mercantil* (19 March 1982).
17. *Veja* (4 May 1983).
18. *Correio da Manhã* (16 May 1965).
19. CVRD, *Carajás 1985* (Rio: CVRD, 1985).
20. Eul-Soo Pang, "Brazil's External Debt: Part II: the Inside View," *UFSI Reports* 1984/No. 38 South America [ESP-2-84] (1985), pp. 1–7, esp., 6. *O Estado de*

S. Paulo (12 February 1984). The journalist who wrote the report also pointed out that much of the goods bought were thrown away or stored in warehouses in Brazil and even overseas.

21. Câmara dos Deputados. Comissão Parlamentar de Inquérito, *Dívida externa e do acordo FMI-Brasil*,a testimony by Mário Henrique Simonsen, Brasília, 10 November 1983 [ms].

22. There are several good works on the world financial market and its relations to the developing world's debt. Michael Moffitt, *The World's Money: International Banking from Bretton Woods to the Brink of Insolvency* (New York: Simon & Schuster, 1983), pp. 93–132, and Jeffry A. Frieden, *Banking on the World: the Politics of American International Finance* (New York: Basil Blackwell, 1989), p. 131. The most recent and highly technical work on the Third World debt is written by: William R. Cline, *International Debt Reexamined* (Washington: Institute of International Economics, 1995), pp. 275–344 deal with Latin America.

23. João Paulo dos Reis Velloso, *A contenção nos investimentos governamentais* (Brasília: SEPLAN, 1976).

24. Gustavo Lins Riberiro, *Transnational Capitalism and Hydropolitics in Argentina: the Yacyretá High Dam* (Gainesville, FL: The University Press of Florida, 1994), pp. 43–5.

25. João Camillo Penna, *A dívida externa e o comércio internacional* (Brasília: SEPLAN, 1984), pp. 7–12.

26. *Jornal da Tarde* (22 December 1987). Eul-Soo Pang, "Brazil's External Debt: Part I: the Outside View," *UFSI Reports*, 1987/No. 37, South America, pp. 1–8, esp., 4–5.

27. *O Estado de S. Paulo* (29 January 1975).

28. Velloso, *O estado e a economia*.

29. Antônio Delfim Netto, *Análise da política econômica nacional* (Brasília: SEPLAN 1980). This was a speech made before the Brazilian Joint Chiefs of Staff, 2 September 1980.

30. *Forum Gazeta Mercantil* (São Paulo, 1983). The Brazilian "Wall Street Journal" convoked a forum of leading businessmen, industrialists, and bankers to review the state of the economy. On Nelson Mortada's view, *O Estado de S. Paulo* (4 January 1984).

31. Jan Tinbergen, coord., *RIO: Reshaping the International Order: a Report to the Club of Rome*, Anthony J. Dolman, editor, and Jan van Eittinger, director (New York: 1976), p. 38.

32. *Correio da Manhã* (1 February 1964) and *Jornal do Brasil* (2 February 1964).

33. Getúlio Carvalho, *Petrobrás: Do monopólio aos contratos de risco* (Rio: FU, 1976).

34. In Chile, many active officers were appointed to manage SOEs, universities, and ministries under Pinochet. In Brazil and Argentina, it was rare that active officers were put in charge of these nonmilitary sectors, except for some governmental agencies and national and state police units.

35. Carvalho, *Petrobrás*, pp. 165–71.

36. Conselho Nacional de Petróleo [Brasil] *Atualidades: Conselho Nacional de Petróleo* (Brasília: January–February 1984), pp. 32–43.

37. Alberto Tamer, *Petróleo: o preço da dependência. O Brasil na crise mundial* (Rio: Editora Nova Fronteira, 1980), pp. 27–38, 123.

38. Petrobrás, *Relatório annual consolidado* (Rio: Petrobrás, 1976), p. 10; *Relatório annual* (Rio: Petrobrás, 1981), p. 19; *Relatório annual* (Rio: Petrobrás, 1979), pp. 6–7. SEST/SEPLAN [Brasil], *Sinopse da atuação da SEST no período 1980/84*, p. 15.
39. A typical leftist paranoia is well articulated in: Maria Augusta Tibiriçá Miranda, *O petróleo é nosso: A luta contra o "entreguismo" pelo monopólio estatal* (Petrópolis: Vozes, 1981), pp. 457–64, and "Nota oficial do MDB contra os 'contratos de risco'," in *Petróleo: Contratos de risco e dependência*, coord. Bernardo Kucinski (São Paulo: Brasiliense, 1977), pp. 213–17.
40. Conselho Nacional de Petróleo [Brasil], *Atualidades* (1984), *passim*.
41. República Federativa do Brasil. Ministério das Minas e Energia, *Balanço energético nacional 1985* (Brasília: CNP, 1985), p. 14. Conselho Nacional de Petróleo [Brasil], *Atualidades*, pp. 29–32.
42. Petrólero Brasileiro [Petrobrás], "True Blue Power," *Latin Finance* (May 1995), p. 26.
43. *Jornal do Brasil* (27 July 1984). Banco Central do Brasil, *Brasil: Programa econômico* 18 (Brasília: BCB, Setembro de 1988), p. 81. For 1988, Petrobrás imported 653 000 bbpd and spent $3.457 billion. For the ill-fated alcohol program, consult: Michael Barzelay, *The Politicized Market Economy: Alcohol in Brazil's Energy Strategy* (Berkeley: University of California Press, 1986), pp. 78–82. For the pricing problem consult: Sérgio Luiz Coutinho Nogueira, "Fatores impeditivos da consolidação do PROALCOOL," *Anais do I Simpósio Nacional sobre álcool combustível* (Brasília: Câmara dos Deputados, 1985), pp. 92–103.
44. "A Petrobrás com medo da concorrência," *Veja* (30 March 1994), pp. 70–9.
45. On Mexico, consult: United States Department of Commerce. International Trade Administration, "Mexico – PEMEX Reorganization – IM1920724," *National Trade Data Bank*, 30 November 1993, CD-ROM. "Mexico – Reorganization of PEMEX – IM1930219," ibid., 30 November 1993. U.S. Department of State, "Industrial Outlook for Petroleum and Natural Gas – Mexico," ibid., 30 November 1993. For the comparisons of Latin American countries, see "A Petrobrás com medo da concorrência," pp. 75, 78.
46. J. Carlos de Assis, *Os mandarins na república: Anatomia dos escândalos da administração pública: 1948–84* (Rio: Paz e Terra, 1984) is a blistering indictment of abuses by parastatals. A Petrobrás commercial director replied to Assis's charges categorically: Assessoria de Promoções da Interbrás, *Resposta a "Os mandarins da república:" Interbrás: Ficção & realidade* (Rio: Editora Lord, 1984).
47. Ibid., pp. 215–16, esp., 220.
48. Assis, *Os mandarins na república*, pp. 69–78, esp., 72–4.
49. Assesoria de Promoções da Interbrás, *Resposta a "Os mandarins da república,"* pp. 123–39.
50. Carvalho, *Petrobrás*, pp. 140–6.
51. Siegfried Marks, "Petroleum: Unfinished Reform," *U.S./Latin Trade* (April 1995), pp. 38–48.
52. Paulo Bastos Tigre, *Technology and Competition in the Brazilian Computer Industry* (New York: St. Martin's Press, 1983), pp. 3–5. Emmanuel Adler, *The Power of Ideology: the Quest for Technological Autonomy in Argentina and Brazil* (Berkeley: University of California Press, 1991), pp. 181–97.

53. Tigre, *Technology*, pp. 66–7. Henrique Rattner, *Informática e sociedade* (São Paulo: Editora Brasiliense, 1985). Christina Tavares and Milton Seligman, *Informática: A batalha do século XXI* (Rio: Paz e Terra, 1984), pp. 66–9.
54. Tigre, *Technology*, pp. 53–5.
55. Laura D'Andrea Tyson, *Who's Bashing Whom? Trade Conflict in High-Technology Industries*, 2nd ed. (Washington, DC: Institute for International Economics, 1992 [1988]).
56. Campos, *Além do cotidiano*, pp. 229–35. David C. Bruce, "Brazil Plays the Japan Card," *Third World Quarterly* (1983), pp. 848–60. For the Japanese experience, consult: Bela Balassa and Marcus Noland, *Japan in the World Economy* (Washington, DC: Institute of International Economics, 1988), pp. 39–40.
57. Tavares and Seligman, *Informática*, pp. 78–86.
58. Even banks entered into computer manufacturing. The ItauTec, a subsidiary of the Itaú Bank, was one of the first makers of personal computers in Brazil. Other banks and civil engineering firms also have been active in the business.
59. Campos, *Além do cotidiano*, pp. 241–50.
60. An excellent critique of the market reserve was published in: "Confusão electrônica," *Veja* (16 July 1986), pp. 96–103. Cláudio Mammana, org., *Informática e a Nova República* (São Paulo: HUCITEC, 1985), lists the complete text of the Lei Informática, pp. 177–294.
61. In the June 1991 visit to the White House, Collor wanted to bring two "gifts" to Bush: the new informatics law and industrial patent law. Neither was ready when the president was about to leave for the US. For the details, see "PMDB decide contra a reserva na informática," *Folha de S. Paulo* (5 June 1991); "PMDB negocia fim da reserva na informática," *Folha de S. Paulo* (6 June 1991); and "Informática continuará com incentivos," *Jornal do Brasil* (14 June 1991). For the continued ban, see "Fugindo do atraso," *Veja* (19 September 1990).
62. In October 1990, Sen. Karsten of Wisconsin added a rider to a budget bill that would have prohibited Embraer from purchasing IBM components to upgrade its supercomputer. Brazil dispatched two pro-US cabinet members to lobby the US congress and succeeded in killing the Karsten rider. For the details, see *Folha de S. Paulo* (21 October 1990).

4   Chile: the Revolution That No One Desired

1. Marcelo J. Cavarozzi and James F. Petras, "Chile," in *Latin America: the Struggle with Dependency and Beyond*, eds. Ronald H. Chilcote and Joel C. Edelstein (New York: John Wiley & Sons, 1974), pp. 495–578.
2. Manuel Antonio Garretón, *The Chilean Political Process*, trans. Sharon Kellum and Gilbert W. Merkx (Winchester, MA: Unwin Hyman, 1989), pp. 4–11.
3. Ibid., pp. 5–7. For some curious reason, Garretón fails to include in his "industrial sector" mining groups.
4. Federico Gil, *The Political System of Chile* (Boston: Houghton Mifflin, 1966), p. 90.

5. Ibid., p. 158.
6. John J. Johnson, *Political Change in Latin America: the Emergence of the Middle Sector* (Stanford: Stanford University Press, 1958), p. 80.
7. Ibid., p. 151.
8. Albert O. Hirschman, *Journeys toward Progress: Studies of Economic Policy-Making in Latin America* (New York: The Twentieth-Century Fund, 1963), pp. 183–4.
9. Ibid., p. 182.
10. Michael Fleet, *The Rise and Fall of Chilean Christian Democracy* (Princeton: Princeton University Press, 1985), pp. 22–3.
11. Robert J. Alexander, *The ABC Presidents: Conversations and Correspondence with the Presidents of Argentina, Brazil, and Chile* (New York: Praeger Publishers, 1992), p. 230 (Conversation with Frei in Havana, 14 May 1950).
12. Tomas Moulian, "Desarrollo político y estado de compromiso: Desajustes y crisis estatal en Chile," *Colección CIEPLAN*, No. 8 (July 1982), pp. 112–13.
13. Ibid., pp. 43–58.
14. Paul E. Sigmund, *The Overthrow of Allende and the Politics of Chile, 1964–1976* (Pittsburgh: University of Pittsburgh Press, 1977), pp. 24–5.
15. Ibid., p. 260.
16. Ibid., p. 31.
17. Dagmar Raczynski, "Determinantes del éxodo rural: Importancia de factores del lugar de origen, Chile, 1965–70," *Colección Estudios CIEPLAN*, No. 8 (July 1982), pp. 61–104, esp., 62–3.
18. Sigmund, *Overthrow of Allende*, pp. 27–8. Kyle Steenland, *Agrarian Reform under Allende: Peasant Revolt in the South* (Albuquerque, NM: University of New Mexico Press, 1977), pp. 7–9. Alexander, *The ABC Presidents*, p. 213 (5 July 1968 conversation with Alessandri).
19. Raczynski, "Determinantes del éxodo rural," p. 67.
20. Seymour M. Hirsch, *The Price of Power: Kissinger in the Nixon White House* (New York: Summit Books, 1983), p. 259. Theodore H. Moran, *Multinational Corporations and the Politics of Dependence: Copper in Chile* (Princeton: Princeton University Press, 1974), pp. 57–152 deal with Chile.
21. Paul W. Moore and Rebecca K. Hunt, "The Andean Pact: In the Forefront," US Department of Commerce/International Trade Administration, Business America, 13 June 1994, and "Andean Pact Restructured," International Market Insight, 12 March 1996, both in *National Trade Data Bank*, CD-ROM (January 1997).
22. Hirsch, *Price of Power*, p. 261, footnote.
23. Sigmund, *Overthrow of Allende*, pp. 19–20, 80–1. Alexander, *ABC Presidents*, p. 245 (conversation with Frei on 1 July 1971, Santiago).
24. Fleet, *Rise and Fall of Chilean Christian Democracy*, pp. 89–99. Sigmund, *Overthrow of Allende*, pp. 50–4.
25. Moulian, "Desarrollo político," p. 135.
26. Ibid., p. 141.
27. Fleet, *Rise and Fall of Chilean Christian Democracy*, pp. 105–13.
28. Alexander, *ABC Presidents*, p. 219 (conversation with Alessandri, 1 July 1971, Santiago). The former president was obviously referring to the PDC's objective of establishing a "communitarian" society in Chile. Hirsch, *Price of Power*, p. 261.

29. Hirsch, *Price of Power*, pp. 258–9.
30. Sigmund, *Overthrow of Allende*, pp. 37–48.
31. "40 Committee" was named after the presidential order No. 40 for the National Security Council. Forty does not represent the number of members on the committee.
32. John Ranelagh, *The Agency: the Rise and Decline of the CIA* (New York: Simon & Schuster, 1987), pp. 514–15.
33. Hirsch, *Price of Power*, pp. 271–73.
34. Ranelagh, *Agency*, pp. 516–19. Hirsch, *Price of Power*, pp. 275–6.
35. Hirsch, *Price of Power*, p. 294 (on NSDM 93 and Kissinger being a Chilean desk officer) and p. 295 (on $8 million).
36. Ranelagh, *Agency*, p. 515.
37. Alexander, *ABC Presidents*, pp. 271–2 (conversation with Allende, 15 January 1947, Santiago).
38. Ibid.
39. Sigmund, *Overthrow of Allende*, pp. 141–7, 152–4. Moran, *Multinational Corporations*, pp. 129–44. Raymond F. Mikesell, "Conflict and Accommodation in Direct Foreign Investment: the Copper Industry," in *Latin American-U.S. Economic Interactions: Conflict, Accommodation, and Policies for the Future*, eds. Robert B. Williamson, William P. Glade, Jr., and Karl M. Schmitt (Washington, DC: American Enterprise Institute, 1974), pp. 185–99, esp., 189–90, 196–7.
40. Stefan de Vylder, *Allende's Chile: the Political Economy of the Rise and Fall of the Unidad Popular* (Cambridge, Eng.: Cambridge University Press, 1976), pp. 126–34.
41. Sigmund, *Overthrow of Allende*, pp. 133–4.
42. Ibid., p. 156.
43. Steenland, *Agrarian Reform under Allende*, pp. 16–18. Sigmund, *Overthrow of Allende*, p. 139. James Petras and Hugo Zemelman Merino, *Peasant in Revolt: a Chilean Case Study 1965–1971*, trans. Thomas Flory (Austin, TX: University of Texas Press, 1972), pp. xi–xiii.
44. Steenland, *Agrarian Reform under Allende*, pp. 25–6. Sigmund, *Overthrow of Allende*, pp. 139–40.
45. Richard J. Barnett and Ronald E. Muller, *Global Reach: the Power of the Multinational Corporations* (New York: Simon & Schuster, 1974), p. 83.
46. Deborah Shapley, *Promise and Power: the Life and Times of Robert McNamara* (Boston: Little Brown, 1993), p. 496. Sigmund, *Overthrow of Allende*, p. 191.
47. Ibid., pp. 191–4.
48. David F. Cusack, *Revolution and Reaction: the Internal Dynamics of Conflict and Confrontation in Chile* (Denver: DU Graduate School of International Studies, 1977), pp. 43–5.
49. Sigmund, *Overthrow of Allende*, pp. 196–7, 226.
50. Vylder, *Allende's Chile*, p. 209.
51. Ricardo Israel Z., *Politics and Ideology in Allende's Chile* (Tempe, AZ: Center for Latin American Studies, Arizona State University, 1989), pp. 173–4.
52. Ibid., pp. 226–35.
53. Cusack, *Revolution and Reaction*, pp. 66–7.
54. Israel Z., *Politics and Ideology*, pp. 231–4.

55. Cusack, *Revolution and Reaction*, p. 69.
56. Brian Loveman, "Military Dictatorship and Political Opposition in Chile," in *Chile: Dictatorship and Struggle for Democracy*, eds. Grinor Rojo and John J. Hassett (Gaithersburg, MD: Hispanoamerica, 1988), pp. 17–52, esp., 44.
57. Barbara Stallings, *Class Conflict and Economic Development in Chile, 1958–1973* (Stanford: Stanford University Press, 1978), pp. 69–79.
58. Gonzalo Martner, *El gobierno del presidente Salvador Allende 1970–1973: una evaluación* (Concepción: Editora Lar, 1988), pp. 369–74, 395–6, Cuadro 23.
59. Furtado, *Os ares do mundo*, pp. 200–5.

5 Argentina's Travails of Democracy and Market Economy

1. World Bank, *World Development Report 1992*, pp. 218–19, 222–3, Tables 1 and 3. Inter-American Development Bank, *Economic and Social Progress in Latin America: 1991 Report*, pp. 23–7, 273 (Tables B-1 and B-2).
2. Felipe A. M. de la Balze, *Remaking the Argentine Economy* (New York: Council on Foreign Relations, 1995), pp. 61–2.
3. "The International 500: the Fortune Directory of the Largest Industrial Corporations outside the U.S.," *Fortune* (20 August, 1984), p. 200. FIEL, *Los costos del estado regulador* (Buenos Aires: FIEL, 1989), pp. 215–16. FIEL, *El fracaso del estatismo: una propuesta para la reforma del sector público argentino* (Buenos Aires: Sudamericana-Planeta, 1987), pp. 11–22. Smith, *Authoritarianism*, p. 270.
4. Leuco and Díaz, *El heredero de Perón*, p. 210.
5. Ibid., p. 232.
6. One Porteño newspaper reported that Argentina transferred $130 billion to international banks between 1982 and 1986. For this figure, consult Galasso, *Gatos y sardinas en la economía argentina*, p. 143. Carlos Menem and Eduardo Duhalde, *La revolución productiva* (Buenos Aires: Peña Nilo Editora, 1989), pp. 65–7.
7. Menem and Duhalde, *La revolución productiva*, pp. 76–7. Gabriela Cerruti and Sergio Ciancaglini, *El octavo círculo: Crónica y entretelones de la Argentina menemista* (Buenos Aires: Planeta, 1991), p. 57.
8. Cerruti and Ciancaglini, *El octavo círculo*, pp. 55–7.
9. Jorge Schvarzer, *Bunge & Born: Crecimiento y diversificación de un grupo económico* (Buenos Aires: CISEA, 1989).
10. Ministerio de Obras y Servicios Públicos [Argentina], "La reforma del estado y el proceso de privatizaciones (Ley 23.696 y Decreto 1105/89): Balance de 120 dias (10 de julio al 10 de noviembre de 1989)" [ms]. Horacio Verbitsky, *Robo para la corona: los frutos prohibidos del árbol de la corrupción* (Buenos Aires: Planeta, Espejo de la Argentina, 1991), pp. 133–5.
11. Luis Majul, *Por qué cayó Alfonsín: el nuevo terrorismo económico: los personajes, las conexiones, las claves secretas* (Buenos Aires: Editorial Sudamericana, 1990), pp. 81–3.
12. Eduardo Luis Curia, *Dos años de la economía de Menem: una etapa de transformaciones* (Buenos Aires: El Cronista, 1991), pp. 36–45.
13. Ibid., pp. 62–7.

14. FIEL, *Regulaciones y estancamiento: el caso argentino* (Buenos Aires: FIEL, 1988), p. 26. Victoria Griffith, "Ironing Out the Wrinkles," *Latin Finance* (September 1992), pp. 71–5. Robert Y. Stebbings, "Carlos Menem in Argentina: Country Focus: Argentina," unpaginated.
15. De la Balze, *Remaking the Argentine Economy*, pp. 70–5.
16. Curia, *Dos años del la economía de Menem*, pp. 70–2.
17. Cerruti and Ciancaglini, *El octavo círculo*, p. 28.
18. Gabriel Cerruti, *El jefe: Vida y obra de Carlos Saul Menem* (Buenos Aires: Planeta, 1993), pp. 319–20.
19. Olga Wornat, "Las confesiones de Manzano," *Somos* (22 February 1993), pp. 4–9. Manzano granted an interview with the Argentinian weekly in La Jolla, California.
20. "Las mil y una caras de Ibrahim," *Somos* (1 March 1993), pp. 4–9.
21. Cerruti, *El jefe*, pp. 369–70.
22. Cerruti and Ciancaglini, *El octavo círculo*, pp. 277–8.
23. Ibid., p. 33. Cerruti, *El jefe*, pp. 349–50. Cerruti reported in a good scandal-mongering style that Amira lived in the same apartment in Madrid where she shared the place with her former husband Col. Ibrahim and her current lover al Kassar.
24. Martín Granovsky, *Misión cumplida: la presión norteamericana sobre la Argentina, de Braden a Todman* (Buenos Aires: Planeta Espejo de la Argentina, 1992), pp. 227–43, 351–4 (the letter).
25. Cerruti and Ciancaglini, *El octavo círculo*, pp. 235–7, 242–55. Emir was also accused of having received a hefty bribe from a Swiss firm supplying the ink to the Casa de Moneda. Cerruti and Ciancaglini even revealed the Citibank account number in New York that the Yoma, Inc. in New York used. See, for the details, pp. 242–3.
26. Cerruti and Ciancaglini, *El octavo círculo*, p. 33. Cerruti, *El jefe*, pp. 349–51, 369–71.
27. Cerruti, *El jefe*, pp. 341–2 for her remarks.
28. Ibid., pp. 341–2.
29. Jorge Greco, "Complot para un divorcio," *Somos* (23 September 1991), pp. 10–11. The article claimed that Seindeldín and Zulema frequently exchanged letters through the colonel's wife and "maintain [*sic*] an excellent relationship."
30. Cerruti, *El jefe*, 340–2.
31. The code name for Seindeldín was the camel, which the Argentinian press popularized during and after the ill-fated Carapintadas coup.
32. Cerruti, *El jefe*, p. 342.
33. Ibid., pp. 364–5.
34. Varela and Zicolillo, *Un domingo en el purgatorio*, pp. 11–13. Enrique N'haux, *Menem-Cavallo: el poder mediterráneo* (Buenos Aires: Ediciones Corregidor, 1993), p. 103. N'haux said that, in 1983, the impoverished Viscovich, out of a job, had to turn to Cavallo for help. The disciple found his old mentor a job. The following year, Visovich died.
35. Ibid., pp. 102–9.
36. James P. Brennan, *The Labor Wars in Córdoba 1955–1976: Ideology, Work, Labor Politics in an Argentine Industrial City* (Cambridge, MA: Harvard University Press, 1996).

37. Javier Corrales, "Why Argentines Followed Cavallo: a Technopol between Democracy and Economic Reform," in *Technopols: Freeing Politics and Markets in Latin America in the 1990s*, ed. Jorge L. Domingues (University Park, PA: The Pennsylvania State University Press, 1997), pp. 49–93, esp., p. 54.
38. Varela and Zicolillo, *Un domingo*, pp. 143–55.
39. The Argentinian Ministry of Foreign Affairs has two functions: foreign relations and the faith (culto), presumeably due to the Vatican diplomatic representation in the country.
40. N'haux, *Menem-Cavallo* is a superb study on the composition of foundation technocrats, their ties to business, and their rise to power.
41. Ibid., p. 197. Galasso, *Gatos y sardinas*, p. 124.
42. Cerruti, *El jefe*, p. 374. Menem often said that "I did not fight all my life just to become president for six years and afterward go away. And we, the Arabs, live for a hundred years." As it turned out, the second term was fixed for four years.
43. Cerruti, *El jefe*, p. 365. Varela and Zicolillo, *Un domingo*, pp. 235–7.
44. Javier Corrales, "Why Argentines Followed Cavallo," pp. 60–1.
45. The economic advisers whom Cavallo brought from the Mediterranean Foundation and its research tank are known as "mediterráneos" to distinguish them from others. The term also denotes trusted aides of Cavallo.
46. Varela and Zicolillo, *Un domingo*, pp. 237–8.
47. Price Waterhouse, *Doing Business in Argentina* (Buenos Aires: Price Waterhouse, May 1992, Diskette), 8:1. USDOC/ITA, "Argentina – Overseas Business Report – Marketing – OBR8907," CD-ROM, IT Market 111110878, *National Trade Data Bank*, 2 October 1992. Inter-American Development Bank, *Economic and Social Progress in Latin America: 1991*, pp. 27–9. Maria Beatriz Nofal, "MERCOSUR and Free Trade in the Americas," in *Integrating the Americas: Shaping Future Trade Policy*, ed. Sidney Weintraub (New Brunswick, NJ: Transaction Publishers, 1994), pp. 137–68. Cavallo, "Argentina: Trade Reform, 1976–1982."
48. Cavallo, "Argentina: Trade Reform, 1976–1982," p. 27. "¿Quál es el plan de Cavallo?" *Novedades Económicas* (March 1991), no pagination, analyzes the plan. "¿Desregulación o picardia?" *Somos* (11 November 1991), p. 17.
49. "Emerging-Market Indicators," *The Economist* (18 July 1998), p. 92.
50. Varela and Zicolillo, *Un domingo*, pp. 251–2.
51. Nicholas Brady, secretary of the treasury of the Bush administration, proposed a plan to reduced Third World debt.
52. De la Balze, *Remaking the Argentine Economy*, pp. 88–99.
53. USDOC/ITA, "Argentina – Menem on Privatization" and "Argentina – Bank Privatization – IMI920630," CD-ROM, *National Trade Data Bank*, 2 October 1992. Inter-American Development Bank, *Economic and Social Progress in Latin America: 1991*, pp. 26–7.
54. "Argentina," *Latin Finance: 1992: Second Annual Privatization in Latin America* (March 1992), pp. 44–6; "Argentina Still Going," *Latin Finance* (October 1996), p. 100.
55. Mary M. Shirley, "Privatization in Latin America: Lessons for Transitional Europe," *World Development* (September 1994), pp. 1313–23, esp., 1319.

56. Martin Redrado, *Tiempo de desafio* (Buenos Aires: Planeta, 1994), pp. 22–5.
57. Ibid., pp. 110–30.
58. De la Balze, *Remaking the Argentine Economy*, pp. 82–3, 91–3.
59. Ibid., pp. 99–105.
60. United Nations Conference on Trade and Development, *World Investment Report 2000: Cross-border Mergers and Acquisitions and Development* (New York: United Nations, 2000), p. 284.
61. World Bank, *2000 World Development Indicators*, www.worldbank.org.
62. *LatinFinance* No. 84 (1996), no pagination.
63. Juan Antonio Zapata, "The Argentine Economic Strategy," speech at the Latin American Mining Conference, Scottsdale, AZ, 23–5 February 1996.
64. Inter-American Development Bank, *Economic and Social Progress in Latin America: 1997 Report: Latin America after a Decade of Reforms* (Washington, DC: IDB, 1997), pp. 251–2.
65. International Monetary Fund, www.imf.org/external/NP/LOI/1999/051099.HTM and www.imf.org/external/NP/LOI/2000/arg/INDEX.HTM.
66. Mark P. Jones, "Argentina: Questioning Menem's Way," *Current History* (February 1998), pp. 71–5; the quote is from p. 71.
67. The first account of deaths was 26. The final tally reached 28. Michelle Wallin and Pamela Druckerman, "Argentina's Beleaguered Government Collapses," *Wall Street Journal* (21 December 2001): A 13; Bill Cormier, "Argentine Peronists Regain Presidency," *Washington Post* (21 December 2001) online: www.washingtonpost.com/wp-dyn/articles/A16383-2001Dec22.html; "Flirting with Anarchy," *The Economist* (5 January 2002), pp. 12–13.
68. "The Bell Tolls for Mercosur," *Latin Trade* (January 2002), p. 20.
69. World Bank, "Poor People in a Rich Country: a Poverty Report for Argentina. Volume I," Document of the World Bank, Report No. 19992 AR (23 March 2000).
70. "IMF Augments Argentina Stand-by Credit to $21.57 Billion, and Completes Fourth Review," Press Release No. 01/37 (7 September 2001), International Monetary Fund, Washington, DC, www.imf.org/external/np/sec/pr/2001/pr0137.html.
71. "Staying Mum," *The Economist* (15 December 2001), p. 30.
72. Mary Anastasia O'Grady, "Play 'Deuda Eterna' and Learn All about the IMF," *Wall Street Journal* (21 December 2001): A15.
73. Michelle Wallin, "Argentine Leader Declares State of Emergency," *Wall Street Journal* (20 December 2001): C12; Thomas Catán and Richard Lapper, "Argentina in Crisis Talks to Head Off Collapse," *Financial Times* (8–9 December 2001), p. 1.
74. Michelle Wallin, "After Devaluation, Argentina Struggles On," *Wall Street Journal* (10 January 2002): A8.

6   "Brazil Is Not a Serious Country"

1. General Charles de Gaulle visited Brazil in the late 1960s and supposedly commented, on his departure from Rio, that "This is not a serious country." The Brazilians, journalists and academics paraphrased the famous saying as "Isso não é um país sério" or "este país não é sério."

2. Nigel Harris, *The End of the Third World: Newly Industrializing Countries and the Decline of an Ideology* (New York: Penguin Books, 1990), p. 148. Harris cites the example: Brazil, a backward economy, was able to "shake off the slump" in the 1930s, while the U.S. was not.
3. Ibid., p. 84.
4. The figures for 1990 came from: World Bank, *World Development Report 1992*, pp. 218–19 (Table 1) and 222–3 (Table 3). The 1995 figures based on purchasing power parity come from: "The Bottom Line," *Asia Week* (26 May 1995), p. 63. Since Taiwan is not a member of the World Bank, its figures are my own estimate based on the data from *Asia Week*.
5. UNCTAD *Trade and Development Report, 1993* (New York: UN, 1993), pp. iv–v.
6. "Cardoso de Mello, Brazil's New Minister for Economics, Begins to Walk Tightrope," *Wall Street Journal* (2 March 1990).
7. Eul-Soo Pang, "Brazil and the United States," in *United States Policy in Latin America*, ed. John D. Martz (Lincoln, NE, and London: University of Nebraska Press, 1995), pp. 144–83, esp. 144–50.
8. "O choque de Zélia," *Veja* (21 March 1990), pp. 60–3.
9. "A saída do nocaute" and "Uma pancada pesada," *Veja* (28 March 1990), pp. 46–9 and 50–2, respectively.
10. "É de tirar o sono," *Istoé Senhor* (28 March 1990), pp. 28–33.
11. Antônio Carlos Pojo do Rêgo and João Paulo M. Peixoto, *A política econômica das reformas administrativas no Brasil* (Rio: Expressão e Cultura, 1998), p. 73.
12. Eul-Soo Pang and Laura Jarnagin, "Brazil's Catatonic Lambada," *Current History* (February 1991), pp. 73–5, 85–7.
13. Regis Bonelli, Gustavo B. Franco, and Winston Fritsch, "Macroeconomic Instability and Trade Performance in Brazil: Lessons from the 1980s to the 1990s," *Bangladesh Development Studies* (June–September 1992), pp. 129–61.
14. On the law of similars, see Robert J. Alexander, *Brazil: Industrial Policies and Manufactured Exports* (Washington, DC: The Brookings Institution, 1983). For the Korean case, see Richard Luedde-Neurath, *Import Controls and Export-Oriented Development: a Reassessment of the South Korean Case* (Boulder, CO: Westview Press, 1986).
15. "A turma do calote," *Veja* (17 May 1995), pp. 30–7.
16. Sebastian Edwards, "The United States and Foreign Competition in Latin America," in *The United States in the World Economy*, ed. Martin Feldstein (Chicago: University of Chicago Press, 1988), pp. 9–75, esp., 41. Sam Laird and Alexander Yeats, "Nontariff Barriers of Developed Countries, 1966–1986," *Finance and Development* (March 1989), pp. 12–13.
17. Bonelli, Franco, and Fritsch, "Macroeconomic Instability," p. 133.
18. Yongil Lim, "Comparing Brazil and Korea," in *Lessons in Development: a Comparative Study of Asia and Latin America*, eds., Seiji Naya, Miguel Urrutia, Shelley Mark, and Alfredo Fuentes (San Francisco: IFCS, 1989), pp. 93–117, esp., 94–6.
19. Annibal V. Villela and Werner Baer, *O setor privado nacional: Problemas e política para seu fortalecimento* (Rio: IPEA/INPES 1980), pp. 159–64.
20. FIESP [Brasil], *Livre para crescer: Proposta para um Brasil moderno* (São Paulo: FIESP, 1990), pp. 135–40, 145–52.
21. Inter-American Development Bank, *Economic and Social Progress in Latin America: 1994 Report*, p. 15.

22. "Pérola aos porcos," *Veja* (27 November 1991), p. 99.
23. Bonelli, Franco, and Fritsch, "Macroeconomic Instability," pp. 133–42.
24. "Confusão electrônica."
25. Ibid.
26. Ibid., p. 97. "Essa é a lei com que o senador Roberto Campos ficou defendendo os interesses dos americanos."
27. Ibid., p. 98.
28. "Nocaute tecnológico," *Veja* (19 June 1991), p. 37.
29. Scott McCartney, "Catching Up: Computer Sales Sizzle as Developing Nations Try to Shrink PC Gap," *Wall Street Journal* (29 June 1995), A1.
30. In early 1980, Peru had 140 parastatals: see Horacio Boneo, ed., *Privatización del dicho al hecho* (Buenos Aires: El Cronista Comercial, 1985), p. 41. For Mexico, see Guillermo Ortiz, "Mexico's Been Bitten by the Privatization Bug," *Wall Street Journal* (15 September 1989). For Argentina, see Alberto J. Ugalde, *Las empresas públicas en la Argentina* (Buenos Aires: El Cronista Comercial, 1984), p. 27. For Brazil, see Pang, "Brazil's External Debt: Part I," pp. 4–5. For Venezuela, see Carlos Ball, "Privatization, Venezuelan Style," *Wall Street Journal* (1 June 1989). For Chile, Pan A. Yotopoulos, "The (Rip) Tide of Privatization: Lessons from Chile," *World Development* (May 1989), pp. 684–91, esp., 684–5, and Alejandro Foxley, *Latin American Experiments in Neo-Conservative Economics* (Berkeley, CA: University of California Press, 1983), pp. 61–71.
31. World Bank, *1998 World Development Indicators* (Washington, DC: World Bank, 1998), pp. 182–4.
32. Celso Luiz Martone, "Expansão do- estado empresário no Brasil," in *A crise do "Bom Patrão*," pp. 59–65. Former US Ambassador to Brazil L. A. Motley estimated that as much as 60 percent of the country's GDP came from the SOEs. See his comments in "Protecionismo existe em qualquer país: Entrevista [com] Anthony Motley," *O Globo* (5 June 1988). *Jornal da Tarde* (7 December 1973, 6 April 1974, and 11 April 1977) published articles on the etiology and growth of Brazil's SOEs.
33. Armando Castelar Pinheiro and Fábio Giambiagi, "Brazilian Privatization in the 1990s," *World Development* (May 1994), pp. 739–59, esp., 739–40, 749.
34. The official census of the federally owned and managed SOEs in 1988 and 1989 was 175 and 230 respectively. See Presidência da República. SEPLAN, *Relatório das empresas estatais–1988: Ano-base 1988* (Brasília: SEPLAN, 1989) and *Perfil das empresas estatais–1989: Ano-base 1989* (Brasília: SEPLAN, 1989).
35. Medida Provisória No. 157, 15 March 1990 – Dispõe sobre criação de Certificados de Privatização e dá outras providências.
36. The government had five representatives on the commission.
37. *Visão* (8 August 1990) and *O Globo* (21 August 1990).
38. Pinheiro and Giambiagi, "Brazilian Privatization."
39. The five privatized SOEs were USIMINAS, CELMA, USIMEC, MAFERSA, and COSINOR. For the details, see "Lenha na privatização," *Veja* (15 January 1992), p. 66.
40. Ibid.
41. "A praça da bagunça," *Veja* (2 October 1991), pp. 18–23.
42. "Os tigres da pensão," *Veja* (20 November 1991), pp. 78–81.
43. "Escándalo federal," *Veja* (4 September 1991), pp. 28–35, esp., 29.
44. "Turbulência no casal presidencial," *Veja* (21 October 1991), pp. 20–6.

45. "Força na larga," *Veja* (20 June 1990), pp. 36–7.
46. "A República que invadiu o Brasil," *Veja* (3 July 1991), pp. 16–23.
47. "As provas bancárias" and "No carro do amigo," *Veja* (8 July 1992), pp. 18–22 and 24–6.
48. "O último vôo," *Veja* (10 May 1995), p. 37. The arrest of PC's pilot was made in Buenos Aires, when Mrs. Bandeira wanted to take their teenaged daughter to see the father in Buenos Aires. According to Brazilian law, a minor must secure a court authorization to travel abroad. Mrs. Bandeira requested the court for permission and the teenager's name was tagged by the Federal Police. The court promptly informed the police that the mother and the daughter were travelling to Buenos Aires.
49. Joaquim de Carvalho, "Fim de caso," *Veja* (7 August 1996), pp. 32–8.
50. Joaquim de Carvalho, "A conta e o conto," *Veja* (19 March 1997), pp. 24–6.
51. Claúdio Humberto Rosa e Silva, *Mil dias de solidão: Collor bateu e levou* (São Paulo: Geração Editora, 1993), pp. 45–50, 83–4, 96–7.
52. Ibid., pp. 26–3.
53. Ibid.
54. "Emerging-Market Indicators," *The Economist* (28 May 1994), p. 108. "Cotações," *Veja* (16 March 1994), p. 102.
55. "Cotações," *Veja* (4 May 1994), p. 99.
56. *Veja: Guia do Real: Como fica sua vida com a nova moeda*, an insert in *Veja* (6 July 1994). Gustavo H. B. Franco, *O Plano Real e outros ensaios* (Rio: Francisco Alves, 1995), is a superb history of the monetary reform. Velloso, coord., *O real e o futuro da economia*. The nation's leading economists and policy makers review the Real Plan and make a forecast.
57. André Lara Resende, "A moeda indexada: uma proposta para eliminar a inflação inercial," *Revista de Economia Política* (April/June 1985), pp. 130–4. Resende said: "The essence of the proposal is, then, the introduction of a new money that would circulate on parallel with the cruzeiro. Such money would be defended from inflationary imposition through its stable tie to the ORTN (a national treasury note) and, at least in the beginning, also tied to the dollar"(p. 132).
58. Rêgo and Peixoto, *A política econômica*, p. 21.
59. "The Disorders of Progress," a survey of Brazil, *The Economist* (27 March 1999).
60. Lincoln Gordon, "Assessing Brazil's Political Modernization," *Current History* (February 1998), pp. 76–81.
61. "Cardoso Hails First Month of Power Saving, despite Target Shortfalls," *Latin American Regional Reports: Brazil Report* (3 July 2001), p. 1; "Energy Crisis Damages Cardoso," *Latin American Regional Reports: Brazil Report* (3 July 2001), p. 2.
62. "Unequal Income Distribution, 'almost unaffected by economic reforms,'" *Latin American Regional Reports: Brazil Report* (24 April 2001), p. 1.
63. Freedom House, "FH Country Ratings: Annual Survey of Freedom Country Scores 1972–73 to 1990–2000," www.freedomhouse.org/ratings/index.html.
64. "Serra and Jereissati Throw Their Hats into the Ring for PSDB Nomination," *Latin American Regional Reports: Brazil Report* (16 October 2001), p. 1.
65. Bolívar Lamounier, "Um é pouco, dois é bom, três é ..." *Exame* (26 December 2001), pp. 10–12.

7   Chile: Pinochet's Not Too Silent Revolution

1. Pamela Constable and Arturo Valenzuela, *A Nation of Enemies: Chile under Pinochet* (New York: W. W. Norton, 1991), p. 52.
2. Valdés, *Pinochet's Economists*, p. 16.
3. Ibid., pp. 19, 64.
4. Ibid., pp. 58, 59, 65–9, 81. Augusto Varas, *Los militares en el poder: Regimen y gobierno militar en Chile 1973–1986* (Santiago: Pehuén/FLACSO, 1987), pp. 29–30.
5. Taylor Branch and Eugene M. Popper, *Labyrinth* (New York: Penguin Books, 1983), pp. 80–2 (on the supposed involvement of MIR) and pp. 411–12 (on forged documents and visas).
6. Delano and Traslaviña, *La herencia de los Chicago Boys*, pp. 28–9.
7. The quote is from Aung San Suu Kyi, the Burmese pro-democracy leader. Alstair Horne, "Battle in Burma," *Wall Street Journal* (25 March 1997), A18.
8. Delano and Traslaviña, *La herencia de los Chicago Boys*, pp. 13–19, 59.
9. Ibid., pp. 27–9, 32–6.
10. The term "neoliberal" is used in the European and Latin American context, defined herein as the one who advocates a small government, less public spending for social programs, and the least interventionist role assigned to the state. A liberal in Europe and Latin America is known as a conservative in American politics.
11. Centro de Estudios Públicos, *"El Ladrillo:" Bases de la política económica del gobierno militar chileno,* prologue by Sergio de Castro (Santiago: CEP, 1992), pp. 27–38.
12. Ibid., pp. 30–2, 120.
13. Ibid., pp. 114–15.
14. Constable and Valenzuela, *A Nation of Enemies*, pp. 172–3, 186–7.
15. Interview with Alejandro Hales, Lima, 15 November 1994. Hales was minister of mines during the Aylwin government (1990–94).
16. Constable and Valenzuela, *A Nation of Enemies*, pp. 172–3.
17. Ibid., pp. 168–71.
18. Ibid., Delano and Traslaviña, *Las herencia de los Chicago Boys*, pp. 29–31, 39.
19. Ibid., p. 45.
20. Oscar Muñoz, "Crecimiento y desequilíbrio en una economía abierta: el caso chileno, 1976–81," *Colección CIEPLAN*, No. 8 (July 1982), pp. 19–41.
21. Ibid., pp. 26–7.
22. Delano and Traslaviña, *La herencia de los Chicago Boys*, pp. 47–9, 53.
23. Joaquín Lavín, *Miguel Kast: Pasión de viver*, 6th ed. (Santiago: Zig-Zag, 1988), pp. 126–8.
24. Foxley, *Latin American Experiments*, pp. 103–9. Dominique Hachette and Rolf Lüders, *Privatization in Chile: an Economic Appraisal* (San Francisco: ICS Press, 1993), pp. 5–6, 31–2. Genaro Arriagada Herrera and Carol Graham, "Chile: Sustaining Adjustment during Democratic Transition," in *Voting for Reform: Democracy, Political Liberalization, and Economic Adjustment*, eds. Stephan Haggard and Steven R. Webb (Washington, DC: IRBD, 1994), pp. 242–89, esp., 244–50.
25. Hachette and Lüders, *Privatization in Chile*, pp. 3–5.

26. Yotopoulos, "The (Rip) Tide of Privatization"; Hachette and Lüders, *Privatization in Chile*, pp. 23–5. Laura A. Hastings, "Regulatory Revenge: the Politics of Free-Market Financial Reforms in Chile," in *The Politics of Finance in Developing Countries*, eds. Stephan Haggard, Chung H. Lee, and Sylvia Maxfield (Ithaca, NY: Cornell University Press, 1993), pp. 201–2.
27. Lavin, *Miguel Kast*, pp. 83–9.
28. Muñoz gives 36.5 percent. See "Crecimiento y desequilíbrios," p. 28, Table 6.
29. José Pablo Arellano and René Cortázar, "Del milagro a la crisis: Reflexiones sobre el momento económico," *Colección CIEPLAN*, No. 8 (July 1982), pp. 43–60, esp., 46–8.
30. Ibid.
31. Arellano and Cortázar, "Del milgaro," pp. 46–8.
32. Alejandro Foxley, "Después del monetarismo," in *Reconstrucción económica para la democracia*, 4th ed. (Santiago: Editorial Aconcagua, 1984), pp. 15–94; also Foxley, "Cinco lecciones de la crisis actual," *Colección CIEPLAN*, No. 8 (July 1982), pp. 161–71, and Ricardo Ffrench-Davis, "El experimento monetarista en Chile: una síntesis crítica," *Colección Estudios CIEPLAN*, No. 9 (December 1982), pp. 5–40, are exhaustive critiques of the Chicago Boys' policy.
33. José Piñera, "Chile," in *The Political Economy of Policy Reform*, ed. John Williamson (Washington, DC: Institute of International Economics, 1994), pp. 225–31.
34. Matt Moffett, "Mexico Might Learn from Fall of the Peso in Chile Last Decade," *Wall Street Journal* (16 January 1995), A1, A6.
35. Hachette and Lüders, *Privatization in Chile*, pp. 15–23; Hastings, "Regulatory Revenge," pp. 213–15. On credit and banking activities, consult: Foxley, "Cinco lecciones de la crisís actual," esp., p. 163.
36. Felipe Larrain B., "El comportamiento del sector público en un país altamente endeudado," in *El sector público y la crisis de la América Latina*, eds. Felipe Larrain and Marcelo Selowsky (Mexico: Fondo de Cultura Económica, 1990), pp. 150–7.
37. Moffett, "Mexico Might Learn."
38. Matias E. Rojas, "Many Chileans Still Lured by Statist's Siren Song," *Wall Street Journal* (27 July 1990), A6.
39. "Australia Launches Investigations of Alan Bond's Business Dealings," *Wall Street Journal* (8 September 1989).
40. Mario Marcel, "Privatización y finanzas públicas: el caso de Chile, 1985–1988," *Colección Estudios CIEPLAN*, No. 26 (June 1989), pp. 5–60, especially, p. 24 for the view that SOEs were operating with profit and hence why privatize them? Juan Foxley, "Financing Chile's Privatization Program," a Paper presented at the Second International Conference on Privatization in Latin America, Institute of the Americas, La Jolla, 14–16 April 1991. Foxley's paper is dated 9 April 1991, however. He is a brother of Alejandro Foxley, Minister of Finance in the Aylwin government, and served as chairman of CORFO. Ernesto Tironi B., "Requirements for Successful International Participation in Privatization: the Chilean Experience," a Paper presented at the Second International Conference on Privatization in Latin America, Institute of the Americas, La Jolla, 14–16 April 1991. Tironi was General Manager of CORFO. Arriaga and Graham, "Chile," p. 245.

41. Hachette and Lüders, *Privatization in Chile*, pp. 46–50.
42. José Pablo Arellano, "Elementos para el análisis de la reforma provisional chilena," *Colección Estudios CIEPLAN*, No. 6 (December 1981), pp. 5–44.
43. Patricio Arrau, "La reforma provisional chilena y su financiamiento durante la transición," *Colección Estudios CIEPLAN*, 32 (June 1991), pp. 5–44, esp., 30–1.
44. Ibid.
45. José Piñera, "Empowering Workers: the Privatization of Social Security in Chile," *Cato Journal* 15:2–3, pp. 1–10, http://www.cato.org/pubs/journal/cjl5n2-3-1.html. Piñera states on p. 2 that "There is no obligation whatsoever to invest in government or any other types of bonds." But AFP fund managers consider it prudent to invest money in government funds. Some funds hold as much as 70 percent of their portfolio in government bonds.
46. Hernán Cheyre V., *La pensión en Chile ayer y hoy: Impacto de una reforma*, 2nd ed. (Santiago: Centro de Estudios Públicos, 1991), pp. 77–97.
47. Piñera, "Empowering Workers," p. 8.
48. For the 1994 figure, consult: U.S. Department of Commerce. International Trade Administration, "Chile – New Capital Market Regs-IM940203," Market Research Reports, 26 December 1994, *National Trade Data Bank*, CD-ROM (February 1995).
49. For the 1994 figure, consult: United States Department of Commerce, International Trade Administration, "Chile - New Capital Market Regs-IM940203," Market Research Reports, Dec. 26, 1994, *National Trade Data Bank*, CD-ROM (February 1995).
50. Ibid., pp. 99–101. Hachette and Lüders, *Privatization in Chile*, pp. 52–55. Oscar Muñoz G. and Hector E. Schamis, "Las transformaciones del estado en Chile y la privatización," in *¿Adonde va América Latina?: Balance de las reforms económicas*, ed. Joaquín Vial (Santiago: CIEPLAN, 1992), p. 292. "Crecimientos sectoriales," *Estrategia*, Santiago (3 June 1994), p. 3.
51. Piñera, "Empowering Workers," pp. 3–4.
52. Stallings, *Class Conflict*, pp. 102–6. Collier and Collier, *Shaping the Political Arena*, pp. 555–65.
53. Stallings, *Class Conflict*, pp. 146–7.
54. Alan Angell, "Unions and Workers in Chile during the 1980s," in *The Struggle for Democracy in Chile, 1982–1990*, eds. Paul W. Drake and Iván Jaksic (Lincoln, NE: University of Nebraska Press, 1991), pp. 188–210, esp., 195–6.
55. Ibid.
56. Alejandro Foxley, "La política económica para la transición," in *Transición a la democracia: Marco político y económico*, ed. Oscar Muñoz G. (Santiago: CIEPLAN, 1994), pp. 101–19. Edgardo Boeninger, "El marco político general e el marco institucional del próximo gobierno," in ibid. pp. 43–67, esp., 43–59, 66–7. Also his speech at Public Policy Forum, Institute of the Americas, La Jolla, 3 March 1994. Boeninger made it clear that for Chile, "capitalism versus socialism" is not an option; rather, "democracy and drive toward market economy" are the country's legitimate alternatives. Boeninger served as Aylwin's minister of the interior and minister of the presidency. He was credited with organizing civil opposition to the military regime. "The End of the Pinochet Era: Chile's Transition to Democracy," an interview with Genaro Arriagada Herrera, *Harvard International Review* (Spring 1990), pp. 19–20, 54. Arriagada was vice-president of the Christian Democratic Party.

57. Manuel Feliu, *Los desfíos de la empresa moderna: la batalla del capital humano* (Santiago: Editorial Renacimiento, 1994), p. 8.
58. Joaquín Vial, Andrea Butelmann, and Carmen Celedon, "Fundamentos de las políticas macroeconómicas del gobierno democrático chileno," *Colección Estudios CIEPLAN*, No. 30 (December 1990), pp. 55–89, esp., 56.
59. Ibid, pp. 56–8, 69–71, 76–82.
60. Perry Ball, "Mining in Chile: 1991," Working Paper No. 3, Latin American Center for Minerals & Energy Development, Colorado School of Mines (April 1991). For the tax rates, consult: United States Department of Commerce, International Trade Administration, "International Business Practices: Region 1: North and South America: Chile," 30 November 1993, *National Trade Data Bank*, CD-ROM. For the 1993 mining investment figure, consult: United States Department of Commerce, International Trade Administration, "Chile – U.S. Investment," 1 March 1994; "Chile – U.S. Investment," 29 June 1994; and "Chile – Economic, Science News," 24 April 1994, all in Market Research Report, *National Trade Data Bank*.
61. United States Department of Commerce, International Trade Administration, "Chile – February Economic Round-Up," 27 September 1994, Market Research Report, *National Trade Data Bank*.
62. Vial, Butelmann, and Celedon, "Fundamentos," p. 70, Table 3. For the figures of the 1990s, United States Department of Commerce, International Trade Administration.
63. United States Department of Commerce, International Trade Administration, "Farmed Salmon Production – IMI940511" and "Chile's Farmed Salmon Production – IMI954012," Market Research Reports, 27 April 1995, *National Trade Data Bank* (May 1995). Interview with the deputy manager of exports, CAP, Santiago, 18 August 1994. United States Department of Commerce, International Trade Administration, "Chile – Forestry Industry Trends – IMI94629," Market Research Reports, 29 June 1994, *National Trade Data Bank* (July 1994).
64. United States Department of Commerce, International Trade Administration, "Argentina – Investment by Chile – IM950212," Market Research Reports, *National Trade Data Bank*, CD-ROM (September 1995).
65. United States Department of Commerce, International Trade Administration, "Chile – Investment in Mexico – IM950119," Market Research Reports, *National Trade Data Bank*, CD-ROM (September 1995).
66. "Perú será miembro de APEC a partir de 1998," *Gestión* (26 November 1996), 1, 18.
67. William Waack, "Não sou o Eduardito," Interview with Eduardo Frei, *Veja* (16 March 1994), pp. 7–9, esp., 8.
68. Ibid.
69. Joseph Collins and John Lear, *Chile's Free-Market Miracle: a Second Look* (Oakland, CA: Food First Book, 1995), pp. 7–9. The book espoused a decidedly leftist perspective. As such, some of the data and interpretation in the book are either out of date or too excessive in logic.
70. United States Department of Commerce, International Trade Administration, "Chile – Shipping Company Privatization – IMI941028," Market Research Reports, 26 December 1994, *National Trade Data Bank*, CD-ROM (February 1995).

71. Boeninger, "The Chilean Political Transition to Democracy."
72. "Pinochet Delays Departure in Defiance of Campaign against His Senatorial Post," *Latin American Weekly Report* (20 January 1998), p. 25.
73. "The Military and Past Rights Abuses: a Problem Which Refuses to Go Away," *Latin American Weekly Report* (27 January 1998), p. 37.
74. "Chile Reacts by Adjusting Dollar Rate, Easing Capital Inflows & Cutting Outlays," *Latin American Weekly Report* (30 June 1998), p. 289.
75. Arturo Valenzuela, "Judging the General: Pinochet's Past and Chile's Future," *Current History* (March 1999), pp. 99–104.
76. Ibid., p. 101.
77. Felipe Aguero, "Chile's Lingering Authoritarian Legacy," *Current History* (February 1998), pp. 66–70.
78. Valenzuela, "Judging the General," p. 102.
79. "Is the Era of Consensus about to Close?" *Latin American Weekly Report* (7 April 1998), pp. 162–3.
80. "Mercosur Maintains United Front despite Row over Chile's Free Trade Talks with US," *Latin American Regional Reports: Southern Cone Report* (19 December 2000), p. 1.
81. Eduardo Gallardo, "Chile's Center-Left Keeps Control," *Washington Post* (17 December 2001), www.washingtonpost.com/wp-dyn/articles/A53036-2001Dec17.html.

Conclusion: Will the Past Overtake the Future in Latin America?

1. Strange, *Retreat of the State*, pp. 3–12. Hirst and Thompson, *Globalization in Question*, pp. 190–4. Reich, *Work of Nations*, pp. 301–15. Benjamin R. Barber, *Jihad vs. McWorld: How Globalism and Tribalism Are Reshaping the World* (New York: Ballentine Books, 1995), p. 39.
2. Daniel Yergin and Joseph Stanislaw, *The Commanding Heights: the Battle between Government and the Marketplace That Is Remaking the Modern World* (New York: Simon & Schuster, 1998), pp. 43–4.
3. Joachim Bamrud, "Summit of the Americas: a Historic Free-Trade Boost?" *U.S. Latin Trade* (December 1994), pp. 28–34. Nora Lustig, Barry P. Bosworth, and Robert Z. Lawrence, eds., *North American Free Trade: Assessing the Impact* (Washington, DC: The Brookings Institution, 1992).
4. Jeffrey A. Frankel, *Regional Trading Blocs in the World Economic System* (Washington, DC: Institute for International Economics, 1997), pp. 248–80, is a concise history of regional trade blocs of the world. Yoichi Funabashi, *Asia Pacific Fusion: Japan's Role in APEC* (Washington, DC: Institute for International Economics, 1995). Gary Clyde Hufbauer and Jeffrey J. Schott, *Western Hemisphere Economic Integration* (Washington, DC: Institute for International Economics, 1994).
5. Jens Bartelson, *A Genealogy of Sovereignty* (Cambridge, England: Cambridge University Press, 1995).
6. Fareed Zakaria, *From Wealth to Power: the Unusual Origins of America's World Role* (Princeton: Princeton University Press, 1998), pp. 4–5, 8–12.

7. "The Bottom Line," *AsiaWeek* (3 July 1998), p. 72. PPP stands for purchasing power parity.
8. UNDP, *Human Development Report 1997* (New York: Oxford University Press, 1997), pp. 208–9. World Bank, *1998 World Development Indicators*, pp. 72–86.
9. World Bank, *East Asian Miracle*, ch. 1. Chris Gay, "A Life of Its Own," *Far Eastern Economic Review* (27 March 1997), pp. 54–60. Edwards, "Why Are Latin America's Saving Rates So Low?"
10. World Bank, *World Development Report 1991*, pp. 3, 28–9.
11. Luiz Carlos Bresser Pereira, "Economic Reforms and Economic Growth: Efficiency and Politics in Latin America," in *Economic Reforms in New Democracies: a Social-Democratic Approach*, eds. Luis Carlos Bresser Pereira, José Maria Maravall, and Adam Przeworski (New York: Cambridge University Press, 1993), pp. 15–76, esp., 15–16.
12. Ken Warn, "The Rise and Fall of Yarbán," *Latin Trade* (August 1998), pp. 26–7.
13. Castañeda, *Utopia Unarmed*, pp. 42–50.
14. Robert Barro, *Determinants of Economic Growth: a Cross-Country Empirical Study* (Cambridge, MA: The MIT Press, 1997), pp. xi–xii, 49–52.
15. Ibid., pp. 52–61.
16. Silvio Borner, Aymo Brunetti, and Beatrice Weder, *Political Credibility and Economic Development* (London: St. Martin's Press, 1995), pp. 37–9.
17. Paul Craig Roberts and Karen LaFollette Araujo, *The Capitalist Revolution in Latin America* (New York: Oxford University Press, 1997), p. 47.
18. Lucian W. Pye, *Asian Power and Politics: the Cultural Dimensions of Authority* (Cambridge, MA: The Belknap Press, 1985), pp. 329–34.
19. Stephan Haggard and Robert R. Kaufman, *The Political Economy of Democratic Transitions* (Princeton: Princeton University Press, 1995), pp. 4–8, 25–44.
20. Douglas A. Chalmers, Maria do Carmo Campello de Souza, and Atilio A. Boron, "Introduction: the Right and Latin American Democracy," in *The Right and Democracy in Latin America*, eds. Douglas A. Chalmers, Maria do Carmo Campello de Souza, and Atilio A. Boron (New York: Praeger, 1992), pp. 1–9, esp., 1–2.
21. Adam Schwarz, "Bigger Is Better," *Far Eastern Economic Review* (20 June 1998), pp. 3–6.
22. "Meet the Global Factory," a survey of manufacturing, *The Economist* (20 June 1998), pp. 3–18, esp. 3–6. Yahya Sadowski, "Ethnic Conflict," *Foreign Policy* (Summer 1998), p. 19.
23. Sachs, "International Economics."
24. "Meet the Global Factory."
25. Nancy Birdsall, "Life Is Unfair: Inequality in the World," *Foreign Policy* (Summer 1998), pp. 76–91.
26. World Bank, *World Development Report 1997*, pp. 222-3.
27. United Nations Conference on Trade and Development, *Trade and Development Report, 1997: Globalization, Distribution and Growth* (New York: 1998), p. 109.
28. Philip F. Kelly and Kris Olds, "Questions in a Crisis: the Contested Meanings of Globalisation in the Asia-Pacific," in *Globalisation and the Asia-Pacific: Contested Territories*, eds. Kris Olds, Peter Dicken, Philip F. Kelly, Lily Kong, and Henry Wai-chung Yeung (London and New York: Routledge, 1999), pp. 1–15, esp., 1.

29. Of the globalization critics, there are several schools: the old socialist-Marxist, environmentalist-ecologists, and opponents of multinational corporations. The following items are worth reading: Henry Veltmeyer and James F. Petras, *The Dynamics of Social Change in Latin America* (London and New York: Palgrave, 2000); Diana Tussie, ed., *The Environment and International Trade Negotiations: Developing Country Stakes* (London and New York: Palgrave, 1999); James H. Mittelman and Mustapha Kamal Pasha, *Out from Underdevelopment Revisited: Changing Global Structures and the Remaking of the Third World* (London and New York: Palgrave, 1996); Robert Gilpin, *The Challenge of Global Capitalism: the World Economy in the 21st Century* (Princeton: Princeton University Press, 2001); Madhu Agrawal, *Global Competitiveness in the Pharmaceutical Industry: the Effect of National Regulatory, Economic, and Market Factors* (London: Haworth Press, 1999); and finally, Thomas J. Biersteker, *Financial Globalization and Democracy in Emerging Markets* (London and New York: Palgrave, 1999).

30. Hugo Chavez of Venezuela and Mohamad Mahathir of Malaysia have been the lightning rods of their respective region's antiglobalization rhetoric.

31. "UMNO General Assembly: We are responsible to the Malays," *The Straits Times* (Singapore: 13 May 2000), p. 53; Ahmad A. Talib, "PM: We'll fight tooth and nail," *New Straits Times* (Kuala Lumpur: 21 June 2000), pp. 1, 4; and "Dr. M: Abuses of globalisation destructive," *The Sun* (Kuala Lumpur: 17 June 2000), p. 2.

32. David F. DeRosa, *In Defense of Free Capital Markets: the Case against a New International Financial Architecture* (Princeton: Bloomberg Press, 2001), pp. 1–21.

33. Morris Goldstein, *The Asian Financial Crisis: Causes, Cures and Systemic Implications* (Washington, DC: Institute for International Economics, 1998), pp. 7–22. Callum Henderson, *Asia Falling: Making Sense of the Asian Crisis and Its Aftermath* (New York: BusinessWeek Books, 1998), chs. 5 and 6. Curiously, Henderson argues that the Mexican meltdown began it all.

34. Jorge G. Castañeda, *The Mexican Shock: Its Meaning for the U.S.* (New York: New Press, 1995), p. 212.

Bibliography

A. Books

Abranches, Sérgio Henrique, et al. *A empresa pública no Brasil: uma abordagem multidisciplinar.* Brasília: IPEA/SEMOR, 1980.

Adler, Emmanuel. *The Power of Ideology: the Quest for Technological Autonomy in Argentina and Brazil.* Berkeley: University of California Press, 1991.

Agrawal, Madhu. *Global Competitiveness in the Pharmaceutical Industry: the Effect of National Regulatory, Economic, and Market Factors.* London: Haworth Press, 1999.

Alexander, Robert J. *The ABC Presidents: Conversations and Correspondence with the Presidents of Argentina, Brazil, and Chile.* New York: Praeger Publishers, 1992.

——. *Juscelino Kubitschek and the Development of Brazil.* Athens, OH: Ohio University Press, 1991.

——. *Brazil: Industrial Policies and Manufactured Exports.* Washington, DC: The Brookings Institution, 1983.

Alves, Maria Helena Moreira. *State and Opposition in Military Brazil.* Austin, TX: University of Texas Press, 1985.

Arruda, Marcos, Herbert de Souza, and Carlos Afonso. *Multinationals and Brazil: the Impact of Multinational Corporations in Contemporary Brazil.* Kitcher, Ont. Canada: Moir Press, 1975.

Assessoria de Promoções da Interbrás. *Resposta a "Os mandarins da república:" Interbrás: Ficção & relaidade.* Rio: Editora Lord, 1984.

Assis, J. Carlos de. *Os mandarins na república: Anatomia dos escândalos da administração pública: l948–84.* Rio: Paz e Terra, 1984.

Aylwin Azocar, Patricio. *La transición chilena: Discurosos escogidos. Marzo 1990–1992.* Santiago: Editorial Andrés Bello, 1992.

Balaam, David N., and Michael Veseth, eds. *Introduction to International Political Economy.* Upper Saddle River, NJ: Prentice Hall, 1996.

Balassa, Bela, and Marcus Noland, *Japan in the World Economy.* Washington, DC: Institute of International Economics, 1988.

Ball, Nicole. *Security and Economy in the Third World.* Princeton: Princeton University Press, 1988.

Barber, Benjamin R. *Jihad vs. McWorld: How Globalism and Tribalism Are Reshaping the World.* New York: Ballentine Books, 1995.

Barnet, Richard J., and Ronald E. Muller. *Global Reach: the Power of the Multinational Corporations.* New York: Simon & Schuster, 1974.

Barro, Robert. *Determinants of Economic Growth: a Cross-Country Empirical Study.* Cambridge, MA: The MIT Press, 1997.

Bartelson, Jens. *A Genealogy of Sovereignty.* Cambridge, Eng.: Cambridge University Press, 1995.

Barzelay, Michael. *The Politicized Market Economy: Alcohol in Brazil's Energy Strategy.* Berkeley: University of California Press, 1986.

Bergsten, C. Fred, Thomas Horst, and Theodore H. Moran, *American Multinationals and American Interests*. Washington, DC: The Brookings Institution, 1978.

Biersteker, Thomas J. *Financial Globalization and Democracy in Emerging Markets*. London and New York: Palgrave, 1999.

Birdsall, Nancy, and Frederick Jaspersen, eds. *Pathways to Growth: Comparing East Asia and Latin America*. Washington, DC: Inter-American Development Bank, 1997.

Boneo, Horacio, ed. *Privatización del dicho al hecho*. Buenos Aires: El Cronista Comercial, 1985.

Borner, Sylvio, Aymo Brunetti, and Beatrice Weder. *Political Credibility and Economic Development*. London: St. Martin's Press, 1995.

Boyer, Robert, and Daniel Drache, eds. *States against Markets: the Limits of Globalization*. London and New York: Routledge, 1996.

Braga, Roberto Saturno. *Política econômica e estatização (debates parlamentares)*. Rio: Civilização Brasileira, 1976.

Branch, Taylor, and Eugene M. Popper. *Labyrinth*. New York: Penguine Books, 1983.

Brecher, Jeremy, and Tim Costello. *Global Village or Global Pillage: Economic Reconstruction from the Bottom Up*. Boston: South End Press, 1994.

Brennan, James P. *The Labor Wars in Córdoba 1995–1976: Ideology. Work. Labor Politics in an Argentine Industrial City*. Cambridge, MA: Harvard University Press, 1994.

Bryan, Lowell, and Diana Farrell. *Market Unbound: Unleashing Global Capitalism*. New York: John Wiley & Sons, 1996.

Burtless, Gary, Robert Z. Lawrence, Robet E. Litan, and Robert J. Shapiro. *Globaphobia: Confronting Fears about Open Trade*. Washington, DC: The Brookings Institution, 1998.

Campos, Roberto. *Reflexões do crepúsculo*. Rio: Topbooks Editora, 1991.

——. *Além do cotidiano*. 2nd ed. Rio: Record, 1985.

Cardoso, Fernando Henrique. *Autoritarismo e democratização*. Rio: Paz e Terra, 1978.

——. *O modelo político brasileiro e outros ensaios*, 2nd ed. São Paulo: DIFEL, 1973.

——. *Análises do modelo brasileiro*. Rio: Paz e Terra, 1972.

——. *O model brasileiro*. São Paulo: DIFEL, 1972.

——. *Política e desenvolvimento em sociedades dependentes*. Rio: Zahar Editores, 1971.

Carnoy, Martin. *The State & Political Theory*. Princeton: Princeton University Press, 1984.

——, Manuel Castells, Stephen S. Cohen, and Fernando Henrique Cardoso. *The New Global Economy in the Information Age: Reflections on Our Changing World*. University Park, PA: The Pennsylvania State University Press, 1993.

Carvalho, Getúlio. *Petrobrás: Do monopólio aos contratos de risco*. Rio: FU, 1976.

Castañeda, Jorge G. *The Mexican Shock: Its Meaning for the U.S.* Trans. Maria Castañeda. New York: New Press 1995.

——. *Utopia Unarmed: the Latin American Left after the Cold War*. New York: Alfred A. Knopf, 1993.

Castells, Manuel. *The Rise of Network Society*. Vol. 1: *The Information Age: Economy, Society and Culture*. Malden, MA: Blackwell, 1996.

Castro, Paulo Rabello de, et al. *A crise do "Bom Patrão."* Rio: CEDES/APEC, 1983.

Centro de Estudios Públicos. *"El Ladrillo": Bases de la politica económica del gobierno military chileno.* Santiago: CEP, 1992.

Cerruti, Gabriela. *El jefe: Vida y obra de Carlos Saul Menem.* Buenos Aires: Planeta, 1993.

——, and Sergio Ciancaglini. *El octavo círculo: Crónica y entretelones de la Argentina menemista.* Buenos Aires: Planeta, 1991.

Chalmers, Douglas A., Maria do Carmo Campello de Souza, and Atilio A. Boron, eds. *The Right and Democracy in Latin America.* New York: Praeger, 1992.

Cheyre V., Hernán. *La pensión en Chile ayer y hoy: Impacto de una reforma.* 2nd ed. Santiago: Centro Estudios Públicos, 1991.

Clark, A. Kim. *The Redemptive Work: Railway and Nation in Ecuador, 1895–1930.* Wilmington, DE: Scholarly Research Books, 1998.

Cline, William R. *International Debt Reexamined.* Washington, DC: Institute for International Economics, 1995.

Cohen, Daniel. *The Wealth of the World and the Poverty of Nations.* Cambridge, MA: MIT Press, 1998.

Collier, David, ed. *The New Authoritarianism in Latin America.* Princeton: Princeton University Press, 1979.

Collier, Ruth Berins, and David Collier. *Shaping the Political Arena: Critical Junctures, the Labor Movement, and Regime Dynamics in Latin America.* Princeton: Princeton University Press, 1991.

Collins, Joseph, and John Lear. *Chile's Free-Market Miracle: a Second Look.* Oakland, CA: Food First Book, 1995.

Congdon, Tim. *The Debt Threat.* Oxford, Eng.: Oxford University Press, 1988.

Constable, Pamela, and Arturo Valenzuela. *A Nation of Enemies: Chile under Pinochet.* New York: W. W. Norton, 1991.

Covre, Maria de Lourdes M. *A fala dos homens: Análise do pensamento tecnocrático 1964–1981.* São Paulo: Editora Brasiliense, 1983.

Cuevas Farren, Gustavo. *Renovación ideológica en Chile: los partidos y su nueva visión estratégica.* Santiago: Universidad de Chile, 1993.

Curia, Eduardo Luis. *Dos años de la economía de Menem: una etapa de transformaciones.* Buenos Aires: El Cronista. 1991.

Cusack, David F. *Revolution and Reaction: the Internal Dynamics of Conflict and Confrontation in Chile.* Denver: DU Graduate School of International Studies, 1977.

D'Araújo, Maria Celina, and Celso Castro, orgs. *Ernesto Geisel.* 2nd ed. Rio: Fundação Getúlio Vargas, 1997.

Davata, Alejandro, and Luis Lorenzano. *Argentina: the Malvinas and the End of the Military Rule.* Trans. Ralph Johnston. London: Verso, 1983.

De la Balze, Felipe A.M. *Remaking the Argentine Economy.* New York: Council on Foreign Relations, 1995.

Deane, Marjorie, and Robert Pringle. *The Central Banks.* New York: Viking, 1995.

Delano, Manuel, and Hugo Translaviña. *La herencia de los Chicago Boys.* Santiago: Ornitorrinco, 1989.

Delfim Neto, Antônio. *Delfim: "Não olhe só a dívida: Veja o que ela representa: Itaipu, Tucuruí, o programa siderúrgico, os metrôs, Caraíba, a petroquímica, Tubarão ..."* Brasília: Secretaria de Planejamento, 1983.

——. *Análise da política econômica nacional.* Brasília: SEPLAN, 1980.

DeRosa, David F. *In Defense of Free Capital Markets: the Case against a New International Financial Architecture*. Princeton: Bloomberg Press, 2001.

Di Tella, Guido, and Carlos Rodriguez Braun. *Argentina, 1946–83: the Economic Ministers Speak*. New York: St. Martin's Press, 1990.

Dicken, Peter. *Global Shift: Transforming the World Economy*. New York: The Guilford Press, 1998.

Dobson, Christopher, John Miller, and Ronald Payne. *The Falklands Conflict*. London: Coronet Books, 1982.

Dominguez, Jorge I., ed. *Technopols: Freeing Politics and Markets in Latin America in the 1990s*. University Park, PA: The Pennsylvania State University Press, 1996.

Drake, Paul W. *Labor Movements and Dictatorships: the Southern Cone in Comparative Perspective*. Baltimore, MD: The Johns Hopkins University Press, 1996.

——, and Iván Jaksic, eds. *The Struggle for Democracy in Chile 1982–1990*. Lincoln, NE: University of Nebraska Press, 1991.

Dreifus, René Armand. *A internacional capitalista: Estratégias e táticas do empresario transnacional 1918–1986*. Rio: Espaço e Tempo, 1987.

——. *1964: a conquista do estado: Ação política, poder e golpe de classe*. Petrópolis: Vozes, 1981.

Droyer, Robert, and Daniel Drache, eds. *States against Markets: the Limits of Globalization*. London and New York: Routledge, 1996.

Editora Abril. *Exame: Melhores e Maiores: As 500 maiores empresas do Brasil 1998*. São Paulo: Exame, 1998.

Erro, Davide G. *Resolving the Argentine Paradox: Politics and Development, 1966–1992*. Boulder, CO: Lynne Rienner Publishers, 1993.

Evans, Peter. *Dependent Development: the Alliance of Multinational, State, and Local Capital in Brazil*. Princeton: Princeton University Press, 1979.

Falcão, Armando. *Tudo a declarar*. Rio: Editora Nova Fronteira, 1989.

Fawcett, Louise, and Andre Hurell, eds. *Regionalism in World Politics: Regional Organizations and International Order*. New York: Oxford University Press, 1995.

Feliu, Manuel. *Los desfios de la empresa moderna: la batalla del capital humano*. Santiago: Editorial Renacimiento, 1994.

FIEL [Argentina]. *Los costos del estado regulador*. Buenos Aires: FIEL, 1989.

——. *Regulaciones y estancamiento: e1 caso argentino*. Buenos Aires: FIEL, 1988.

——. *El fracaso del estatismo: una propuesta para la reforma del sector público, argentino*. Buenos Aires: Sudamericana-Planeta. 1987.

FIESP [Brasil]. *Livre para crescer: Proposta para um Brasil moderno*. São Paulo: FIESP, 1990.

Fleet, Michael. *The Rise and Fall of Chilean Christian Democracy*. Princeton: Princeton University Press, 1985.

Fontana Aldunate, Arturo. *Los economistas y el presidente Pinochet*. Santiago: Zig-Zag, 1988.

Foster, Harry F. *If You Go to South America*. New York: Dodd, Mead & Company, 1928.

Fox, Robert. *Eyewitness Falklands: a Personal Account of the Falklands Campaign*. London: Methuen, 1982.

Foxley, Alejandro: *Latin American Experiments in Neo-Conservative Economics*. Berkeley: University of California Press, 1983.

Franco, Gustavo H. B. *O Plano Real e outros ensaios*. Rio: Francisco Alves, 1995.

Frank, Andre Gunder. *Re-Orient: Global Economy in the Asian Age*. Berkeley: University of California Press, 1998.

——. *Critique and Anti-Critique: Essays on Dependence and Reformism*. New York: Praeger, 1984.

——. *Capitalism and Underdevelopment in Latin America: Historical Studies of Chile and Brazil*. New York: Monthly Review, 1967.

Frankel, Jeffrey A. *Regional Trading Blocs in the World Economic System*. Washington, DC: Institute for International Economics, 1997.

Freiden, Jeffrey A. *Debt, Development, & Democracy: Modern Political Economy and Latin America, 1965–1985*. Princeton: Princeton University Press, 1991.

——. *Banking on the World: the Politics of American International Finance*. New York: Basil Blackwell, 1989.

Friedman, Thomas L. *The Lexus and the Olive Tree*. New York: Farr, Straus and Giroux, 1999.

Funabashi, Yoichi. *Asia Pacific Fusion: Japan's Role in APEC*. Washington, DC: Institute for International Economics, 1995.

Furtado, Celso. *Os ares do mundo*. Rio: Paz e Terra, 1991.

——. *A fantasia organizada*. Rio: Paz e Terra, 1985.

Galasso, Norberto. *Gatos y sardinas en la economía argentina: De Martinez de Hoz a Cavallo*. Buenos Aires: Editorial Fraterna, 1992.

Garcia, Alexandre. *Nos bastidores das notícias*. 5th ed. Rio: Editora Globo, 1990.

Garretón, Manuel Antonio. *The Chilean Political Process*. Winchester, MA: Unwin Hyman, 1989.

Gerschenkron, Alexander. *Economic Backwardness in Historical Perspective*. New York: Frederick A. Praeger, 1962.

Gil, Federico. *The Political System of Chile*. Boston: Houghton Mifflin, 1966.

Gilpin, Robert. *The Challenge of Global Capitalism: the World Economy in the 21st Century*. Princeton: Princeton University Press, 2001.

Giussani, Pablo. *¿Por qué, doctor Alfonsín?* Buenos Aires: Sudamericana-Planeta, 1987.

Goldstein, Morris. *The Asian Financial Crisis: Causes, Cures and Systemic Implications*. Washington, DC: Institute for International Economics, 1998.

Gonçalves, Reinaldo. *Globalização e desnacionalização*. São Paulo: Paz e Terra, 1999.

Granovsky, Martín. *Misión cumplida: la presión norteamericana sobre la Argentina de Braden a Todman*. Buenos Aires: Planeta Espejo de la Argentina, 1992.

Greider, William. *One World, Ready or Not: the Manic Logic of Global Capitalism*. New York: Simon & Schuster, 1997.

Grimwade, Nigel. *International Trade: New Patterns of Trade, Production and Investment*. New York: Routledge, 1989.

Guéhenno, Jean-Marie. *The End of the Nation State*. Minneapolis: University of Minnesota Press, 1995.

Hachette, Dominique, and Rolf Lüders. *Privatization in Chile: an Economic Appraisal*. San Francisco: ICS Press, 1993.

Haggard, Stephan. *Pathways from the Periphery: the Politics of Growth in the Newly Industrializing Countries*. Ithaca, NY: Cornell University Press, 1990.

——, and Robert Kaufman. *The Political Economy of Democratic Transitions*. Princeton: Princeton University Press, 1995.

Harris, Nigel. *The End of the Third World: Newly Industrializing Countries and the Decline of an Ideology*. New York: Penguin Books, 1990.

Hastings, Max, and Simon Jenkins. *The Battle for the Falklands.* London: Michael Joseph Publishers, 1983.

Hausman, Ricardo, and Liliana Rojas-Suárez, eds. *Volatile Capital Flows: Taming Their Impact on Latin America.* Washington, DC: Inter-American Development Bank, 1996.

Held, David. *Democracy and the Global Order: From the Modern State to Cosmopolitan Governance.* Stanford: Stanford University Press, 1996.

———, Anthony McGrew, David Goldblatt, and Jonathan Perraton. *Global Transformation: Politics, Economics and Culture.* Stanford: Stanford University Press, 1999.

Henderson, Cullum. *Asia Falling: Making Sense of the Asian Crisis and Its Aftermath.* New York: Business Week Books, 1998.

Hilton, Stanley E. *Hitler's Secret War in South America, 1939–1945: German Military Espionage and Allied Counter-Espionage in Brazil.* Baton Rouge, LA: Louisiana State University Press, 1981.

Hirsch, Seymour. *The Price of Power: Kissinger in the Nixon White House.* New York: Summit Books, 1983.

Hirschman, Albert O. *Journeys toward Progress: Studies of Economic Policy-Making in Latin America.* New York: The Twentieth Century Fund, 1963.

Hirst, Paul, and Grahame Thompson. *Globalization in Question: the International Economy of the Possibilities of Governance.* Cambridge, UK: Polity Press, 1996.

Hodges, Donald C. *Argentina's "Dirty War": an Intellectual Biography.* Austin, TX: University of Texas Press, 1991.

———. *Argentina, 1943–1987: the National Revolution and Resistance.* Rev. ed. Albuquerque, NM: University of New Mexico Press, 1988.

Hufbauer, Gary Clyde, and Jeffrey J. Schott. *Western Hemisphere Economic Integration.* Washington, DC: Institute for International Economics, 1994.

II, Sakong. *Korea in the World Economy.* Washington, DC: Institute for International Economics, 1992.

Israel Z., Ricardo. *Politics and Ideology in Allende's Chile.* Tempe, AZ: Center for Latin American Studies, Arizona State University, 1989.

Johnson, John J. *Political Change in Latin America: the Emergence of the Middle Sector.* Stanford: Stanford University Press, 1958.

Julius, DeAnne. *Global Companies & Public Policy: the Growing Challenge of Foreign Direct Investment.* New York: Council on Foreign Relations, 1990.

Kenen, Peter B., ed. *Managing the World Economy: Fifty Years after Bretton Woods.* Washington, DC: Institute for International Economics, 1994.

Kennedy, Paul. *The Rise and Fall of the Great Powers: Economic Change and Military Conflicts from 1500 to 2000.* New York: Random House, 1987.

Krugman, Paul. *The Return of Depression Economics.* New York: W. W. Norton, 1999.

Kucinski, Bernado, coord. *Petróleo: Contratos de risco e dependência.* São Paulo: Brasiliense, 1977.

Kuttner, Robert. *The End of Laissez-Faire: National Purpose and the Global Economy after the Cold War.* Philadelphia, PA: University of Pennsylvania Press, 1991.

Larrain, Felipe, and Marcelo Selowisky, eds. *El sector político y la crisis de la América Latina.* Mexico: El Trimestre Economico, 1990.

Lavin, Joaquín. *Miguel Kast: Pasión de viver.* 6th ed. Santiago: Zig-Zag, 1988.

Leuco, Alfredo, and José Díaz. *El herdero de Perón, entre dios e el diablo.* Buenos Aires: Planeta, 1989.

Lewis, Paul H. *The Crisis of Argentine Capitalism*. Chapel Hill, NC: University of North Carolina Press, 1992.

List, Friedrich. *The National System of Political Economy*. Trans. Sampson S. Lloyd. Fairfield, NJ: August M. Kelley Publishers, 1991.

Luedde-Neurath, Richard. *Import Controls and Export-Oriented Development: a Reassessment of the South Korean Case*. Boulder, CO: Westview Press, 1986.

Lustig, Nora, Barry P. Bosworth, and Robert Z. Lawrence, eds. *North American Free Trade: Assessing the Impact*. Washington, DC: The Brookings Institution, 1992.

Lyons, Gene M., and Michael Mastanduno, eds. *Beyond Westphalia? State Sovereignty and International Intervention*. Baltimore, MD, and London: The Johns Hopkins University Press, 1995.

Majul, Luis. *Por qué cayó Alfonsín: el nuevo terrorismo económico: los personajes, las conexiones, las claves secretas*. Buenos Aires: Editorial Sudamericana, 1990.

Mammana, Claúdio, org. *Informática e a Nova República*. São Paulo: HUCITEC, 1985.

Mander, Jerry, and Edward Goldsmith, eds. *The Case against the Global Economy and for a Turn toward the Local*. San Francisco: Sierra Club, 1996.

Manzetti, Luigi. *The International Monetary Fund and Economic Stabilization: the Argentine Case*. New York: Preager, 1991.

Martner, Gonzalo. *El gobierno del presidente Salvador Allende 1970–1973: una evaluación*. Concepción, Chile: Editora Lar, 1988.

Melman, Seymour. *The Permanent War Economy: American Capitalism in Decline*. New York: A Touchstone Book, 1985.

Menem, Carlos, and Eduardo Duhalde. *La revolución productiva*. Buenos Aires: Peña Nilo Editora, 1989.

Miranda, Maria Augusta Tibiriçá. *O petróleo é nosso: a luta contra o "entreguismo" pelo monopólio estatal*. Petrópolis: Vozes, 1981.

Mittelman, James H., and Mustapha Kamal Pasha. *Out from Underdevelopment Revisited: Changing Global Structures and the Remaking of the Third World*. London and New York: Palgrave, 1996.

Moffitt, Michael. *The World's Money: International Banking from Bretton Woods to the Brink of Insolvency*. New York: Simon & Schuster, 1983.

Moran, Theodore H. *Multinational Corporations and the Politics of Dependence: Copper in Chile*. Princeton: Princeton University Press, 1974.

Mortada, Nelson. *Estatais: Menores gastos, maior produtividade*. Brasília: Secretaria de Planejamento, 1984.

Munck, Ronaldo. *Argentina: From Anarchism to Peronism*. London: Zed Press, 1987.

N'haux, Enrique. *Menem-Cavallo: el poder mediterraneo*. Buenos Aires: Ediciones Corregidor, 1993.

Norden, Deborah L. *Military Rebellion in Argentina: Between Coups and Consolidation*. Lincoln, NE, and London: University of Nebraska Press, 1996.

Nunn, Frederick M. *The Military in Chilean History: Essays on Civil-Military Relations, 1810–1973*. Albuquerque, NM: University of New Mexico Press, 1976.

O'Donnell, Guillermo. *Bureaucratic-Authoritarianism: Argentina 1966–1973 in Comparative Perspective*. Berkeley: University of California Press, 1988.

——. *Modernization and Bureaucratic-Authoritarianism: Studies in South American Politics*. Berkeley: University of California Institute of International Studies, 1973.

Ohmae, Kenichi. *The End of the Nation State: How New Engines of Prosperity Are Reshaping Global Markets*. New York: The Free Press, 1995.

——, ed. *The Evolving Global Economy: Making Sense of the New World Order.* Cambridge, MA: Havard Business School Press, 1995.

Ostiguy, Pierre. *Los capitanes de la industria: Grandes empresarios, política y economía en la Argentina de los años 80.* Buenos Aires: Editorial Legasa, 1990.

Page, Joseph. *Perón: a Biography.* New York: Random House, 1983.

Passarinho, Jarbas. *Um hídrido fértil.* 3rd. ed. Rio: Expressão e Cultura, 1996.

Pastore, José Dagnino. *Crónicas económicas: Argentina, 1969–1988.* Buenos Aires: Editorial Crespillo, 1989.

Penna, João Camillo. *A dívida externa e o comércio internacional.* Brasília: SEPLAN, 1984.

Peralta-Ramos, Monica, and Carlos H. Waisman, eds. *From Military Rule to Liberal Democracy in Argentina.* Boulder, CO: Westview Press, 1987.

Perdia, Roberto Cirilo, and Fernando Vaca Narvaja. *Plano Austral: Nova estratégia do FMI.* Trans. Maria Isabel Ekhvanossafa. Porto Alegre: Editora Tschê, 1986.

Petras, James F. *Politics and Social Forces in Chilean Development.* Berkeley: University of California Press, 1972.

——, and Hugo Zemelman Merino. *Peasant in Revolt: a Chilean Case Study 1965–1971.* Trans. Thomas Flory. Austin, TX: University of Texas Press, 1972.

Pion-Berlin, David. *Through Corridors of Power: Institutions and Civil-Military Relations in Argentina.* University Park, PA: The Pennsylvania State University Press, 1997.

Polanyi, Karl. *The Great Transformation: the Political and Economic Origin of Our Time.* Boston: Beacon Press, 1957 [1944].

Prestowitz, Jr., Clyde V. *Trading Places: How We Are Giving Our Future to Japan and How to Reclaim It.* New York: Basic Books, 1988.

Price, David. *Before the Bulldozer: the Nambiquara Indians and the World Bank.* New York: Seven Locks Press, 1989.

Price Waterhouse. *Doing Business in Argentina.* Buenos Aires: Price Waterhouse, May 1992 [diskette].

Przeworski, Adam. *Democracy and the Market: Political and Economic Reforms in Eastern Europe and Latin America.* New York: Harper Collins, 1991.

——, et al. *Sustainable Democracy.* New York: Cambridge University Press, 1995.

Purcell, Susan Kaufman, and Riordan Roett, eds. *Brazil under Cardoso.* Boulder, CO: Lynn Rienner Publishers, 1997).

Pye, Lucian W. *Asian Power and Politics: the Cultural Dimensions of Authority.* Cambridge, MA: The Belknap Press, 1985.

Ranelagh, John. *The Agency: the Rise and Decline of the CIA.* New York: Simon & Schuster, 1987.

Rattner, Henrique. *Informática e sociedade.* São Paulo: Editora Brasiliense, 1985.

Redrado, Martín. *Tiempo de desafío.* Buenos Aires: Planeta, 1994.

Rêgo, Antônio Carlos Pojo do, and João Paulo M. Peixoto. *A política econômica das reformas administrativas no Brasil.* Rio: Expressão e Cultura, 1998.

Reich, Robert B. *The Works of Nations: Preparing Ourselves for 21st-Century Capitalism.* New York: Vintage Books, 1991.

Ribeiro, Gustavo Lins. *Transnational Capitalism and Hydropolitics in Argentina: the Yacyretá High Dam.* Gainesville, FL: The University Press of Florida, 1994.

Roberts, Paulo Craig, and Karen LaFollette Araujo. *The Capitalist Revolution in Latin America.* New York: Oxford University Press, 1997.

Rock, David. *Authoritarian Argentina: the Nationalist Movement, Its History and Its Impact.* Berkeley: University of California Press, 1995.

——. *Argentina 1516–1987: From Spanish Colonization to Alfonsín.* Berkeley: University of California Press, 1987.

Rodriguez, Octavio. *Teoria do subdesenvolvimento da Cepal.* Rio: Forense-Universitário, 1981.

Rodrik, Dani. *Has Globalization Gone Too Far?* Washington, DC: Institute for International Economics, 1997.

Roquié, Alain. *The Military and the State in Latin America.* Trans. Paul E. Sigmund. Berkeley: University of California Press, 1987.

Rosenau, James, and Ernst-Otto Czempiel, eds., *Governance without Government: Order and Change in World Politics.* New York: Cambridge University Press, 1992.

Rozas, Patricio. *Inversión estranjera y empresas transnacionales en la economia de Chile (1974–1989): Práctica de inversión y estrategia de las empresas transnacionals.* Santiago: CEPAL, 1992.

Sakong, Il. *Korea in the World Economy.* Washington, DC: Institute of International Economics, 1992.

Schott, Jeffrey J. *Western Hemisphere Economic Integration.* Washington, DC: Institute for International Economics, 1994.

Schvarzer, Jorge. *Bunge & Born: Crecimiento y diversificación de un grupo económico.* Buenos Aires: CISEA, 1989.

Schwartz, Herman M. *States versus Markets: History, Geography, and the Development of the International Political Economy.* New York: St. Martin's Press, 1994.

Shapley, Deborah. *Promise and Power: the Life and Times of Robert McNamara.* Boston: Little Brown, 1993.

Sigmund, Paul E. *The Overthrow of Allende and the Politics of Chile, 1964–1976.* Pittsburgh: University of Pittsburgh Press, 1977.

Silva, Cláudio Humberto Rosa e. *Mil dias de solidão: Collar bateu e levou.* São Paulo: Geração Editora, 1993.

Skidmore, Thomas E. *The Politics of Military Rule in Brazil, 1964–85.* New York: Oxford University Press, 1988.

——. *Politics in Brazil 1930–1964: an Experiment in Democracy.* New York: Oxford University Press, 1967.

Smith, William C. *Authoritarianism and the Crisis of the Argentine Political Economy.* Stanford: Stanford University Press, 1991.

Solomon, Steve. *The Confidence Game: How Unelected Central Bankers Are Governing the Changed World Economy.* New York: Simon & Schuster, 1995.

Soros, George. *The Crisis of Global Capitalism (Open Society Endangered).* New York: Public Affairs, 1999.

Spruyt, Hendrik. *The Sovereign State and Its Competitors.* Princeton: Princeton University Press, 1994.

Stallings, Barbara. *Class Conflict and Economic Development in Chile, 1958–1973.* Stanford: Stanford University Press, 1978.

Steenland, Kyle. *Agrarian Reform under Allende: Peasant Revolt in the South.* Albuquerque, NM: University of New Mexico Press, 1977.

Stepan, Alfred. *The State and Society: Peru in Comparative Perspective.* Princeton: Princeton University Press, 1978.

——. *The Military in Politics: Changing Patterns in Brazil.* Princeton: Princeton University Press, 1971.

——, ed. *Democratizing Brazil: Problems of Transition and Consolidation*. New York: Oxford University Press, 1989.

Stopford, John, and Susan Strange, with John S. Henley. *Rival States, Rival Firms: Competition for World Market Shares*. New York: Cambridge University Press, 1992.

Strange, Susan. *The Retreat of the State: the Diffusion of Power in the World Economy*. New York: Cambridge University Press, 1996.

The Sunday Times Insight Team, *The Falklands War: the True Story* (London: Sphere Books, 1982).

Tamer, Alberto. *Petróleo: o preço da dependência. O Brasil na crise mundial*. Rio: Editora Nova Fronteira, 1980.

Tavares, Christina, and Milton Seligman. *Informática: a batalha do século XXI*. Rio: Paz e Terra, 1984.

Thurow, Lester C. *The Future of Capitalism: How Today's Economic Forces Shape Tomorrow's World*. New York: William Morrow and Company, 1996.

Tigre, Paulo Bastos. *Technology and Competition in the Brazilian Computer Industry*. New York: St. Martin's Press, 1983.

Timerman, Jacobo. *A Prisoner without a Name, Cell without a Number*. Trans. Toby Talbot. New York: Vintage Books, 1981.

Tinbergen, Jan, coord. *RIO: Reshaping the International Order: a Report to the Club of Rome*. New York: 1976.

Tolchin, Martin, and Susan J. Tolchin. *Selling Our Security: the Erosion of America's Assets*. New York: Penguin Books, 1992.

Trebat, Thomas J. *Brazil's State-Owned Enterprises: a Case Study of the State as Entrepreneur*. New York: Cambridge University Press, 1983.

Tussie, Diana, ed. *The Environment and International Trade Negotiations: Developing Country Stakes*. London and New York: Palgrave, 1999.

Tyson, Laura D'Andrea. *Who's Bashing Whom? Trade Conflict in High-Technology Industries*. 2nd ed. Washington, DC: Institute for International Economics, 1992 (1988).

Ugalde, Alberto J. *Las empresas públicas en la Argentina*. Buenos Aires: El Cronista Comercial, 1984.

Uriarte, Claudio. *Almirante Cero: Biografía no autorizada de Emilio Eduardo Massera*. Buenos Aires: Planeta, 1992.

Valdés, Juan Gabriel. *Pinochet's Economists: the Chicago School in Chile*. New York: Cambridge University Press, 1995.

Valenzuela, J. Samuel, and Arturo Valenzuela, eds. *Military Rule in Chile: Dictatorship and Oppositions*. Baltimore, MD: The Johns Hopkins University Press, 1986.

Varas, Augusto. *La política de las armas en la América Latina*. Santiago: FLACSCO, 1988.

——. *Los militares en el poder: Regimen y gobierno militar en Chile 1973–1986*. Santiago: Pehuén FLACSO, 1987.

Varela, Luis, and Jorge Zicolillo. *Un Domingo en el purgatorio*. Buenos Aires: Ediciones Beas, 1992.

Vargas Llosa, Mario. *A Fish in the Water*. Trans. Helen Lane. London: Faber & Faber, 1993.

Veja. *Veja: Guia do Real: Como fica sua vida com a nova moeda*. An insert in *Veja*. 6 July 1994.

Véliz, Claudio. *The Centralist Tradition of Latin America*. Princeton: Princeton University Press, 1980.

Velloso, João Paulo dos Reis, et al. *O real e o futuro da economia*. Rio: José Olympio, 1995.

——. *O último trem para Paris: De Getúlio a Sarney: "Milagres," chogues e crises do Brasil moderno*. Rio: Editora Nova Fronteira, 1986.

——. *Brasil: Solução positiva*. São Paulo: Abril/Tec Editora, 1978.

——. *A contenção nos investimentos governamentais*. Brasilia: SEPLAN, 1976.

——. *O estado e a economia*. Brasília: SEPLAN, 1975.

——. *Os 20 anos do BNDE*. Brasília: SEPLAN, 1972.

Veltmeyer, Henry, and James F. Petras. *The Dynamics of Social Change in Latin America*. London and New York: Palgrave, 2000.

Verbitsky, Horacio. *El vuelo*. Buenos Aires: Planeta–Espejo de la Argentina, 1995.

——. *Robo para la corona: los frutos prohibidos del árbol de la corrupción*. Buenos Aires: Planeta-Espejo de la Argentina, 1991.

——. *La educación presidencial: De la derrota del '70 al desguace del estado*. Buenos Aires: Editorial 12, 1990.

Vieira, David Teixeira, and Lenita Correa Camargo, *Multinacionais no Brasil: Diagnóstico e prognóstico*. Rio: Saraiva, 1976.

Villela, Annibal V., and Werner Baer. *O setor privado nacional: Problemas e política para seu fortalecimento*. Rio: IPEA/INPES, 1980.

Volcker, Paul, and Toyoo Gyohten. *Changing Fortunes: the World's Money and the Threat to American Leadership*. New York: Times Books, 1992.

Vylder, Stefan de. *Allende's Chile: the Political Economy of the Rise and Fall of the Unidad Popular*. Cambridge, Eng.: Cambridge University Press, 1976.

Waisman, Carlos H. *Reversal of Development in Argentina: Postwar Counterrevolutionary Policies and Their Structural Consequences*. Princeton: Princeton University Press, 1987.

Weiss, Linda. *The Myth of the Powerless State*. Ithaca, NY: Cornell University Press, 1998.

Williamson, John, ed. *Latin American Adjustment: How Much Has Happened?* Washington, DC: Institute for International Economics, 1990.

Yergin, Daniel, and Joseph Stanislaw. *The Commanding Heights: the Battle between Government and the Marketplace That Is Remaking the Modern World*. New York: Simon & Schuster, 1998.

Zakaria, Fareed. *From Wealth to Power: the Unusual Origins of America's World Role*. Princeton: Princeton University Press, 1998.

B. Journal articles and chapters in anthologies

Aguero, Felipe. "Chile's Lingering Authoritarian Legacy." *Current History*. February 1998. 66–70.

Angell, Alan. "Unions and Workers in Chile during the 1980s." In *The Struggle for Democracy in Chile, 1982–1990*. Eds. Paul W. Drake and Iván Jaksic. Lincoln, NE: University of Nebraska Press, 1991. 188–210.

"ANP Takes Office Talking Tough." *Latin American Weekly Report*. 20 January 1998. 33.

Arellano, José Pablo. "Elementos para el análisis de la reforma previsional chilena." *Colección Estudios CIEPLAN.* No. 6. December 1981. 5–44.

——, and René Cortázar. "Del milagro a la crisis: Reflexiones sobre el momento económico." *Colección CIEPLAN.* No. 8. July 1982. 43–60.

"Argentina." *Latin Finance: 1992: Second Annual Privatization in Latin America.* March 1992. 44–6.

"Argentina Still Going." *Latin Finance.* October 1996. 100.

"Argentina's Economic Chief Replaced in Bid to Boost Radical's Election Chances." *Latin American Regional Reports: Southern Cone Report.* 20 April 1989. 1.

Arrau, Patricio. "La reforma previsional chilena y su financiamiento durante la transición." *Colección Estudios CIEPLAN.* No. 32. June 1991. 5–44.

Arriagada Herrera, Genaro, and Carol Graham. "Chile: Sustaining Adjustment during Democratic Transition." In *Voting for Reform: Democracy, Political Liberalism, and Economic Adjustment.* Eds. Stephan Haggard, and Steven R. Webb. Washington, DC: IRBD, 1994. 242–89.

Bamrud, Joachim. "Summit of the Americas: a Historic Free-Trade Boost?" *U.S./Latin Trade.* December 1994. 28–34.

Barre, Raymond. "La privatización en Francia." In *Privatización: Experiencias mundiales.* Instituto de Estudios Contemporáneos. Buenos Aires: El Cronista Comercial, 1988. 101–16.

"The Bell Tolls for Mercosur." *LatinTrade.* January 2002. 20.

Birdsall, Nancy. "Life Is Unfair: Inequality in the World." *Foreign Policy.* Summer 1998. 76–91.

Bocco, Arnaldo, and Naúm Minsburg. "Políticas económicas en torno al papel del estado." In *Privatizaciones: Reestructuración del estado y de la sociedad (del Plan Pinedo a los Alsogaray).* Eds. Arnaldo Bocco, and Naúm Minsburg. Buenos Aires: Ediciones Letra Buena, 1991. 19–53.

Boeninger, Edgardo. "El marco político general y el marco institucional del próximo gobierno." In *Transición a la democracia: Marco político y económico.* Ed. Oscar Muñoz. G. Santiago: CIEPLAN, 1994. 43–67.

——. "The Chilean Political Transition to Democracy." In *From Dictatorship to Democracy: Rebuilding Political Consensus in Chile.* Ed. Joseph S. Tulchin, and Augusto Varas. Boulder, CO: Lynne Rienner, 1991. 50–61.

Bonelli, Regis, Gustavo B. Franco, and Winston Fritsch. "Macroeconomic Instability and Trade Performance in Brazil: Lessons from the 1980s to the 1990s." *Bangladesh Development Studies.* June–September 1992. 129–61.

Bruce, David C., "Brazil Plays the Japan Card." *Third World Quarterly.* 1983. 848–60.

Calvo, Guillermo A. "Fractured Liberalism: Argentina under Martínez de Hoz." *Economic Development and Culture Change.* April 1986. 511–33.

Capriles, Ruth, and Marisol Rodriguez de Gonzalo. "Economic and Business History in Venezuela." In *Business History in Latin America: the Experience of Seven Countries.* Eds. Carlos Dávila and Rory Miller. Liverpool, UK: Liverpool University Press, 1999. 158–75.

Cardoso, Fernando Henrique. "North–South Relations in the Present Context: a New Dependency?" In *The New Global Economy in the Information Age: Reflections on Our Changing World.* Martin Carnoy, Manuel Castells, Stephen S. Cohen, and Fernando Henrique Cardoso. University Park, PA: The Pennsylvania State University Press, 1993. 149–59.

——. "Associated-Dependent Development and Democratic Theory." In *Democratizing Brazil: Problems of Transition and Consolidation*. Ed. Alfred Stepan. New York: Oxford University Press, 1989. 299–326.

——. "On the Characteristics of Authoritarian Regimes in Latin America." In *The New Authoritarianism in Latin America*. Ed. David Collier. Princeton: Princeton University Press, 1979. 33–57.

——. "Associated-Dependent Development: Theoretical and Practical Implications." In *Authoritarian Brazil: Origins, Policies, and Future*. Ed. Alfred Stepan. New Haven, CT: Yale University Press, 1973. 142–76.

"Cardoso Hails First Month of Power Saving, despite Target Shortfalls." *Latin American Regional Reports: Brazil Report*. 3 July 2001. 1.

Cavallo, Domingo F. "Argentina: Trade Reform, 1976–1982." In *Trade Reform: Lessons from Countries*. Eds. Geoffrey Shepherd and Carlos Geraldo Langoni. San Francisco: ICS Press, 1991. 27–39.

——. "Argentina." In *The Open Economy: Tools for Policymakers in Developing Countries*. Eds. Rudiger Dornbusch and Leslie C. H. Helmers. New York: Oxford University Press, 1988. 267–84.

Cavarozzi, Marcelo J., and James F. Petras. "Chile." In *Latin America: the Struggle with Dependency and Beyond*. Eds. Ronald H. Chilcote and Joel C. Edelstein. New York: John Wiley, 1974. 495–578.

Chalmers, Douglas A., Maria do Carmo Campello de Souza, and Atilio A. Boron. "Introduction: the Right and Latin American Democracy." In *The Right and Democracy in Latin America*. Eds. Douglas A. Chalmers, Maria do Carmo Campello de Souza, and Atilio A. Boron. New York: Praeger, 1992. l–9.

Codevilla, Angelo. "Is Pinochet the Model?" *Foreign Affairs*. November–December 1993. 127–41.

Collier, David. "Overview of the Bureaucratic-Authoritarian Model." In *The New Authoritarianism in Latin America*. Ed. David Collier. Princeton: Princeton University Press, 1979. 20–32.

Conniff, Michael L. "Introduction: Toward a Comparative Definition of Populism." In *Latin American Populism in Comparative Perspective*. Albuquerque, NM: University of New Mexico Press, 1980. 5–13.

Corrales, Javier. "Why Argentines Followed Cavallo: a Technopol between Democracy and Economic Reform." In *Technopols: Freeing Politics and Markets in Latin America in the 1990s*. Ed. Jorge I. Dominguez. University Park, PA: Pennsylvania State University Press, 1997. 49–93.

Dennis, Geoffrey. "Still Bullish in Buenos Aires." *LatinFinance*. September 1992. 76–81.

Dominguez, Jorge. "Latin America's Crisis of Representation." *Foreign Affairs*. January–February 1997. 100–13.

Dornbusch, Rudiger, and Sebastian Edwards. "The Macroeconomics of Populism." In *The Macroeconomics of Populism in Latin America*. Eds. Rudiger Dornbusch, and Sebastian Edwards. Chicago: University of Chicago Press, 1991. 7–13.

——, and Juan Carlos de Pablo. "Debt and Macroeconomic Instability in Argentina." In *Developing Country Debt and the World Economy*. Ed. Jeffrey D. Sachs. Chicago: The University of Chicago Press, 1989. 37–56.

Drake, Paul. "Requiem for Populism?" In *Latin American Populism in Comparative Perspective*. Ed. Michael L. Conniff. Albuquerque, NM: University of New Mexico Press, 1982. 217–45.

Durand, Francisco. "The New Right and Political Change in Peru." In *The Right and Democracy in Latin America*. Eds. Douglas A. Chalmers, Maria do Carmo Campello, and Atilio A. Boron. New York: Praeger, 1992. 239–58.

Edwards, Gertrude G. "The Frondizi Contracts and Petroleum Self-Sufficiency in Argentina." In *Foreign Investment in the Petroleum and Mineral Industries: Case Studies Investor-Host Country Relations*. Eds. Raymond F. Mikesell, and William Bartsch. Baltimore, MD: The Johns Hopkins University Press, 1971. 157–215.

Edwards, Sebastian. "Why Are Latin America's Saving Rates So Low?" In *Pathways to Growth: Comparing East Asia and Latin America*. Eds. Nancy Birdsall, and Frederick Jaspersen. Washington, DC: Inter-American Development Bank, 1997. 131–60.

——. "The United States and Foreign Competition in Latin America." In *The United States in the World Economy*. Ed. Martin Felstein. Chicago: University of Chicago Press, 1988. 9–75.

"The End of the Pinochet Era: Chile's Transition to Democracy." An Interview with Genaro Arriagada Herrera. *Harvard International Review*. Spring 1990. 19–20, 54.

"Energy Crisis Damages Cardoso." *Latin American Regional Reports: Brazil Report*. 3 July 2001. 2.

Evans, Peter B., and Paulo Bastors Tigre. "Going beyond Clones in Brazil and Korea: a Comparative Analysis of NIC Strategies in the Computer Industry." *World Development*. November 1989. 1751–68.

Feinberg, Richard. "Economic Themes for the 1990s." In *Setting the North–South Agenda*. Miami: North–South Center, 1991. 33–8.

Ffrench-Davis, Ricardo. "El experimento monetarista en Ch.le: una síntesis crítica." *Colección Estudios CIEPLAN*. 9 December 1982. 5–40.

Fishlow, Albert. "Some Reflections on Post-1964 Brazilian Economic Policy." In *Authoritarian Brazil: Origin, Policies, and Future*. Ed. Alfred Stepan. New Haven: Yale University Press, 1973. 299–326.

Foxley, Alejandro. "La politica económica para la transición." In *Transición a la democracia: Marco politico y económico*. Ed. Oscar Muñoz G. Santiago: CIEPLAN, 1994. 101–19.

——. "Neoconservative Economic Experiment in Chile." In *Military Rule in Chile: Dictatorship and Oppositions*. Eds. J. Samuel Valenzuela, and Arturo Valenzuela. Baltimore, MD: The Johns Hopkins University Press, 1986. 13–50.

——. "Después del monetarismo." *Reconstrucción económica para la democracia*. 4th ed. Santiago: Editorial Aconcagua, 1984. 15–94.

——. "Cinco lecciones de la crisis actual." *Colección Estudios CIEPLAN*. No. 8. July 1982. 161–71.

"Front Notes." *LatinFinance*. July/August 1997. 9.

Galbraith, John Kenneth. "Preface." *New Political Economy*. March 1997. 5–9.

Gallo, Ezequiel, and Estabán F. Thomsen. "Electoral Evolution of the Political Parties of the Right: Argentina, 1983–1989." In *The Right and Democracy in Latin America*. Eds. Douglas A. Chalmers, Maria do Carmo Campello, and Atilio A. Boron. New York: Praeger, 1992. 142–60.

Garretón, Manuel Antonio. "Political Processes in an Authoritarian Regime: the Dynamics of Institutionalization and Opposition in Chile, 1973–1980. In *Military Rule in Chile: Dictatorship and Oppositions*. Eds. J. Samuel Valenzuela, and Arturo Valenzuela. Baltimore, MD: The Johns Hopkins University Press, 1986. 144–83.

Germani, Gino. "States of Modernization in Latin America." *Studies in Comparative International Development*. 1969–70. 155–74.

Giraldo, Jenne Kinney. "Development and Democracy in Chile: Finance Minister Alejandro Foxley and the Concertación's Project for the 1990s." In *Technopols: Freeing Politics and Markets in Latin America in the 1990s*. Ed. Jorge I. Dominguez. University Park, PA: Pennsylvania State University Press, 1997. 229–75.

Gordon, Lincoln. "Assessing Brazil's Political Modernization." *Current History*. February 1998. 76–81.

Griffith, Victoria. "The Challenge Ahead." *LatinFinance*. May 1995. 24, 29–30.

——. "Ironing Out the Wrinkles." *LatinFinance*. September 1992. 71–5.

Hastings, Laura A. "Regulatory Revenge: the Politics of Free-Market Financial Reforms in Chile." In *The Politics of Finance in Developing Countries*. Eds. Stephan Haggard, Chung H. Lee, and Sylvia Maxfield. Ithaca, NY: Cornell University Press, 1993. 201–29.

Hirschman, Albert O. "The Case against 'One Thing at a Time.'" *World Development*. August 1990. 1119–22.

——. "The Turn to Authoritarianism in Latin America and the Search for Its Economic Determinism." In *The New Authoritarianism in Latin America*. Ed. David Collier. Princeton: Princeton University Press, 1979. 61–98.

Hoge, James F., Jr. "A Conversation with President Cardoso." *Foreign Affairs*. July–August 1995. 62–75.

Jackson, John H. "Managing the Trading System: the World Trade Organization and the Post-Uruguay Round GATT Agenda." In *Managing the World Economy: Fifty Years after Bretton Woods*. Ed. Peter B. Kenen. Washington, DC: Institute for International Economics, 1994. 131–51.

Jameson, Kenneth P. "Dollar Bloc Dependency in Latin America: Beyond Bretton Woods." *International Studies Quarterly*. 1990. 519–41.

Jones, Charles. "Commercial Banks and Mortgage Companies." In *Business Imperialism 1840–1930*. Ed. D. C. M. Platt. Oxford, Eng.: Oxford University Press, 1977. 17–52.

Jones, Mark P. "Argentina: Questioning Menem's Way." *Current History*. February 1998. 71–5.

Kauffman, Robert, and Barbara Stallings. "The Political Economy in Latin American Populism." In *The Macroeconomics of Populism in Latin America*. Eds. Rudiger Dornbusch, and Sebastian Edwards. Chicago: University of Chicago Press, 1991. 15–35.

Kelly, Philip F., and Kris Olds. "Questions in a Crisis: the Contested Meanings of Globalisation in the Asia-Pacific." In *Globalisation and the Asia-Pacific: Contested Territories*. Eds. Kris Olds, Peter Dicken, Philip F. Kelly, Lily Kong, and Henry Waichung Yeung. London and New York: Routledge, 1999. 1–15.

Kruger, Ann O. "Import Substitution versus Export Promotion." In *International Economies and International Economic Policy: a Reader*. Ed. Philip King. New York: McGraw Hill, 1990. 155–65.

Krugman, Paul. "Dutch Tulips and Emerging Markets." *Foreign Affairs*. July–August 1995. 28–40.

Laird, Sam, and Alexander Yates. "Nontariff Barriers of Developed Countries, 1966–1986." *Finance and Development*. March 1989. 12–13.

Larrain B., Felipe. "El comportamiento del sector público en un país altamente endeudado." In *El sector público y la crisis de la América Latina*. Eds. Felipe Larrain, and Macrelo Selowsky. Mexico: Fondo de Cultura Económica, 1990. 150–7.

Lim, Yongil. "Comparing Brazil and Korea." In *Lessons in Development: a Comparative Study of Asia and Latin America.* Eds. Seiji Naya, Miguel Urrutia, Shelley Mark, and Alfredo Fuentes. San Francisco: IFCS, 1989. 93–117.

Loveman, Brian. "Military Dictatorship and Political Opposition in Chile." In *Chile: Dictatorship and Struggle for Democracy.* Eds. Grinor Rojo, and John H. Hassett. Gaithersburg, MD: Hispanoamerica, 1988. 17–52.

Lowenthal, Abraham, "Latin America: Ready for Partnership?" *Foreign Affairs. America & the World 1993.* 1993. 74–92.

Marcel, Mario. "Privatización y finanzas públicas: el caso de Chile, 1985–1988." *Colección Estudios CIEPLAN.* No. 26. June 1988. 5–60.

Marks, Siegfried. "Petroleum: Unfinished Reform." *U.S./Latin Trade.* April 1995. 38–48.

Martone, Celso Luiz. "Expansão do estado empresário no Brasil." In *A crise do "Bom Patrão."* Castro et al. 59–65.

Maxfield, Sylvia, and James H. Nolt. "Protectionism and the Internationalization of Capital: U.S. Sponsorship of Import Substitution Industrialization in the Philippines, Turkey, and Argentina." *International Studies Quarterly.* March 1990. 49–81.

"Mercosur Maintains United Front despite Row over Chile's Free Trade Talks with US." *Latin American Regional Reports: Southern Cone Report.* 19 December 2000. 1.

Mikesell, Raymond F. "Conflict and Accommodation in Direct Foreign Investment: the Copper Industry." In *Latin America-U.S. Economic Interactions: Conflict, Accommodation, and Policies for the Future.* Eds. Robert B. Williamson, William P. Glade, Jr., and Karl M. Schmitt. Washington, DC: American Enterpise Institute, 1974. 185–99.

Montero, Cecilia. "La evolución del empresariado chileno. ¿Surge un nuevo actor?" *Colección Estudios CIEPLAN.* December 1990. 91–122.

Moore, Paul W., and Rebecca K. Hunt. "The Andean Pact: In the Forefront." United States Department of Commerce/International Trade Administration, *Business America.* 13 June 1994. *National Trade Data Bank.* CD-ROM (January 1997).

——. "Andean Pact Restructured." International Market Insight. 12 March 1996. *National Trade Data Bank.* CD-ROM (January 1997).

Moulian, Tomás. "Desarrollo político y estado de compromiso: Desajustes y crisis estatal en Chile." *Colección CIEPLAN.* No. 8. July 1982. 112–13. [Earlier issues did not include *Estudios* in the title.]

Muñoz G., Oscar. "Crecimiento y desequilíbrios en una economía abierta: el caso chileno, 1976–81." *Colección CIEPLAN.* No. 8. July 1982. 19–41.

——, and Hector E. Schamis. "Las transformaciones del estado en Chile y la privatización." In *¿Adónde vá América Latina? Balance de las reformas económicas.* Ed. Joaquín Vial. Santiago: CIEPLAN, 1992. 277–301.

Nader, Ralph, and Lori Wallach. "GATT, NAFTA, and the Subservsion of the Democratic Process." In *The Case against the Global Economy and for a Turn toward the Local.* Eds Jerry Mander, and Edward Goldsmith. San Francisco: Sierra Club, 1996. 92–107.

Nofal, Maria Beatriz. "MERCOSUR and Free Trade in the Americas." In *Integrating the Americas: Shaping Future Trade Policy.* Ed. Sidney Weintraub. New Brunswick, NJ: Transaction Publishers, 1994. 137–68.

Nogueira, Sérgio Luiz Coutinho. "Fatores impeditivos da consolidação do PROÁLCOOL." *Anais do I Simpósio Nacional sobre álcool combustível.* Brasília: Câmara dos Deputados, 1985. 92–103.

O'Donnell, Guillermo. "On the State, Democratization and Some Conceptual Problems: a Latin American View with Glances at Some Postcommunist Countries." *World Development.* August 1993. 1355–69.

——. "Reflections on the Patterns of Change in the Bureaucratic-Authoritarian State." *Latin American Research Review.* 1978. 3–38.

Ohmae, Kenichi. "Putting Global Logic First." In *The Evolving Global Economy: Making Sense of the New World Order.* Ed. Kenichi Ohmae. Cambridge, MA: Harvard, Business School Press, 1995. 129–37.

Pang, Eul-Soo. "Brazil Opens the Last Frontier." *Hemisfile.* November/December 1996. 10–11.

——. "Brazil and the United States." In *United States Policy in Latin America.* Ed. John D. Martz. Lincoln, NE: University of Nebraska Press, 1995. 144–83.

——. "The Darker Side of Brazil's Democracy." *Current History.* January 1988. 21–4, 40.

——. "Brazil's External Debt: Part I: the Outside View." *UFSI Reports.* 1984/No. 37. South America. ESP-1-84. 1985. 1–8.

——. "Brazil's External Debt: Part II: the Inside View." *UFSI Reports.* 1984/No. 38. South America. ESP-2-84. 1985. 1–7.

——. "Modernization and Slavocracy in Nineteenth-Century Brazil." *Journal of Interdisciplinary History.* Spring 1979. 667-88.

——, and Laura Jarnagin. "Brazil's Catatonic Lambada." *Current History.* February 1991. 73–5, 85–7.

Peralta-Ramos, Monica. "Economic Policy and Distributional Conflict among Business Groups in Argentina: From Alfonsín to Menem (1989–1990)." In *The New Argentine Democracy: the Search for a Successful Formula.* Ed. Edward C. Epstein. Wesport, CT: Praeger, 1992. 97–123.

Pereira, Luiz Carlos Bresser. "Economic Reforms and Economic Growth: Efficiency and Politics in Latin America." In *Economic Reforms in New Democracies: a Social-Democratic Approach.* Eds. Luiz Carlos Bresser Pereira, José Maria Maravall, and Adam Przeworkski. New York: Cambridge University Press, 1993. 15–76.

"Petrobrás Loses Control over More than 90% of Potential Oil-Producing Areas." *Latin American Regional Report: Brazil Report.* 7 July 1998. 1.

Piñera, José. "Chile." In *The Political Economy of Policy Reform.* Ed. John Williamson. Washington, DC: Institute for International Economics, 1994. 225–31.

——. "Chile: el proder de una idea." In *El desafío neoliberal: el fin del tercermundismo en América Latina.* Ed. Barry B. Levine. Buenos Aires: Grupo Editorial Norma, 1992. 77–92.

——. "Empowering Workers: the Privatization of Social Security in Chile." *Cato Journal.* 15: 2–3. 1–10, http:/www/cato.org/pubs/journal/cj15n2-3-1.html.

Pinheiro, Armando Castelar, and Fábio Giambiagi. "Brazilian Privatization in the 1990s." *World Development.* May 1994. 739–59.

Prebisch, Raul. "Five Stages in My Thinking on Development." In *Pioneers in Development.* Eds. Gerald M. Meier, and Dudley Sears. New York: Oxford University Press, l984. 175–91.

"Quál es el plan de Cavallo?" *Novedades Económicas*. March 1991. No pagination.

Raczynski, Dagmar. "Determinantes del éxodo rural: Importancia de factores del lugar de origen, Chile, 1965–1970." *Colección Estudios CIEPLAN*. No. 8. July 1982. 61–104.

Resende, André Lara. "A moeda indexada: uma proposta para eliminar a inflação inercial." *Revista da Economia Política*. April/June 1985. 130–4.

Rezende, Fernando. "O crescimento (descontrolado) da intervenção governamental na economia brasileira." In *Seminário sobre planejamento e controle do setor de empresas estatais: Casos nacionais*. Eds. IPEA and CEPAL. Brasília: IPEA, 1983. 151–91.

Rothschild, Emma. "Globalization and the Return of History." *Foreign Policy*. Summer 1999. 106–17.

Sachs, Jeffrey. "International Economics: Unlocking the Mysteries of Globalization." *Foreign Policy*. Spring 1998. 97–111.

Sadowski, Yahya. "Ethnic Conflict." *Foreign Policy*. Summer 1998. 12–23, esp., 19–20.

Sáez, Raúl E. "Las privatizaciones de empresas de Chile." In *Después de las privatizaciones: Hacia el estado regulador*. Ed. Oscar Muñoz G. Santiago: CIESPLAN, 1993. 75–109.

Schneider, Ben Ross. "Privatization in the Collor Government: Triumph of Liberalism or the Collapse of the Developmental State?" In *The Right and Democracy in Latin America*. Eds. Douglas A. Chalmers, Maria do Carmo Campello, and Atilio A. Boron. New York: Praeger, 1992. 225–38.

Schenone, Osvaldo H. "El comportamiento del sector público en la Argentina." In *El sector público y la crisis de la América Latina*. Eds. Felipe Larrain, and Marcelo Selowsky. Mexico City: El Trimestre Econômico, 1990. 16–66.

"Serra and Jereissati Throw Their Hats into the Ring for PSDB Nomination." *Latin American Regional Reports: Brazil Report*. 16 October 2001. 1.

Shirley, Mary. "Privatization in Latin America: Lessons for Transitional Europe." *World Development*. September 1994. l313–23.

"Slaying of a Mammoth Monopoly." *Petroleum Economists*. April 1995. 9–11.

Stebbings, Robert Y. "Carlos Menem in Argentina: Country Focus: Argentina." *Latin Finance*. September 1992. Unpaginated.

Stepan, Alfred. "O que estão pensando os militares." *Novos Estudos Cebrap*. July 1983. 2–7.

"The Technopols." *Latin Trade*. April 1997.

Tricoulat Filho, Renato. "Apresentação e síntesis." In *A crise do "Bom Patrão."* Rio: CEDES, 1984. 13–22.

"Unequal Income Distribution, 'almost unaffected by economic reforms'." *Latin American Regional Reports: Brazil Report*. 24 April 2001. 1.

Valenzuela, Arturo. "Judging the General: Pinochet's Past and Chile's Future." *Current History*. March 1999. 99–104.

Varas, Augusto. "Latin America: Toward a New Reliance on the Market." In *Global Change, Regional Response: the New International Context of Development*. Ed. Barbara Stallings. New York: Cambridge University Press, 1995. 272–308.

Vera Ferrer, Oscar Humberto. "The Political Economy of Privatization in Mexico." In *Privatization of Public Enterprises in Latin America*. Ed. William Glade. San Francisco: ICSG, 1991. 35–57.

Vial, Joaquín, Andrea Butelmann, and Carmen Celedon. "Fundamentos de las políticas macroeconómicas del gobierno democrático chileno." *Colección Estudios CIEPLAN.* No. 30. December 1990. 55–89.

Wallin, Michelle. "After Devaluation, Argentina Struggles On." *Wall Street Journal.* 10 January 2002. A8.

——. "Argentine Leader Declares State of Emergency." *Wall Street Journal.* 20 December 2001. C12.

Wallin, Michelle, and Pamela Druckerman. "Argentina's Beleaguered Government Collapses." *Wall Street Journal.* 21 December 2001. A 13.

Walters, Sir Alan A. "La privatización en el Reino Unido." In *Privatización: Experiencias mundiales.* Buenos Aires: El Cronista Comercial, 1988. 15–46.

Warn, Ken. "The Rise and Fall of Yarbán." *Latin Trade.* August 1998. 26–7.

Weeks, Scott. "Debt Research on the Rise." *Latin Finance.* July/August 1997. 21–2.

Weiss, Linda. "Globalization and the Myth of the Powerless State." *New Left Review.* September–October, 1997. 2–37.

Wyatt-Walter, Andres. "Regionalism, Globalization, and World Economic Order." In *Regionalism in World Politics: Regional Organizations and International Order.* Eds. Louise Fawcett, and Andrew Hurell. New York: Oxford University Press, 1995. 74–121.

Yotopoulos, Pan A. "The (Rip) Tide of Privatization: Lessons from Chile." *World Development.* May 1989. 684–91.

Zapata, Juan Antonio. "The Argentine Economic Strategy," speech at the Latin American Mining Conference, Scottsdale, AZ, 23. 5 February 1996.

C.   Newspapers and weeklies

"O amor fulminante." *Veja.* 17 October l990. 3–35.

"A empresa estatal, no Brasil, não nasceu por motivos ideológicos e, sim, para preencher espaços que estavam vazios." *O Estado de S. Paulo.* 29 January 1975.

"Argentina Prepares Plan for the Economy." *Wall Street Journal.* 4 April 1989.

"Australia Launches Investigations of Alan Bond's Business Dealings." *Wall Street Journal.* 8 September 1989.

Ball, Carlos. "Privatization, Venezuelan Style." *Wall Street Journal.* 1 June 1989.

Baum, Julian. "The Money Machine." *Far Eastern Economic Review.* 11 August 1994. 62–5.

"Betting on Brazil." *The Economist.* 8 October 1994. 17.

"Big is Back." A Survey of Multinationals. *The Economist.* 24 June 1995 (Insert).

"Bolero de jaquetão." *Veja.* 18 June 1990. 35–6.

"The Bottom Line." *AsiaWeek.* 3 July 1998. 72.

"The Bottom Line." *AsiaWeek.* 14 March 1997. 61.

"The Bottom Line." *AsiaWeek.* 26 May 1995. 63.

"Brazil Completes Debt Pact with Banks, Argentina Resisting Creditors' Demand." *Wall Street Journal.* 3 November 1988.

"Canhedo baixa crista." *Veja.* 15 January 1992. 63–4.

"Cardoso de Mello, Brazil's New Minister for Economics, Begins to Walk Tightrope." *Wall Street Journal.* 2 March 1990.

Carvalho, Joaquim de. "A conta e o conto." *Veja.* 19 March 1997. 24–6.

———. "Fim de caso." *Veja*. 7 August 1996. 32–8.
Catán, Thomas, and Richard Lapper. "Argentina in Crisis Talks to Head Off Collapse." *Financial Times*. 8–9 December 2001. 1.
"Chile Reacts by Adjusting Dollar Rate, Easing Capital Inflows & Cutting Outlays." *Latin American Weekly Report*. 30 June 1998. 289.
"O choque de Zélia." *Veja*. 21 March 1990. 60–3.
Cohen, Margot. "Tackling a Bitter Legacy." *Asia Week*. 2 July 1998. 22–7.
"Conexões aéreas." *Veja*. 1 July 1992. 24–5.
"Confusão electrônica." *Veja*. 16 July 1986. 96–103.
"O congresso dá volta por cima." *Veja*. 26 January 1994. 28–35.
Cormier, Bill. "Argentine Peronists Regain Presidency." *Washington Post*. 21 December 2001. online: www.washingtonpost.com/wp-dyn/articles/A16383-2001Dec22.html.
Correa, Marcos de Sá. "Fleury ou não Fleury." *Veja*. 10 May 1995. 35.
"Cotações." *Veja*. 16 March 1994. 102.
"Cotações." *Veja*. 4 May 1994. 99.
"Crecimientos sectoriales." *Estrategia*. Santiago. 3 June 1994. 3.
D'Amico, Hector, Silvia Fesquet, Gustavo González, and Maria Grinstein. "Onganía: 30 años no es nada." *Noticias*. 19 February 1995. 50–6.
"A Daring Economic Plan Arouses Debate in Brazil." *The New York Times*. 18 March 1990.
"Desregulación o picardia?" *Somos*. 11 November 1991. 17.
"A difícil arte de ser Itmar." *Veja*. 16 November 1994. 36.
"The Disorders of Progress," a survey of Brazil. *The Economist*. 27 March 1999.
"Dr. M: Abuses of Globalisation Destructive." *The Sun*. Kuala Lumpur: 17 June 2000. 2.
"É de tirar o sono." *Istoé Senhor*. 28 March 1990. 28–33.
"Emerging-Market Indicators." *The Economist*. 18 July 1998. 92.
"Emerging-Market Indicators." *The Economist*. 28 May 1994. 108.
Enough, Eduardo. "Só um romantic." *Veja*. 4 December 1991. 7–10.
"Escándalo federal." *Veja*. 4 September 1991. 25–35.
"Estado em disparada." *Veja*. 26 April 1995. 104–5.
"Flirting with Anarchy." *The Economist*. 5 January 2002. 12–13.
"Força na larga." *Veja*. 20 June 1990. 36–7.
"Fugindo do atraso." *Veja*. 19 September 1990.
Gallardo, Eduardo. "Chile's Center-Left Keeps Control." *Washington Post*. 17 December 2001. www.washingtonpost.com/wp-dyn/articles/A53036-2001 Dec17.html.
Gaspari, Elio. "Eu não quis colaborar." An interview with Luís Octávio Motta Veiga, President of Petrobrás. *Veja*. 17 June 1992. 7–11.
Gay, Chris. "A Life of Its Own." *Far Eastern Economic Review*. 27 March 1997. 59–60.
"Global Banks." *Business Week* International Edition. 24 May 1994.
Greco, Jorge. "Complot para un divórcio." *Somos*. 23 September 1991. 10–11.
"A guerra ao turbante." *Veja*. 23 March 1988. 38–44.
"A guerra do leite." *Veja*. 25 July 1990. 30–3.
Horne, Alstair. "Battle in Burma." *The Wall Street Journal*. 25 March 1997. A18.
"IMF Reluctance Blocks Progress by Argentina." *The Wall Street Journal*. 2 February 1989.
"Informática continuará com incentivos 5." *Jornal do Brasil*. 14 June 1991.

"The International 500: the Fortune Directory of the Largest Industrial Corporations outside the U.S." *Fortune.* 20 August 1984. 200.

"Is the Era of Consensus about to Close?" *Latin American Weekly Report.* 7 April 1998. 162–3.

Lamounier, Bolívar. "Um é pouco, dois é bom, três é ..." *Exame.* 26 December 2001. 10–12.

"Lenha na privatização." *Veja.* 15 January 1992. 66.

"A linha quente de PC." *Veja.* 8 July 1992. 28–31.

McCartney, Scott. "Catching Up: Computer Sales Sizzle as Developing Nations Try to Shrink PC Gap." *Wall Street Journal.* 29 June 1995. A1.

"Man of the Year." *Latin Finance.* May 1995. 19–21.

"Market Value: Total Capitalization." *Asia Week.* 20 May 1998. 104.

"Meet the Global Factory." A Survey of Manufacturing. *The Economist.* 20 June 1998. 3–18.

"Las mil y una caras de Ibrahim." *Somos.* 1 March 1993. 4–9.

"The Military and Past Rights Abuses: a Problem Which Refuses to Go Away." *Latin American Weekly Report.* 27 January 1998. 37.

"Modest Man, Immodest Task." *The Economist.* 8 October 1994. 42.

Moffett, Matt. "Mexico Might Learn from Fall of the Peso in Chile's Lost Decade." *Wall Street Journal.* 16 January 1995. A1, A6.

"Um motorista no médio de caminho." *Veja.* 8 July 1992. 22.

"New Ideas for the Old Left." *The Economist.* 17 January 1998. 29–30.

"No carro do amigo." *Veja.* 8 July 1992. 24–6.

"Nocaute tecnológico." *Veja.* 19 June 1991. 37.

O'Grady. Mary Anastasia. "Play 'Deuda Eterna' and Learn All about the IMF." *Wall Street Journal.* 21 December 2001. A15.

Ortiz, Guillermo. "Mexico's Been Bitten by the Privatization Bug." *Wall Street Journal.* 15 September 1989.

"O país dos barnabés." *Veja.* 20 June 1990. 12–35.

"Uma pancada pesada." *Veja.* 28 March 1990. 50–2.

"Pérola aos porcos." *Veja.* 27 November 1991. 99.

"Perú será miembro de APEC a partir de 1998." *Gestión.* Lima. 26 November 1996. 1, 18.

"A Petrobrás com medo da concorrência." *Veja.* 30 March 1994. 70–9.

Petrolero Brasileiro [Petrobrás]. "True Blue Power." *Latin Finance.* May 1995. 26.

"Pinochet Delays Departure in Defiance of Campaign against His Senatorial Post." *Latin American Weekly Report.* 20 January 1998. 25.

"O Planalto sacou primeiro." *Veja.* 31 May 1995. 20–7.

"PMDB decide contra a reserva na informática." *Folha de S. Paulo.* 5 June 1991.

"PMDB negocia fim da reserva na informática." Folha de S. Paulo. 6 June 1991.

Policarpo, Jr. "O burocrata abre a mala da corrupção." *Veja.* 20 October 1993. 20–7.

"A praça da bagunça." *Veja.* 2 October 1991. 18–23.

"Protecionismo existe em qualquer país: Entrevista [com] Antony Motley." *O Globo.* 5 June 1988.

"As provas bancárias." *Veja.* 8 July 1992. 18–22.

"Quál es el plan de Cavallo?" *Novedades Económicas.* March 1991. No pagination.

"A República que invadiu o Brasil." *Veja*. 3 July 1991. 16–23.
"A Reserva mascarada." *Veja*. 12 June 1991. 72.
Rojas, Matias E. "Many Chileans Still Lured by Statist's Siren Song." *Wall Street Journal*. 27 July 1990. A6.
"A saída do nocaute." *Veja*. 28 March 1990. 46–69.
Schwarz, Adam. "Bigger Is Better." *Far Eastern Economic Review*. 20 June 1998. 3–6.
——— "Bigger Is Better." *The Far Eastern Economic Review*. 28 July 1994. 24.
"Staying Mum." *The Economist*. 15 December 2001. 30.
Talib, Ahmad A. "PM: We'll fight tooth and nail." *New Straits Times* (Kuala Lumpur: 21 June 2000). 1, 4.
Tasker, Rodney, and Adam Schwarz. "ASEAN: Growing Pains." *The Far Eastern Economic Review*. 28 July 1994. 22–3.
"A terra treme." *Veja*. 27 October 1995. 32–5.
"Os tigres dapensão." *Veja*. 20 November 1991. 78–81.
Toledo, Roberto Pompeu de. "Enfim, um presidente que deu certo." *Veja*. 16 November 1994. 34–45.
"Turbulência no casal presidencial." *Veja*. 21 October 1991. 20–6.
"A turma do calote." *Veja*. 17 May 1995. 30–7.
"O último vôo." *Veja*. 10 May 1995. 37.
"UMNO General Assembly: We are responsible to the Malays." *The Straits Times* (Singapore: 13 May 2000). 53.
"Venceu a tradição." *Veja*. 21 December 1994. 40–1.
Waack, William. "Não sou o Eduardito." Interview with Eduardo Frei. *Veja*. 16 March 1994. 7–9.
"World Stocks," *AsiaWeek*. 9 April 1999. 67.
Wornat, Olga. "Las confesiones de Manzano." *Somos*. 22 February 1993. 4–9.
"Zélia sae e rouba a cena." *Veja*. 15 May 1991. 14–19.

D.   Government and multilateral agencies

Banco Central do Brasil. *Brasil: Programa econômico* 18. Brasília: BCB, Setembro de 1998.
BNDES [Brasil]. *BNDE System: Annual Report*. Rio: BNDE, 1981. Various years.
Câmara dos Deputados [Brasil]. Comissão Parlamentar de Inquérito. *Dívida externa e do acordo FMI-Brasil*. Brasília: CD, 10 November 1983. [ms].
CEPAL/CET. *Las empresas transnacionales en la Argentina*. Estudios e Informes de la CEPAL, No. 56. Santiago: CEPAL, 1986.
Conselho Nacional de Petróleo [Brasil]. *Atualidade: Conselho Nacional de Petróleo*. Brasília: January–February 1984.
CVRD [Brasil]. *Carajás 1985*. Rio: CVRD, 1985.
Freedom House. "FH Country Ratings: Annual Survey of Freedom Country Scores 1972–73 to 1990–2000." www.freedomhouse.org/ratings/index.htm.
Inter-American Development Bank. *Economic and Social Progress in Latin America: 1997 Report: Latin America after a Decade of Reforms*. Washington, DC: IDB, 1997.
———. *Economic and Social Progress in Latin America: 1994 Report: Special Report: Fiscal Decentralization*. Washington, DC: IDB, 1994.

———. *Economic and Social Progress in Latin America: 1991 Report: Special Edition – Social Security*. Washington, DC: IDB, 1991.

———. *Economic and Social Progress in Latin America: 1988 Report*. Washington, DC: IDB, 1988.

International Monetary Fund www.imf.org/external/NP/LOI/1999/051099.HTM and www.imf.org/external/NP/LOI/2000/arg/INDEX.HTM.

———. "IMF Augments Argentina Stand-by Credit to \$21.57 Billion, and Completes Fourth Review," Press Release No. 01/37 (7 September 2001), International Monetary Fund, Washington DC, www.imf.org/external/np/sec/pr/2001/pr0137.htm.

IPEA [Brasil] and CEPAL. *Seminário sobre planejamento e controle do setor de empresas estatais: Debates e reflexões*. Brasília: IPEA/CEPAL, 1983.

Ministerio de Economía e Obras y Servicios Públicos [Argentina]. *Argentina en crecimiento: 1993–1995. III. Políticas Sectoriales*. Buenos Aires: MEOSP, 1993.

Ministerio de Obras y Servicios Públicos [Argentina]. "La reforma del estado y el processo de privatizaciones (Ley 23.696 y Decreto 1105/89): Balance de 120 dias (10 de julio al 10 de noviembre de 1989). [ms].

Petrobrás [Brasil]. *Relatório Anual and Relatório Anual Consolidado*. Rio: Petrobrás. Various years.

Presidência da República [Brasil]. Secretaria de Planejamento. *Razões para acreditar em 1984: Apesar dos dez anos de crise mundial*. Brasília: SEPLAN, 1984.

———. Secretaria de Orçamento e Controle de Empresas Estatais. *Cadastro das empresas estatais. Atualizado em setembro – 1983*. Brasília: SEST, 1983.

República Federativa do Brasil. Ministério das Minas e Energia. *Balanço energético nacional 1985*. Brasília: CNP, 1985.

Sábato Commission [Argentina]. *Nunca Más: Informe da Comissão Nacional sobre o desaparecimento de pessoas na Argentina, presidida por Ernesto Sábato*. Porto Alegre: L&PM Editores, 1984. A Brazilian edition.

SEPLAN [Brasil]. *Perfil das empresas estatais – 1989: Ano-base 1989*. Brasília: SEPLAN, 1989.

———. *Relatório das empresas estatais – 1998: Ano-base 1988*. Brasília: SEPLAN, 1989.

———. CNPq [Brasil]. *Setor produtivo estatal: Dispêndio em ciências e tecnologia 1978/82*. Brasília: SEPLAN, 1982.

SEST/SEPLAN [Brasil], *Cadastro das empresas estatais 1984*. Brasília: SEST, 1984.

———. *Legislação básica*. Brasília: SEST, 1984.

———. *Sinopse da atuação da Sest no período 1980/84*. Brasília: SEST, 1984.

United Nations Conference on Trade and Development. *World Investment Report 2000: Cross-border Mergers and Acquisitions and Development*. New York: United Nations, 2000.

———. *Trade and Development Report, 1997: Globalization, Distribution and Growth*. New York: United Nations, 1998.

———. *World Investment Report 1997: Transnational Corporations, Market Structure and Competition Policy*. New York: United Nations, 1997.

———. *Trade and Development Report, 1993*. New York: United Nations, 1993.

United Nations Development Programme [UNDP]. *Human Development Report 1997*. New York: Oxford University Press, 1997.

United Nations Economic Commission for Latin America. *El desarrollo económico de la Argentina*. Santiago: CEPAL, 1958.

United States Department of Commerce: International Trade Administration. *National Trade Data Bank.* CD-ROM. Various years.

World Bank. "Poor People in a Rich Country: a Poverty Report for Argentina. Volume I." Document of the World Bank, Report No. 19992 AR. 23 March 2000.

——. *2000 World Development Indicators.* www.worldbank.org.

——. *World Development Report 1999/2000: Entering the 21st Century.* New York: Oxford University Press, 1999.

——. *1999 World Development Indicators.* Washington, DC: The World Bank, 1999.

——. *1988 World Development Indicators.* Washington, DC: The World Bank, 1998.

——. *World Development Report 1997: the State in a Changing World.* New York: Oxford University Press, 1997.

——. *The East Asian Miracle: Economic Growth and Public Policy.* New York: Oxford University Press, 1993.

——. *World Development Report 1992: Development and the Environment.* New York: Oxford University Press, 1992.

——. *World Development Report 1991: the Challenge of Development.* New York: Oxford University Press, 1991.

E.   Unpublished papers and websites

Azevedo, Wagner Canhedo. "Pronouncement of Mr. Wagner Canhedo Azevedo of VASP–Viação Aérea São Paulo, S/A." A Paper given at the Second International Conference on Privatization in Latin America. Institute of the Americas, La Jolla, CA, 15 April 1991.

Ball, Perry. "Mining in Chile: 1991." Working Paper No. 3, Latin American Center for Minerals & Energy Development, Colorado School of Mines. April 1991.

FIEL (Fundación de Investigaciones Económicas Latino-Americanas). "El regimen de compre nacional: una aplicación a la industria petrolera." Buenos Aries. October 1988. FIEL Library [ms].

Foxley, Juan. "Financing Chile's Privatization Program." A Paper presented at the Second International Conference on Privatization in Latin America, Institute of the Americas, La Jolla 14–16 April 1991.

Pang, Eul-Soo, and Laura J. Pang. "Argentine Mining Development Project for the Province of Mendoza: a Provincial Mining Development Strategy: Deregulatory and Decentralization Approaches." Prepared for Dr. Rodolfo F. Gabrielli, Governor of the Province of Mendoza and Dr. Juan Antonio Zapata, the then Undersecretary of Provincial Public Sector Reform Assistance, Ministry of the Interior, Government of Argentina. 1993. [ms].

Piñera, José. "Empowering Workers: the Privatization of Social Security in Chile." *The Cato Journal.* Vol. 15, No. 2–3. No date. 1–10. http://www.cato.org/pubs/journal/cj15n2-3-1.html.

Tironi B., Ernesto. "Requirements for Successful International Participation in Privatization: the Chilean Experience." A Paper presented at the Second International Conference on Privatization in Latin America, Institute of the Americas, La Jolla, 14–16 April 1991.

Index